Youth, Jobs, and the Future

Youth, Jobs, and the Future
Problems and Prospects

EDITED BY
Lynn S. Chancer
Martín Sánchez-Jankowski
Christine Trost

OXFORD
UNIVERSITY PRESS

UNIVERSITY PRESS

Oxford University Press is a department of the University of Oxford. It furthers
the University's objective of excellence in research, scholarship, and education
by publishing worldwide. Oxford is a registered trade mark of Oxford University
Press in the UK and certain other countries.

Published in the United States of America by Oxford University Press
198 Madison Avenue, New York, NY 10016, United States of America.

Library of Congress Cataloging-in-Publication Data
Names: Chancer, Lynn S., 1954– editor. | Sánchez-Jankowski, Martín, 1945– editor. |
Trost, Christine, 1964– editor.
Title: Youth, jobs, and the future: problems and prospects /
edited by Lynn Chancer, Martín Sánchez-Jankowski, Christine Trost.
Description: New York, NY: Oxford University Press, [2019] |
Includes index. Identifiers: LCCN 2018008314 | ISBN 9780190685904 (pbk) |
ISBN 9780190685898 (hbk) | ISBN 9780190685911 (updf) | ISBN 9780190685928 (epub)
Subjects: LCSH: Youth—Employment—United States. |
Unemployed youth—United States. | Youth—United States—Social conditions. |
Youth—United States—Economic conditions.
Classification: LCC HD6273.Y6556 2019 | DDC 331.3/470973—dc23
LC record available at https://lccn.loc.gov/2018008314

9 8 7 6 5 4 3 2 1

Paperback printed by WebCom, Inc., Canada
Hardback printed by Bridgeport National Bindery, Inc., United States of America

This book is dedicated to our sons
Alex, Reed, Javier, Julián, and Andrés
who inspire us to envision a better world for their
and future generations of youth.

Contents

PART III. SOCIOECONOMIC PRECARITY AND YOUTH UNEMPLOYMENT

PART IV. WHAT IS TO BE DONE?

Illustrations

Acknowledgments

We wish to express our sincere appreciation to several parties without whom this edited volume—and the conference on which it is based—would not have been possible.

Many thanks to the staff of Roosevelt House, Hunter College's excellent public policy institute, for providing space, expertise, technical assistance, and serious enthusiasm for the "Youth, Jobs, and the Future" conference that was a great success when held there on October 22–23, 2015. In particular, we are most appreciative for the assistance provided by Harold Holzer, Shyama Venkateswar, and Rafael Munoz. Of course, a special thank you is also due to President Jennifer Raab of Hunter College for financial as well as programmatic advice and assistance: her interest in "public sociological" endeavors was evident and extremely helpful.

In addition, we wish to acknowledge the support provided at the Roosevelt House conference from the University of California at Berkeley's Institute for the Study of Societal Issues (ISSI) and from New York University's Center for Advanced Social Science Research. Again, without the conference and the participation of many excellent speakers, many of whose ideas have been expanded upon within this volume, *Youth, Jobs, and the Future: Problems and Prospects* would not have made it into print.

At Hunter, over the last three to four years, research assistants Kevin Moran and Omar Montana assisted with culling data and background information as well as with practical administrative matters. At Berkeley, Melody Ng provided valuable research assistance.

Last but not least, we are very grateful to Oxford University Press for their support of this topic and book. We wish to thank James Cook for commissioning the volume and his understanding of the issue's importance. Many thanks, too, to Emily MacKenzie for prompt editorial assistance and to Rajesh Kathamuthu for careful attention to detail and overall assistance through the production process.

Contributors

Richard Alba is a distinguished professor of sociology at the Graduate Center of the City University of New York. He is the author of *Strangers No More: The Challenge of Integration in North America and Western Europe* (with Nancy Foner, Princeton University Press, 2015) and *The Next Generation: Immigrant Youth in a Comparative Perspective* (with Mary Waters, New York University Press, 2011), along with many other books and articles on immigration, race, and ethnicity in comparative perspective.

Yasemin Besen-Cassino is a professor of sociology at Montclair State University and the book review editor of *Gender & Society*. She received her Ph.D. from SUNY Stony Brook in 2005, and her research focuses on work, labor, and gender.

Shawn D. Bushway is a professor of public administration and policy at the Rockefeller College of Public Affairs and Policy with a courtesy appointment in the School of Criminal Justice. He is a member of New York State's Permanent Commission on Sentencing Reform, and his primary research interests involve criminal justice policy, the desistance process, and the effect of background check policies on employment for individuals with criminal history records.

Patrick J. Carr is associate professor of sociology and director of the Program in Criminal Justice at Rutgers University-New Brunswick. He is the author of *Clean Streets: Controlling Crime, Maintaining Order and Building Community Activism* (NYU Press, 2005) and coauthor, with Maria Kefalas, of *Hollowing Out the Middle: The Rural Brain Drain and What It Means for America* (Beacon, 2009). His current research focuses on why "college for all" fails many and on witnesses in the criminal justice system.

Lynn S. Chancer is a professor at Hunter College and executive officer of the Ph.D. Program in Sociology, Graduate Center of the City University of New York. She has written books that include *Sadomasochism in Everyday*

Life: Dynamics of Power and Powerlessness, High-Profile Crimes: When Legal Cases Become Social Causes, and *Gender, Race and Class: An Overview,* as well as many articles about social and cultural theory.

Nancy Foner is a distinguished professor of sociology at Hunter College and the Graduate Center, City University of New York. She has more than a dozen books on immigration to her credit, most recently, *Strangers No More: Immigration and the Challenges of Integration in North America and Western Europe,* written with Richard Alba.

Ari Grant-Sasson is a graduate of Middlebury College, where he studied labor history with a focus on the Industrial Revolution.

David J. Harding is associate professor of sociology and director of the Social Sciences Data Lab at the University of California, Berkeley. His research interests include incarceration and prisoner reentry, urban poverty, education, mixed methods, and causal inference. He is the author of *Living the Drama: Community, Conflict and Culture Among Inner-City Boys* (University of Chicago Press, 2010).

Michael Hout is a professor of sociology at New York University. He is known for research on social change in the United States and comparative studies of educational and occupational mobility.

Arne L. Kalleberg is Kenan Distinguished Professor of Sociology at the University of North Carolina at Chapel Hill. His most recent book is *Precarious Lives: Job Insecurity and Well-Being in Rich Democracies* (Polity Press, 2018). He is the editor of *Social Forces: An International Sociological Journal.*

Maria Kefalas is a professor of sociology at Saint Joseph's University. She writes about marriage and the family, youth and the transition to adulthood, and rural and urban communities. Her essays have appeared in the *Washington Post, Slate, The Root,* and *The Chronicle of Higher Education.*

Robert Kuttner is cofounder and coeditor of *The American Prospect* and professor of social policy at Brandeis University's Heller School. He was a founder of the Economic Policy Institute and serves on its executive committee. He is the author of ten books on politics and economics, most recently *Debtors' Prison: The Politics of Austerity Versus Possibility.* His newest book is, *Can Democracy Survive Global Capitalism?* (W.W. Norton & Company, 2018).

Stanley S. Litow is president emeritus of the IBM Foundation and IBM vice president of Corporate Affairs and Corporate Citizenship. Prior to his time at IBM he served as deputy schools chancellor for the City of New York; as president of Interface, the think tank he founded; and as executive director of the Urban Corps in the mayor's office. He has served on multiple presidential and gubernatorial commissions, including the president's Welfare to Work Commission, and serves as a trustee of the State University of New York, where he chairs the Academic Affairs Committee.

Katherine Eva Maich is a postdoctoral scholar at the Center for Global Workers' Rights in the School of Labor and Employment Relations at The Pennsylvania State University. She received her Ph.D. in sociology from the University of California, Berkeley, in 2017, where she was a Berkeley Empirical Legal Studies Fellow. Her research uses ethnographic methods to explore labor informality and the reproduction of gender and racial inequality.

Jamie K. McCallum is an assistant professor of sociology at Middlebury College. His book *Global Unions, Local Power* (Cornell, 2013) won the best book award on labor from the American Sociological Association.

Jeffrey D. Morenoff is a professor in the Department of Sociology, the Gerald R. Ford School of Public Policy, and the Institute for Social Research at the University of Michigan, and the director of the Population Studies Center at the University of Michigan. His research straddles the fields of sociology, demography, and criminology, including work on the influence of the criminal justice system on the health and well-being of people with criminal records, the challenges people face upon returning from prison to the community, and how neighborhood environments and the process of neighborhood change influence the health and well-being of neighborhood residents.

Anh P. Nguyen is a Ph.D. candidate in sociology at the University of Michigan. His research focuses on punishment, inequality, race, and health. His current project examines the determinants and consequences of solitary confinement.

Sarah Reibstein is a Ph.D. student in the Department of Sociology at Princeton University. She has conducted quantitative and qualitative research on the Alaska Permanent Fund dividend program and is planning to study universal income policies more broadly in her dissertation work.

Martín Sánchez-Jankowski is a professor of sociology and director of the Institute for the Study of Societal Issues at the University of California at Berkeley. His research focuses on inequality in advanced and developing societies and has been directed toward understanding the social arrangements and behavior of people living in poverty. He is the author of award-winning books including *Islands in the Street: Gangs and American Urban Society* and *Cracks in the Pavement: Change and Resilience in Poor Neighborhoods.*

Andrew Stern is the president emeritus of the Service Employees International Union and a senior fellow at the Economic Security Project.

Grace Suh is director of Education and Corporate Citizenship at IBM. Prior to IBM Grace worked at the Children's Defense Fund and has worked on education and children's issues in both city and state government. She serves on a number of education committees and boards including the Cahn Fellows Program and Schools That Can.

Christine Trost is associate director of the Institute for the Study of Societal Issues at the University of California at Berkeley, where she also completed a Ph.D. in political science. She has written journal articles and edited volumes on topics related to political ethics, campaign practices, civic and political engagement, and the emergence of the Tea Party including *Steep: The Precipitous Rise of the Tea Party* (co-edited with Lawrence Rosenthal).

Youth, Jobs, and the Future

Introduction

Lynn S. Chancer, Martín Sánchez-Jankowski,
and Christine Trost

In most societies, moving from school to work—entering the labor market and landing a job—is viewed as essential to making a successful transition from youth to adulthood. Jobs provide young adults with financial independence, an avenue for social and geographic mobility, a source of identity and self-worth, and an opportunity to make significant contributions to the society in which they live. Indeed, the promise of a job is woven into the fabric of American life and plays an essential role in achieving the upward mobility that lies at the heart of the American dream. Study hard, do well in school, and you will be rewarded with a good-paying job and prosperity beyond what your parents achieved.

The sudden and massive economic downturn known as the Great Recession (2007–2009) shattered this dream for a generation of American youth. Youth unemployment in the United States soared to a postwar record of 19 percent. By 2010, unemployment rates were highest among young people, averaging more than 25 percent for 16- to 19-year-olds and over 15 percent among 20- to 24-year-olds (Sum et al. 2014). Even youth able to secure jobs were likely to experience "scarring" in the form of lower levels of earnings (for 10 years or more), lower-quality jobs, and lower levels of job satisfaction and career progression due to having entered the job market during a severe economic downturn (Kalleberg and von Wachter 2017).

In spite of a partial economic recovery, American youth continue to experience high unemployment and underemployment. In April 2015, although the overall unemployment rate in the United States declined to 5.4 percent, the unemployment rate for youth remained significantly higher (10.5 percent for 16- to 19-year-olds; 16.8 percent for 20- to 24-year-olds) (Desilver 2015). Millions more youth remain underemployed or are "disconnected" from school and work. A 2016 Brookings Institute report estimated that 3 million young people aged 16–24 are neither in school nor working, and black and Latino youth are three to six times more likely to be disconnected than white youth (Ross and Svajlenka 2016).

While the widespread job destruction and losses in earnings precipitated by the Great Recession have had an unprecedented impact on American teens and young adults, their employment prospects have been declining for more than two decades as a result of significant changes in the structure and nature of work. The rise of the "24/7 economy" and nonstandard work schedules (Presser 2003), polarization between "good jobs" and "bad jobs" (Kalleberg 2009, 2012), the replacement of routine manual work with automation, the steady decline in manufacturing jobs, and the rise in low-wage insecure jobs without benefits, which rely on nonstandard schedules, unpredictable work hours, and other cost-saving measures to shift risk from corporations to the individual (Hacker 2006), all contribute to diminished employment prospects for American youth.

The problem of youth joblessness is not restricted to the United States but is shared by youth globally. The disadvantages faced by young people seeking work are many. Their relative lack of skills and work experience, smaller social networks, and limited knowledge about how and where to look for work make securing employment, especially during economic downturns, more difficult. They are also likely to have fewer financial resources to draw on during their job search, creating a dependence on parental or family support if this is available (International Labour Office 2010, 28). It is no longer uncommon for young people to move home and rely on family or social networks to get by. As a result, young people are more likely to accept lower wages and jobs below their skill set or to move into the informal economy and be among the working poor (International Labour Office 2010, 3).

As in the United States, youth unemployment rates across the globe are more sensitive to economic shocks than adult rates (International Labour Office 2010, 5), especially in countries with developed economies. The International Labour Office estimated that 81 million youth were unemployed at the end of 2009, representing the largest ever cohort of unemployed youth and an increase of 7.8 million from 2 years earlier when the global economic crisis began (2010, 1). While some regions of the world have experienced a partial recovery, there is no sign of improvement in others (e.g., Middle East and North Africa); and the recovery has lasted longer than expected, with significant consequences for youth (International Labour Office 2010, 6). In all regions of the world youth unemployment rates are two to three times higher than adult rates and are projected to take longer to recover (International Labour Office 2010, 3, 6). Even before the Great Recession, there was a steady decline in youth labor force participation globally, from 54.7 percent in 1998 to 50.8 percent in 2008 (International Labour Office 2010, 3). Especially impacted are young women, who have a harder time finding work than young men (International Labour Office 2010, 5), as do poor youth, youth who are members of ethnic minorities, and youth with less educational attainment or with disabilities.

A recent study of joblessness in Europe found that irrespective of country youth are more likely to be unemployed than adults and are more likely to be in temporary employment (O'Reilly et al. forthcoming, see chapter 5). Since the Great Recession, unemployment rates for youth in Europe have hovered around 20 percent (Caliendo and Schmidl 2015, 1). Concentration of youth in temporary or part-time jobs is growing, along with discouragement among those who are jobless. On average, between 20 percent and 30 percent of all youth aged 15–29 in Organisation for Economic Co-operation and Development countries (especially France, Greece, Spain, and Italy), although qualified, "experience persistent difficulties in accessing stable employment" and are "caught in a series of precarious jobs interspersed by relatively short periods of unemployment or economic inactivity" (O'Reilly et al. 2015, 2). A smaller but still significant percentage of European youth are not engaged in any form of employment, education, or training (O'Reilly et al. forthcoming).

Economists and other scholars have documented the economic, social, and individual costs of youth unemployment. Youth who are unemployed do not contribute to generating the wealth needed to fuel the nation's economy and replenish the tax base used to fund government programs. Instead, they represent a waste of productive and creative potential and a loss of investment in education. They become financially dependent on their families or claim early reliance on public benefits and other government support measures. The social and individual costs of not working are equally significant for youth and include social exclusion and isolation, alienation, loss of hope in the future, and a sense of uselessness, which "can lead to increased crime, mental health problems, violence, conflicts and drug taking" (International Labour Office 2010, 6).

European responses to youth joblessness have been relatively swift and comprehensive. They include expansion and improvement in the quality of apprenticeship programs, greater investments in vocational education and training "plus" programs that link in-classroom instruction and on-the-job training, job search assistance and monitoring, training and wage subsidies, public works programs, and promoting youth mobility across Europe. In addition to country-specific initiatives such as New Deal for Young People in the United Kingdom, Jugend mit Perspektive in Germany, and the Youth Unemployment Program in Demark, the European Union launched a wide range of new policy initiatives from 2010 to 2014 targeted at unemployed youth. These included, among others, Youth on the Move, an initiative directed at enhancing the quality of education and training systems and promoting youth mobility across Europe; Youth Opportunities Initiative, which funds apprenticeship and entrepreneurship programs and provides assistance to youth and employers seeking transnational recruitment and job placement; Youth Guarantee, which includes funding and asks member states to make a commitment to young people under the age of 25 to receive a good-quality offer of employment, continued education, apprenticeship, or training within 4 months of leaving formal education or becoming un-employed; and Youth Employment Initiative, which provides funding and support to young people who are not in education, employment, or training programs and live in areas of Europe where youth unemployment was higher than 25 percent in 2012 (O'Reilly et al. 2015, 9–12).[1]

These and other initiatives have been met with varying degrees of success (Caliendo and Schmidl 2015; O'Reilly et al. 2015).[2] For example, research shows that countries with a substantial dual apprenticeship system (which combines apprenticeships and vocational education), such as Austria, Denmark, Germany, and Switzerland, have fewer disconnected youth and lower rates of youth unemployment than other countries (O'Reilly et al. 2015, 12). Transferring these successes and resource-intensive schemes to other countries and regions in Europe, however, is proving challenging, not only because of the substantial public and private sector investment required to ensure successful implementation but also due to institutional factors and resource differences between and even within countries (e.g., differ-ences in the quality and capacity of public employment agencies required to provide youth with advice on job, education, and training opportunities) (O'Reilly et al. 2015, 10–12). European Union policies designed to encourage the free movement of labor across Europe helped to lower rates of unem-ployment in some member countries but came at the cost of young migrant workers (especially those traveling east to west) finding employment in low-paying, low-skilled jobs for which they were overeducated and overqualified (O'Reilly et al. 2015, 6–7). Although the "youth guarantee" scheme has had some success in Nordic countries, implementation in other parts of Europe has been uneven (O'Reilly et al. 2015, 11).

While youth unemployment has received significant attention across Europe, it remains relatively overlooked as an area of study and policy in-tervention in the United States.[3] Can anything be learned from European responses to youth unemployment? For example, might Germany's highly regarded dual apprenticeship system, which relies on "the broad support of employers, trade unions and the government for regulation and financing" (Cahuc et al. 2013), provide a viable model for aiding American youth? Comparisons between Europe and the United States are helpful to a point, but as we argue below, there are significant differences—such as relatively low levels of public support for government assistance, weaker trade unions and government protections, different immigration and racial–ethnic patterns, and other cultural characteristics distinctive to the United States—that mark the United States as "exceptional" and limit the ability to easily adopt European solutions.

In the US context, the harmful effects of unemployment are measured mostly in terms of simple loss of earnings, whereas scholars have shown that early-life unemployment creates a harmful multiplier effect, engendering a wide range of negative adult-life outcomes and attendant social problems for youth. Most worrisome, perhaps, is the significant increase in American youth who feel insecure and disconnected from work and education and who believe that their life chances and opportunities are depressingly uncertain or declining. Missing is a sociological analysis of what is often viewed as a solely economic problem. What is distinctive about American *youth's* experience with unemployment? How does the rise of precarious employment affect young people in particular? And how do culture and agency, along with structure, shape youth (un)employment in the United States and responses to it? As several authors in this volume point out, the development of precarious work and technological changes that impact job availability, especially for young people, has brought traditional assumptions about work itself into question. Are any jobs worth taking, no matter how poorly paid? Are young people willing to undertake what sociologist Benjamin Hunnicutt (1988) has called "work without end" such that no time is left for socializing, leisure, and/or pursuing their education? (See also Schor 1993.)

Indeed, youth today face heightened socioeconomic precariousness and insecurity not only in the realm of work but also in school as the cost of a college education continues to skyrocket. At the same time, these experiences vary greatly with differing circumstances and backgrounds. Yet within sociology, little discussion has occurred between scholars interested in political economy, culture, work, labor, and family about this issue. In addition, the problem of youth joblessness has not been tackled in the American context with the focused aim of influencing policymakers, politicians, and legislators. In the realm of policy, public debate is taking place about surrounding issues affecting youth such as student debt and increasing the minimum wage. For example, Bernie Sanders' presidential campaign called attention to both rising student debt and unaffordable tuition (Sanders proposed making community colleges tuition-free). In general, though, little attention has been paid to the availability of jobs and the problem of secure employment in the primary labor market over decades to come.

This book aims to fill this gap through chapters that take a wide range of interdisciplinary perspectives on young people, jobs, and socioeconomic precarity. The chapters address both structural causes of youth unemployment in the United States and the role of culture and agency in shaping how jobs and work are currently defined and how they are being redefined in the swiftly changing US economy. The volume grows out of a 2-day conference, "Youth, Jobs and the Future," held at the Roosevelt House of Hunter College of the City University of New York in October 2015. Each chapter tackles a specific aspect of the problem and makes policy recommendations; some of these recommendations involve economic and political changes, while others focus on changes in cultural attitudes needed to understand and ameliorate the problem of worsened youth prospects.

The first part of the book features chapters providing an overview of general structural trends in youth employment and unemployment in the United States. The second part contains chapters on cultural and social changes that have affected youth and includes research on young people's normative attitudes about what comprises a good job and work. The third part focuses on social impediments and strains relevant to how diverse groups of young people navigate unemployment and socioeconomic precarity. Chapters in the last section of the volume turn to the key question of "what is to be done?" and examine proposals ranging from new forms of vocational training and education for underprivileged youth to shorter hours, universal basic income, and full employment. Each chapter in Part IV offers ideas aimed, alone or in combination, at ameliorating the problems elaborated in Parts I, II, and III.

Together we hope this book fills an important gap in the literature, as well as contributing to public sociological debates, by illuminating what is distinctive about youth unemployment and socioeconomic precarity in the US context. This includes our own emphasis on the combined and simultaneous role played by structure, agency, and culture in shaping youth problems and prospects in America. We do not intend to simply reiterate past arguments about "American exceptionalism" as though the United States does not partake of many analogous economic and cultural processes that are happening globally. Clearly, this is not the case as youth unemployment and socioeconomic precarity are international problems urgently facing many countries around the world that are also experiencing broad processes of privatization and "neoliberal" capitalism. Nonetheless, perhaps it can be safely said that, from a scholarly perspective, noticeably less attention has been paid to this issue in the US context; in this respect, a certain "exceptionalism" has arisen through this very scholarly and sociological omission. We aim to fill this this gap by thinking, and rethinking, about problems of work, jobs, and culture that impact this generation's future and the cohesiveness of American society in decades to come.

For this book's purposes, we argue that the distinctiveness of the US case necessitates taking cultural influences and structural features into account so as to fully and comprehensively explore youth unemployment and socio-economic precarity. Yet most attention paid to these problems in the United States has prioritized discussion of structural causes (Bell and Blanchflower 2011). While many scholars believe the "natural" place to begin is with the contribution of structural factors to youth unemployment, the chapters to come evidence the equal significance of cultural factors. Giving an equally central role to culture entails looking at two aspects of it in relation to structural conditions. One aspect involves looking at how young people *react* as individual agents to the challenging situation facing them. The other aspect involves examining attitudes that people bring in *response* to youth unemployment when it comes to recommending changes at more collectively political levels. This raises the question of how stuck we are (or are not) in traditional concepts of work and economy that no longer seem to fully and accurately describe socioeconomic processes occurring in our present historical situation. Consequently, this book looks to culture to probe attitudes toward a worsening problem that may well require a combination of traditional and freshly creative ideas to ameliorate it.

To best understand the phenomena at hand, then, we begin with deeply entrenched ideological aspects of American thought that have affected aspirations and hopes about work: namely, the ongoing influence of the "American dream." Even though our socioeconomic structures have altered, still culturally persistent and widespread in the late 2010s is the "rags to riches" myth of Horatio Alger. The potent symbol of the "American dream" is the notion that anyone in America, regardless of background or age, can achieve his or her desired goals in life through hard work and effort.

Whether consciously or not, the overwhelming majority of youth in the United States continue to believe in the current political economic system that promises to reward those who follow its rules and work hard toward self-improvement. While not everyone believes that the system guarantees success, the conviction persists that the United States is committed to maximizing an individual's opportunity to achieve success regardless of race, ethnicity, class, gender, and/or other social distinctions (Hochschild 1996; Young 2006).

The American dream ideology is instilled and reinforced in the activities of the family, the education and legal systems, as well as the media and popular cultural venues. In point of fact, young people in the United States are constantly provided examples of the "riches" and "statuses" made available to individuals. Moreover, they are encouraged to accept that achieving wealth and high status is possible for everyone and that to be successful, resentment and envy must be replaced by desire and effort. As a result, American youth are encouraged to embrace a set of values and norms associated with specific individual behaviors needed to realize material aspirations and goals. However, problems arise for youth when they—as agents acting for and often by themselves—have to translate aspirations arising from American dream ideology into a set of concrete strategies.

Stressing the potent and ongoing cultural influence of the American dream in no way takes away from the simultaneous importance of the structural framework within which young people's cultural aspirations and goals circulate. Indeed, structural conditions provide the boundaries within which individual youth exercise their choices and achieve their goals. It is for precisely this reason (i.e., structure as the overarching framework within which agents operate) that more attention has been paid to economics than culture by scholars interested in the youth unemployment problem in local, national, and international contexts. The consensus has been that at all economic levels profound institutional transformations have occurred, with clear effects on job opportunities available to everyone, especially youth.

Turning to structure, then, there are at least four conditions that have dramatically affected problems of youth unemployment and socioeconomic precarity. The first is that the primary labor market has changed from requiring semi-skilled (as in prior factory work) to demanding highly skilled service work and advanced levels of human capital. Given that youth are in the developmental stage of accumulating human capital, this has made them effectively unable to compete for many jobs.

The second condition is that few vacancies exist for young people to fill since the primary labor market (which previously generated jobs with higher wages, benefits, and relative security) has been in an extended period of decline. In previous decades, particularly in the 1960s through the 1980s, youth graduating high school could be far more confident about securing such primary labor market jobs that had potential to form the bases of their careers. Moreover, young people going to college could much more easily acquire 2–3 months' summer work experience before restarting their college educations in the fall. This is no longer the case, however, leaving young people who presently want temporary short-term jobs—let alone full-time ones—with little, and with historically very diminished, access to these occupations.

A third structural condition affecting young people involves the low-skilled secondary market production sectors wherein some expansion has occurred. Despite expansion, this sector has not proved itself capable of significantly increasing employment opportunities for youth. One reason is that this sector typically offers low wages, long hours, no benefits, difficult working conditions, and no job security. Another factor involves the salience of cultural expectations: for young people brought up to believe in the American dream, participation in these sectors becomes unattractive because they are jobs with little chance for acquiring income security and social mobility.

Last, the expansion of low-skilled secondary sector jobs has not helped youth in that even if young people are willing to take "gig" (or insecure) jobs for the short term, competition sometimes arises from a workforce often deemed more attractive by employers. This competition can often be from immigrant workers who have been more willing to accept whatever conditions are presented to them and who may commit to staying at such jobs until they are no longer needed. Often, immigrant workers are prepared to do this because of economic insecurities related to their immigration status. They may also be responsible for providing for family dependents and may desire to work multiple jobs so as to save money for the purchase of a single-family home or to invest in the educations of their children. In other words, willingness to take insecure jobs results from structural impediments that immigrants also face. Employers may favor immigrants over youth due to a perception that immigrant workers are more likely to remain longer term, come to work on time, be productive while working, and not miss work because of sickness, whereas youth who may not want to get up and work on a given day may leave to find something better and may lack the same level of discipline. This impression persists even though, as a later chapter demonstrates, the Millennial generation has often been unfairly and inaccurately portrayed as being "lazy." In this way, the category of "youth" is placed in structural competition with the category of "immigrants," who may be older and more willing to "settle" for low-paying, low-benefit jobs. For both groups, though, the ideology of the American dream remains alive and well, even though it may be unfulfilled.

In sum, both cultural ideologies and structural conditions work together to impact the likelihood of the American dream coming to fruition (or not) given that employers, immigrant groups, and young people often continue to operate under its sway. However, what constitutes the American dream for a given individual varies, and people react differently to the dilemmas and disparities they face in ways that often reinforce and reproduce the structural conditions that contribute to high levels of youth unemployment. Take the practices of young people at the level of "agency," for the American dream goes hand in hand with the ethos that a person must work hard throughout life to improve her or his socioeconomic position. Of course, this ethos is predicated on a belief that everything and anything is possible and that metaphorically speaking "the world is one's oyster." However, individuals vary in assessing the probability of realizing their grandest dreams. Moreover, when this assessment involves considerable disparity between what one wants and what can be achieved, the incentive to maintain the discipline to drive oneself to meet the schedules of punishing jobs and/or production levels is severely challenged.

What results is a form of cognitive dissonance that is likely to affect the kind of job a young person is willing to take after assessing if its requirements meet the expectations of his or her short- or long-term goals, the social significance of having a job, the status associated with doing it, and the economic costs of not taking a particular gig. Thus, some young people will only take a job that does not violate their social assessment of its face value (i.e., the social status associated with a job). For other individuals, the pay or number of hours required may be perceived as "not worth it."

Each of these points—the ongoing influence of the American dream qua cultural ideology; structural changes that differentiate this generation's situation from those of previous generations; competition that may occur between younger and older groups across different immigrant/nonimmigrant, race, gender, and/or ethnic categories; and the range of individual reactions and considerations that go into youth deciding if the job market is even worth it—impacts the youth unemployment situation in the United States. The ensuing chapters speak to all of these issues. Contributors address factors related to the role that diverse backgrounds play in affecting both young people's employment situation and unequal economic outcomes, both of which are often at odds with the alleged American dream.

Before turning to the empirical chapters, we argue for an array of solutions to potentially redress the problems the contributors pose in this book. A complex social problem like youth unemployment and socioeconomic precarity cannot be redressed simplistically. Rather, we suggest measures that need to be simultaneously implemented in order to diminish the predicament many young people now face.

In advocating a multipronged approach, we hold that advocacy for shorter- and longer-term measures is needed. Indeed, ideas developed in this book's fourth and final "what is to be done?" section would work well in combination. To begin, jobs—good jobs—are needed to provide young people with well-founded rather than unrealistic expectations about finding meaningful, secure employment and high-quality and affordable educations. School-to-work transitions need to become a stronger part of the missions of high schools, colleges, and universities; and fighting for free tuition at not only community colleges but 4-year colleges and universities is a political goal worth pursuing. Strong education and job preparation are closely interrelated. Moreover, technical and vocational learning as well as liberal arts educations do not have to be spuriously separated, as the American Sociological Association has recently argued in urging undergraduate and graduate departments to provide broad liberal arts, critical writing, and quantitative skills career training that links undergraduate work and specific job opportunities and paths.

What also needs to happen is increasing investment by the private sector in school-to-job programs aimed directly—especially, if not exclusively—at young people from low-income backgrounds, as well as youth of color given the combined racial and class biases they encounter. As previously described, many of these school-to-work links are being made in programs operating in countries like Germany. In some cases, these offer models worth investigating and possibly emulating in the United States through significant expansion of corporate, state, and non-profit organizational involvement in well-defined programs.

Will such links happen through the initiatives of industry and corporations alone? The importance of government involvement cannot be overstated in dealing with issues of youth unemployment and socioeconomic precarity. Rather than acceding to steady attacks on the welfare state, the situation of young people—and their doubled rates of unemployment, as well as their well-founded feelings of precarity and insecurity—offers good reason, and potentially a culturally-based impetus, to push for government involvement in job creation at levels encompassing local, state, as well as federal measures and legislation.

Among other progressive economists, Robert Kuttner calls for returning to the goal of full employment—an idea that, as he elaborates in his chapter, recycles the Keynesian insistence on state involvement. Full employment is not a new idea, even if it currently is rendered a more "radical" one, in the contemporary political context of America. The benefits of full employment are significant and not just for youth but for the broader political collective. Massive jobs programs, involving interesting and useful jobs, are badly needed to replace sagging infrastructure, develop new energy sources, and build rail transportation of the kind and speed other countries have long had in place, among other socially useful and constructive objectives. Jobs are also certainly needed in education, more than ever, both to develop critical skills and cultural awareness about contemporary life and to increase skills in myriad fields like mathematics, science, and computer science where the United States at present continues to lag. In all these ways, addressing new and older identified needs through legislation aimed at job creation is potentially capable of ameliorating the depressing picture young people otherwise face when coming onto the job market.

Let us go even further in this analysis. Let us assume that, even if the private sector and local, state, and federal governments become more actively involved in job creation as per "full employment" goals, other social factors—notably, technological change with its job-displacing tendencies including the introduction of drones, robotization, and driverless cars—may displace the need for many kinds of jobs, even "good" jobs, that we envision being created going forward. What then? Indeed, a debate between Robert Kuttner and labor leader Andrew Stern, both writing in Part IV, counterposes two positions. Is it the case, as Kuttner argues, that contemporary job losses are political at their core (i.e., they reflect loss of collective will about creating jobs that could exist but are simply not being created)? Or, as Reibstein and Stern contend, are technological developments themselves bequeathing job losses in job categories that cannot simply be replaced?

In fact, it is impossible to know for sure how many jobs technology will displace and how many others that are created will take their place by way of substitution or whether newly created "substitutive" jobs will happen in places and for people who most need them when class, gender, race, ethnicity, and other social biases are co-considered. What we can know for sure is that the very fact of uncertainty is part and parcel related to the cultural and structural changes that have simultaneously occurred and that contribute to feelings of socioeconomic precarity that young people understandably experience and are reacting to—for it is young people who, by the sheer fact of their age, most likely over time will feel the effects of technologically related job losses given the rapid rate that some people predict.

Consequently, in addition to advocating for important measures like private sector involvement in school-to-work transitions and programs and for government job creation to fulfill well-identified national needs—all of which will, of course, assist young people's prospects—we argue for new forms of "social insurance" that not only are germane for young people but have the benefit of potentially protecting everyone against technologically caused job displacements. What kind of protections, though, ought scholars, activists, and members of the concerned public envision?

As more fully elaborated in Part IV, it seems reasonable to suggest that basic income provisions along with shorter hours and work-sharing measures (as the latter are currently called for, and organized around, by some groups of young people) are important policy changes to pursue in addition to, not instead of, job creation and expanded school-to-work programs. Indeed, both basic income and shorter hours add newly creative and innovative ideas to the mix of traditionally established measures needed to address youth unemployment and socioeconomic precarity in the contemporary American context.

Basic income involves paying people a certain amount of "guaranteed" pay necessary for sustenance if jobs cannot be found and have been technologically displaced. Strikingly, both in the United States and in many places around the world, including France and The Netherlands, basic or guaranteed income has become simultaneously popular and debated. The United States is not exceptional insofar as this idea—as with full employment—has a surprisingly long history, going back to Milton Friedman and the proposals about basic income made in the Nixon administration. Presently, the state of Alaska provides eligible residents with a yearly cash payment ($1,022 in 2016) in line with a small "basic" income. Outside the United States, a referendum to institute a basic income appeared on Switzerland's ballot in the last decade; while this measure failed, it received 22 percent of the votes and continued to catapult the issue into greater public awareness all over Europe. Indeed, in France in 2017, Benoit Hamon sought the presidency on the French Socialist Party ticket following François Hollande's descent in popularity; while Hamon lost, his campaign continued to call guaranteed/ basic income to social attention as one solution to unemployment of young and older Europeans.

Why this renewed interest in guaranteed/basic income lately, and what does this have to do with youth unemployment and socioeconomic precarity? Two main reasons can be cited for the upsurge of cultural visibility. First, in an age of technological displacement and what Jamie McCallum refers to as a "gig economy" of more and more part-time, low-paying jobs (with fewer, if any, benefits), a guaranteed income would at least provide a floor for young people whose job prospects have been placed in jeopardy by high rates of unemployment and the loss of even part-time job possibilities. In this respect, basic income could be envisioned as a contemporary form of social security—not only for people of retirement age, who in past eras were perhaps the only ones in need of social security, but now, especially, for youth. Presently, an advantage of basic income is that it allows people to accept part-time jobs or jobs involving shorter hours (whether or not these jobs give them sufficient income to live on), knowing that they have another steady source of governmentally provided income. The notion thus nicely dovetails with Maich, McCallum, and Grant-Sasson's call for shorter hours and work sharing of "good" jobs to ameliorate problems of unemployment and underemployment.

The second reason for advocating basic income, as a significant component of an array of measures needed to redress youth unemployment and socioeconomic precarity, is as much cultural as structural in character. Like shorter hours and work sharing, basic income speaks to another persistent byproduct of socioeconomic processes discussed throughout this volume. This is the advent of seeming work-without-end, a situation wherein—given the increasingly gig-like character of jobs—people work longer hours, and often two or three jobs, just to get by; here, too, one finds a direct repercussion of the structural conditions enumerated earlier that now affect all workers, young and old. As a result, people may feel like they are working themselves "to death" figuratively, if not also literally—a situation against which, according to several chapters, many young people from the middle or working class with low incomes have rebelled by waiting to see if "good" jobs come along or by turning to alternative unregulated markets.

Despite allegations to the contrary, there is evidence that the Millennial generation is hard-working. Although they have been just as influenced by the American dream as prior generations, this book gives evidence of a particular kind of cultural and structural crisis. Arguably, the crisis facing young people may have had the effect of making youth think about questions of life's purpose and the quality of one's possibly short or hopefully longer life spans. Their experience underscores the importance of cultural (as well as structural) approaches for thinking—and rethinking—our ideas of work and its qualitative as well as quantitative place in our lives. It is here that the idea of guaranteed income, combined with job creation and other measures, has the advantage of providing not only an insurance policy but a floor limit to the possibility that young people, compelled by callous structural conditions, will work hours and hours, with lessened time for leisure perhaps than ever before, in decades to come. Thus, guaranteed income schemes offer one way to ensure cultural progress that could genuinely protect against people feeling compelled to work endless hours whether to survive or to achieve the (perhaps unachievable and elusive) American dream.

What will it take, politically, for changes to be enacted in the form of a multidimensional program aimed at the problems associated with youth unemployment and socioeconomic precarity? How might this be achieved in public and private sector initiatives that encompass both the shorter and longer terms and the need for both traditionally established measures, like job creation and private/public expansion of school-to-work programs, as well as adoption of new basic income and shorter hours/work-sharing programs?

Obviously, there are no guarantees that politics will shift in the direction needed to enact, socially and individually and at the level of culture as well as structure, the combined recommendations highlighted here. However, what is clear in the chapters that make up this volume is that a problem exists that is not going to go away until young people's job losses and experiences of socioeconomic precarity have been given the attention and redress they require in the United States. As to how American society should go about paying for the new initiatives suggested in this volume, the answer is that government will need to lead. Not only has this been a traditional way that social change has been initiated throughout American history, starting with Alexander Hamilton's vision of a federal government that is active in providing infrastructure for an advancing economy, but because the problem is a "national" one. Nonetheless, the private sector can also provide significant investment in developing programs that contribute to a more productive future for America's youth, as the chapter by Stanley Litow and Grace Suh points out; in those cases where the private sector has taken the initiative, a reasonable policy of granting federal tax relief would be appropriate.

Unemployment is not going to end unless it is directly addressed; technological job displacement and the gig economy, with its production of only insecure and low-paid jobs, are not going to disappear even if we could specify their exact quantitative and qualitative effects. We also know that young people are our future and that they are in need—for the promises made to them by American dream ideology seem farther away and more elusive than ever before. Something has to be done, and the sooner the better. Our young people deserve to reap the benefits of our most creative ideas as well as our most established policies. With this volume we aim to beam a spotlight on the nature of the problems that exist for American youth and by extension our future, while also advocating strongly for further thought and action.

NOTES

1. More information about these initiatives can be found at "Youth Employment," European Commission, http://ec.europa.eu/social/main.jsp?langId=en&catId=1036.

2. O'Reilly et al. (2015) note the difficulty involved in making cross-country comparisons to determine "what works" due to "the variation of program design, national framework conditions, and targeted groups" (12). Even so, Caliendo and Schmidl's (2015) cross-country analysis of active labor market programs for European youth finds mixed results: "While job search assistance (with and without monitoring) results in overwhelming positive effects, we find more mixed effects for training and wage subsidies, whereas the effects for public work programs are clearly negative."

3. Harry Holzer's work is an important exception.

REFERENCES

Bell, David N. F., and David G. Blanchflower, "Young People and the Great Recession," *Oxford Review of Economic Policy* 27, no. 2 (2011): 241–67.

Cahuc, Pierre, Stéphane Carcillo, Ulf Rinne, and Klaus F. Zimmermann. "Youth Unemployment in Old Europe: The Polar Cases of France and Germany." *IZA Journal of European Labor Studies* 2 (2013): 18. https://doi.org/10.1186/2193-9012-2-18.

Caliendo, Marco, and Ricarda Schmidl. "Youth Unemployment and Active Labor Market Policies in Europe." IZA Discussion Papers 9488, Institute for the Study of Labor (IZA), Bonn, Germany, 2015. http://hdl.handle.net/10419/125004.

Desilver, Drew. "For Young Americans, Unemployment Returns to Pre-Recession Levels." Pew Research Center, May 8, 2015. http://www.pewresearch.org/fact-tank/2015/05/08/for-young-americans-unemployment-returns-to-pre-recession-levels/.

Hacker, Jacob S. *The Great Risk Shift: The New Economic Insecurity and the Decline of the American Dream*. New York: Oxford University Press, 2006.

Hochschild, Jennifer L. *Facing Up to the American Dream: Race, Class and the Soul of the Nation*. Princeton, NJ: Princeton University Press, 1996.

Hunnicutt, Benjamin. *Work Without End: Abandoning Shorter Hours for the Right to Work*. Philadelphia: Temple University Press, 1988.

International Labour Office. *Global Employment Trends for Youth: August 2010*. Geneva, Switzerland: International Labour Office, 2010.

Kalleberg, Arne L. "Good Jobs, Bad Jobs: The Rise of Polarized and Precarious Employment Systems in the United States, 1970s to 2000s." *Social Forces* 91, 3: 1105–1109.

———. "Precarious Work, Insecure Workers: Employment Relations in Transition." *American Sociological Review* 74, no. 1 (2009): 1–22.

Kalleberg, Arne L., and Till M. von Wachter. "The U.S. Labor Market During and After the Great Recession: Continuities and Transformations." *RSF: Russell Sage Foundation Journal of the Social Sciences* 3, no. 3 (2017): 1–19.

O'Reilly, Jacqueline, Werner Eichhorst, András Gábos, Kari Hadjivassiliou, David Lain, Janine Leschke, Seamus McGuinness, Lucia Mytna Kureková, Tiziana Nazio, Renate Ortlieb, Helen Russell, and Paola Villa. "Five Characteristics of Youth Unemployment in Europe: Flexibility, Education, Migration, Family Legacies, and EU Policy." *SAGE Open* 5, no. 1 (2015): 1–19.

O'Reilly, Jacqueline, Janine Leschke, Renate Ortlieb, Martin Seeleib-Kaiser, and Paola Villa. Eds. *Youth Labour in Transition*. New York: Oxford University Press, forthcoming.

Presser, Hariett B. *Working in a 24/7 Economy: Challenges for American Families*. New York: Russell Sage Foundation, 2003.

Ross, Martha, and Nicole Prchal Svajlenka. *Employment and Disconnection Among Teens and Young Adults: The Role of Place, Race, and Education*. Washington, DC: Brookings Institution, May 24, 2016. https://www.brookings.edu/research/employment-and-disconnection-among-teens-and-young-adults-the-role-of-place-race-and-education/.

Schor, Juliet. *The Overworked American: The Unexpected Decline of Leisure*. New York: Basic Books, 1993.

Sum, Andrew, Ishwar Khatiwada, Mykhaylo Trubskyy, and Martha Ross. *The Plummeting Labor Market Fortunes of Teens and Young Adults*. With Walter McHugh and Sheila Palma. Washington, DC: Brookings Institution, 2014.

Young, Alford A., Jr. *The Minds of Marginalized Black Men: Making Sense of Mobility, Opportunity, and Future Life Chances*. Princeton, NJ: Princeton University Press, 2006.

Part I

SETTING THE STAGE

Trends and Macrocontexts

1

The Employment Patterns of Young Adults, 1989–2014

Michael Hout

INTRODUCTION

Social science research established long ago that young workers fare worse than their elders; they have higher unemployment and less job security. Some young workers' troubles come from a lack of experience endemic to their youth. Employers value young workers less because mostly they know less about the job; similarly, employers start with younger workers when they have to make layoffs because they can usually find replacements of equivalent skill when business picks up again. Older workers have learned the ropes, and it becomes harder to substitute one for another. Young workers are also less experienced in a broader sense. They make life mistakes as well as work mistakes. Deficits in life experiences as well as work experience put younger workers at a disadvantage. Most of this was known 30 years ago (Freeman and Holzer 1986).

This chapter focuses on differences among young workers. Age, race, and education all affect young people's employability and labor force experiences. First, just a few years can make a big difference among the young. Twenty-four-year-olds are not nearly as raw as 18-year-olds; they may have more education as well. The employment gradient from the late teen years to the mid-20s is upward and pretty straight, as original results presented in this chapter show. Second, gender matters. Young women have different employment patterns from young men. This chapter quantifies this important difference. Third, black and Hispanic youth have more employment difficulties than white and Asian youth. Some of the racial differences simply pass through differences due to residential segregation, differential school quality, criminal justice issues like policing and sentencing, and social networks. But race matters directly as well. Fourth, college graduates have much better employment prospects than people with less education, even among 22-year-olds, even though, at any given age, high school graduates tend to have more employment experience than college graduates. Evidence presented here indicates that credentials outweigh experience, partly because so much employment growth is limited to occupations that require a college degree; but this probably applies in other occupations as well.

All of these broad patterns replicate year after year, but the magnitude depends on the economic conditions at the time. Age, gender, race, and education differences tend to shrink as the labor market tightens. Tight labor markets give employers less choice, so the difference between young workers and older workers becomes smaller in good times. Nonetheless, employers continue to distinguish among types of young workers in good times, just somewhat less so than in bad times.

My goals in this chapter are descriptive. Descriptive research on the employment experience of young people was a mainstay of demographic research in the 1970s and 1980s (see Freeman and Holzer 1986 for a summary). A thorough accounting of trends since 2000, with a focus on the recession years 2007–2010, is overdue.

DATA, STATISTICAL METHODS, AND VARIABLE DEFINITIONS

This chapter quantifies several key relationships. To do so, I have compiled monthly data from the Current Population Survey (CPS) on the principal activities for persons 18–24 years old, focusing on school enrollment and employment, starting in January 1989 and continuing through the most recent available data (from the spring of 2014). The monthly CPS is the standard source for tracking basic labor force indicators. In this chapter I follow as closely as possible the procedures used to produce official statistics such as the monthly employment reports so that the subgroup analyses that appear here accord with the aggregate data in official reports. In conducting the CPS, the Census Bureau selects a representative sample of households and gathers information about all the people living in the selected homes. In most households, one person answers the questions on behalf of all residents, so there is some clustering of reporting errors within households. Respondents occasionally leave data fields blank; the Census Bureau imputes missing data. I use weights provided by the Census Bureau to offset complexities in the CPS sampling design. The integration of Census Bureau data into a coherent time series by the Minnesota Population Center (Flood et al. 2015) was essential to the research reported here.

A household sample excludes the young people who live in what are known as "group quarters." Military barracks and college dormitories are group quarters; prisons are the largest and most significant group quarters. Mass incarceration is its own field of study (Pettit 2012). Suffice to say here that excluding prisoners leaves the most disadvantaged segment of the young adult population out of the calculations (Western and Beckett 1999). Unfortunately, there is no substitute source of monthly data that includes the incarcerated.

Monthly employment data reflect seasonal fluctuation, especially for people under 20 years old, as labor force participation rises when school is not in session during the summer. That seasonal variation is of less interest here than the longer-term trends and differences, so I applied a mix of parametric and nonparametric methods to remove seasonal variation. First, I regressed each dependent variable on month and the independent variables of interest plus an interaction between month and the independent variable, using March as the reference month. I then subtracted the month effects from the observed outcome and applied the nonparametric smoother (locally estimated regression; Cleveland 1994). In smoothing, I set the bandwidth at 0.25; that is narrower than usual, but it is appropriate given my substantive interest in timing labor force changes relative to the Great Recession and subsequent recovery (such as it is).

General economic conditions are a special concern for this chapter. Three recessions have disrupted the labor market since 1989, according to the National Bureau of Economic Research Business Cycle Dating Committee[1]: from July 1990 to March 1991, from March 2001 to November 2001, and from December 2007 to June 2009 (the Great Recession). All charts in this chapter highlight recession months with added gray shading.

The other principal independent variables are gender, race, Hispanic origin, and education. The key dependent variables are "gainful activity" scored 1 if the person was employed, enrolled in school or college, or serving in the military, and 0 otherwise for all persons; employed scored 1 if the person was employed and 0 otherwise for persons not in school or college or the military; underemployed scored 1 for persons working part-time for economic reasons and 0 otherwise among employed persons. Means on all variables (for all years combined) are in Table 1.1.

GAINFUL ACTIVITY: EMPLOYMENT, EDUCATION, AND MILITARY SERVICE

Young adults who are still enrolled in school, pursuing a college degree, serving in the military, or working for pay are moving toward a successful transition to adulthood. My analysis begins with a summary measure that considers the percentage of people engaged in any of those positive activities by month, single year of age, and gender between January 1989 and the

Table 1.1 Means and Standard Deviations of Activity
Indicators and Their Predictors by Gender: Persons 18–24
Years Old, United States, 1989–2014

Variable	All	Men	Women
Gainful activities			
School or college	0.385	0.373	0.398
	(0.487)	(0.484)	(0.489)
Army	0.0005	0.0009	0.0001
	(0.023)	(0.030)	(0.012)
Employed	0.623	0.650	0.597
	(0.485)	(0.477)	(0.490)
Any gainful activity	0.822	0.852	0.793
	(0.382)	(0.355)	(0.405)
Race–ethnicity (%)			
African American	15	14	16
Hispanic	16	17	15
White (non-Hispanic)	64	64	64
Other	5	5	5
Education (%)			
No credentials	20	22	18
High school diploma	33	34	31
Some college	38	36	41
College degree	9	7	10

Note: Numbers in parentheses are standard deviations. Percentages
were rounded independently, so they may not sum to 100 percent.
Age is also an important predictor; the age distribution is nearly flat
within the 18–24 year range (that is, each percentage is very close to
one-seventh or 14.3 percent).
Source: Author's calculations from Flood et al. (2015).

most recent data. Summer months are substantially different from the other
9 months of the year because school is out of session in the summer. The
main trends are easier to see when the summer months and other months
are separated than when the summer dips are part of a single line, so I show
the summer data separated from the other months.

I contrast gainful activity with the employment of young people who are
neither enrolled in school or college nor enlisted in the military. For consist-
ency I show summer months and the rest of the year as separate trends in
employment, too, even though the seasonal fluctuations in employment are
much narrower than the seasonal fluctuations in enrollment.

Figure 1.1 shows the results. Men's and women's activities were quite
different from each other, so I discuss each gender separately.

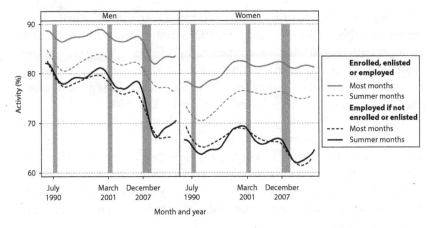

Figure 1.1 Percentage Enrolled in Education, Enlisted in the Military, or
Employed and Percentage Employed if Not Enrolled or Enlisted by Season and
Gender: Household Residents, 18–24 Years Old

Notes: Vertical gray lines indicate recessions, as determined by the National Bureau of
Economic Research. Data smoothed by locally estimated regression. The household-resident
population excludes people living in group quarters, including prisons, dormitories, and
military barracks.

Source: Author's calculations from Flood et al. 2015.

The vast majority of young men engaged in gainful activity; the rate fluc-
tuated between 77 and 89 percent throughout the quarter-century covered in
Figure 1.1. Gainful activity slumped by a couple of percentage points during
and after the 1990 recession (more so in summer), rebounded through the
1990s, dipped again during and after the 2001 recession, recovered some
of the loss during the 2000s, and then fell dramatically during the Great
Recession. Recovery from 2011 through 2014 was steady but recouped only
half of the recession-related loss.

The economic conditions during this quarter-century affected young men's
employment even more than their overall gainful activity. The dip in young
men's employment was deeper in each recession than was the dip in men's
gainful activity. The net effect of the three recessions was to drive the employment rate among young men who were neither students nor soldiers down
from 82 percent to 70 percent in the most recent data. To say the same thing
in a more dramatic way: in the winter of 1989, 18 percent of young men who
were not in school or the army were also not employed; at the bottom of the
Great Recession in 2010, 33 percent of young men who were not in school or
the army were also not employed. Post-recession recovery has reduced that to
30 percent in the most recent data (March 2014), a share substantially worse
than the 18 percent of January 1989 and the 19 percent of fall 2000.

Young women's activities were different. Their gainful activities were much less affected by economic conditions and probably reflect domestic gender relations and what was happening in colleges and universities more than what was going on in the job market. Gainful activity among women rose about 5 percentage points from 78 to 83 percent during the decade of the 1990s. It has not changed significantly since late 1999.

Young women's employment dropped during recessions and recovered some but not all in between. The peak employment among young women was in late 1999—just as it was for 25- to 54-year-old women (Hout and Cumberworth 2015). It did not fully recover from the 2001 recession before falling sharply during the Great Recession. Young women's employment increased from 62 percent after the end of the recession to 65 percent in the most recent data.

Employment patterns vary more sharply with age and time once we separate the single year of age—note that the vertical range of the data in Figure 1.2 is 50 percentage points compared to just 30 percentage points in Figure 1.1.

The trends affecting all young men and women were more pronounced among the 18-year-olds than among the 24-years-olds, as shown in Figure 1.2.

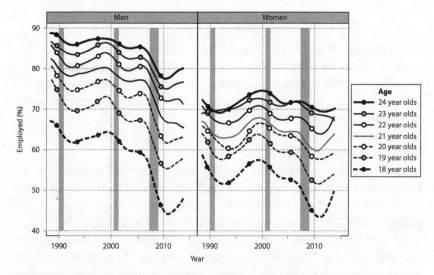

Figure 1.2 Percentage Employed by Time, Age, and Gender: Household Residents, 18–24 Years Old, Not Enrolled in School or College, and Not in the Military

Notes: Vertical gray lines indicate recessions, as determined by the National Bureau of Economic Research. Data smoothed by locally estimated regression. The household-resident population excludes people living in group quarters, including prisons, dormitories, and military barracks.

Source: Author's calculations from Flood et al. 2015.

Sixty-seven percent of 18-year-old men were employed in January 1989. That fell to 61 percent by the time the 1991 recession was over, got back to 64 percent before the 2001 recession, failed to recover any during the early 2000s, fell to 44 percent during the Great Recession, and rose 4 points to 48 percent in the most recent data. The net fall from 1989 to the end of the Great Recession was 23 percentage points.

Other young men experienced similar ups and downs in their employment prospects as the economy fell and recovered, but their net changes from peak to trough were less at each successive age. Among 19-year-olds, the net change from January 1989 to the low point after the Great Recession was 22 percentage points; among 20-year-olds, it was 19 percentage points; among 21-year-olds, it was 17 percentage points; among 22-year-olds, it was 14 percentage points; among 23-year-olds, it was 12 percentage points; among 24-year-olds, it was 11 percentage points.

Economic fluctuations also tempered with age among the young women, as shown in the right-hand panel of Figure 1.2. The over-time variation in employment was significantly less for the women than the men at each age, but the fluctuations were greatest for the 18-year-olds and least for the 24-year-olds, just as among the men. For women the peak was 1999, not 1989, as the historic rise of women's employment at all ages continued up to that point.

The 18-year-olds who are neither enrolled nor enlisted are a much more select subset of all men and women of a cohort than is true by age 24. At 18 years old we are looking at a slice of the cohort that is less educated and more likely to be either African American or Hispanic. So we cannot say from this evidence alone whether it is age, race, or lack of education that exposes 18-year-olds to stronger effects of economic conditions. For that, we further condition the data—first on race and ethnicity and then on education.

EMPLOYMENT TRENDS BY RACE AND EDUCATION

Racial disparities in either educational attainment or employment can make the age profiles of men's and women's employment in any given year differ by race and ethnic group. Because whites and Asians enroll in college at higher rates, they are a higher percentage of the students over 20 years old and, consequently, a smaller percentage of the population we are looking at here—people who are neither students nor soldiers. That might distort the age patterns in Figure 1.2. If the youngest blacks or Hispanics face larger or smaller barriers in employment than older people of the same group, then those differences could compound any statistical bias lurking in Figure 1.2.

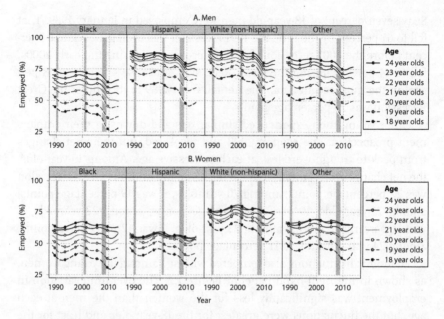

Figure 1.3 Percentage Employed by Time, Age, Race-Ethnicity, and Gender: Persons 18–24 Years Old, Residing in a Household, Not Enrolled in School or College, and Not in the Military

Notes: Vertical gray lines indicate recessions, as determined by the National Bureau of Economic Research. Data smoothed by locally estimated regression. The household-resident population excludes people living in group quarters, including prisons, dormitories, and military barracks.

Source: Author's calculations from Flood et al. 2015.

To gauge the relevance of this combination of biasing factors, Figure 1.3 presents data for four racial and ethnic groups. The CPS follows the standard procedures of the US Census Bureau, so race and Hispanic origin are separate questions; in addition, after 2000, people could name any number of races in answer to the race question. So I had to make decisions about how to classify people who gave more than one answer. The "black/ African American" category includes anyone who claimed black race alone or in mixture, regardless of how they answered the Hispanic-origin question. "Hispanic" includes people who answered the Hispanic origin question affirmatively, provided they did not say they were black on the race question. "White" includes people who gave white as their only answer on the race question, provided that they said they were not of Hispanic origin. "Other" is anyone not classified as black, Hispanic, or non-Hispanic white; most are Asians, but the category also includes Native Americans, Pacific Islanders, and Alaskan natives.

Even in a survey as large as the CPS, the "other" category is quite small; trends combine real change and sampling variability more for this residual group than for the three larger ones. Sampling variability became a problem when I applied the nonparametric smoother to the trends, so I used a nonparametric–parametric hybrid. I regressed employment status on the nonparametrically smoothed data from Figure 1.2 by age, gender, and race–ethnicity, including an interaction term for differences in age- and gender-specific trends (captured in the Figure 1.2 data) by race–ethnicity. The expected values from the hybrid smoothing model are shown in Figure 1.3.

Separating the data by race–ethnicity reveals substantially more variation in employment by age than was visible in Figure 1.2 (the range of age-, gender-, and race-specific employment rates in Figure 1.3 is 75 percentage points compared with 45 percentage points in Figure 1.2). The youngest black men and women had employment rates following the Great Recession that were between 25 and 30 percent, far below the minimum of 45 percent obtained when we failed to take account of racial–ethnic variation.

Among men, blacks had the lowest rate of employment at each age and in each year, ranging from 15 to 24 percentage points lower than the employment rate of whites of the same age in a given year. Less than half of the black men under 20 years old who were neither enrolled nor enlisted were working in any but the first year. At the bottom of the Great Recession only one-fourth of 18-year-old black men were employed; only one-third of the 19-year-olds were. The employment rates of white male 18- and 19-year-olds were just about double the ones for blacks during the recession—one-half and two-thirds, respectively.

Whites' rate of decline in employment from 2001 to 2011 was about 8 percent steeper than the overall rate of decline[2]; the decline for the other groups was not as steep as the overall rate.[3]

Employment rates were uniformly lower among young women than among men in all four racial–ethnic groups, and the change over time was much less. White women were more likely to be employed than were women in the other three groups. Among the youngest women, blacks were least likely to be employed; among women 22 and older, it was Hispanic women who had the lowest employment. Black women's employment rose most sharply with age; age differences were also substantial among "other" women. Age was less of a factor for Hispanic and white women. Thus, the lowest employment was among black women at the youngest ages and among Hispanic women after age 22.

Education affects employment and mediates some of the effects of race–ethnicity and age on employment prospects. Figure 1.4 summarizes the results. I classified education according to credentials: none, high school diploma, some college, and college degree. The data contain information on

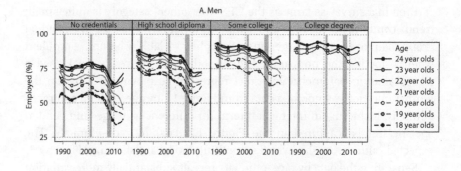

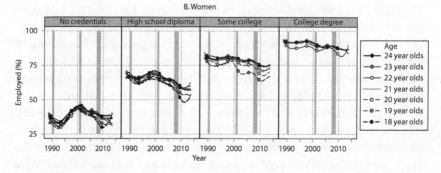

Figure 1.4 Percentage Employed by Time, Age, Education, and Gender: Persons 18–24 Years Old, Residing in a Household, Not Enrolled in School or College, and Not in the Military

Notes: Vertical gray lines indicate recessions, as determined by the National Bureau of Economic Research. Data smoothed by locally estimated regression. The household-resident population excludes people living in group quarters, including prisons, dormitories, and military barracks.

Source: Author's calculations from Flood et al. 2015.

advanced degrees as well, but I will not be analyzing the most educated because the sample is restricted to people less than 25 years old—too young a cutoff to reveal much about the advantages of advanced degrees. We do not observe college graduates younger than 22 years or 18-year-olds with some college either.

Young people's employment prospects rose sharply with education, not surprisingly (Hout 2012). Among 24-year-old men, the rate of employment before the Great Recession was 74 percent among men with no credentials, 82 percent among high school graduates, 88 percent among men with some college, and 91 percent among college graduates. By the beginning of 2011, those rates had all fallen due to the Great Recession, but they had fallen much less for the college graduates. Employment among 24-year-old men in January 2011 was 64 percent for men with no credentials, 72 percent for men with a high school diploma, 82 percent for men with some college, and 89 percent for college graduates; employment declined 10 percentage points for men with no credentials or a high school diploma, 6 percentage points for men with some college, and only 2 percentage points for college graduates.

Employment prospects for younger, less educated men were even more dire. Before the Great Recession, only 50 percent of 18-year-olds with no diploma were employed; similarly, only 61 percent of 18-year-olds with a high school diploma were employed. After the recession, in January 2011, just 34 percent of the men with no diploma and 49 percent of those with a high school diploma were employed. Said another way, after the recession, the employment prospects of 18-year-old men with a high school diploma were on a par with the prospects of men without credentials before the recession; meanwhile, almost two-thirds of uncredentialed 18-year-olds were out of work.

Young women's employment prospects were even more closely tied to their education than young men's were. Strikingly, very little of the age differences in women's employment appear within educational categories; schooling differences explain women's age differences. At the peak of women's employment in 1999 and 2000, 44 percent of women with no credentials were employed, as were 69 percent of women with high school diplomas, 80 percent of women with some college, and 85 percent of women with college degrees. After the Great Recession, all of those percentages were lower: 36 percent among women with no credentials, 59 percent for high school graduates, 72 percent for women with some college, and 80 percent for college graduates; the declines were 8, 10, 8, and 5 percentage points, respectively. As with men, higher education protected most women from the worst consequences of the Great Recession.

QUALITY OF EMPLOYMENT BY EDUCATION

We also care about the quality of employment. Many of the jobs lost during the Great Recession were being done by educated men and women. But when the educated workers got laid off, the less educated young people suddenly found themselves competing with more educated job seekers. Thus, some of the increasing educational differential in employment was attributable to educated workers moving from more to less demanding occupations, while the less educated encountered more obstacles to finding any work.

To explore these kinds of dynamics in these static data, I classified occupations according to their pay and hours. According to the definition I adopt here, a job has "decent" pay if most people employed in that occupation earned more than the lowest quartile of full-time, full-year workers in the whole labor force. The job has "decent" hours if the worker being interviewed was working full-time or, if she or he was working part-time, reported that the reason for part-time work was something other than economic conditions at work. Figure 1.5 shows the results by education for young people who were employed at the time of the survey.

Education paid off in quality of employment for both men and women. About half of the 23- and 24-year-old men with no credentials but a job had a job with decent pay and hours compared to 70 percent of the young men with high school diplomas or some college, and over 80 percent of men with college degrees. The long-term trend after 2001 was downward for all education groups, slightly more so for the least educated. But the long-term trend and the recession effects on quality of employment among the employed were definitely weaker than those trends on overall employment.

Young women's employment quality declined, especially after 2001, in all four education groups. The declines were substantial, averaging 12 percentage points in a 15-year period.

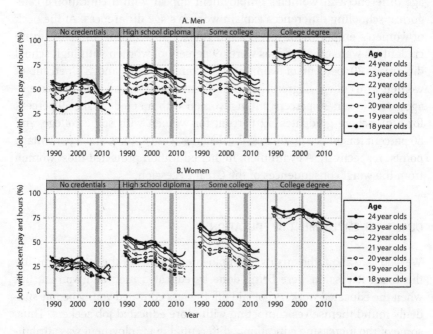

Figure 1.5 Percentage Employed in a Job with Decent Pay and Hours by Education, Age, and Gender: Persons 18–24 Years Old, Residing in a Household and Employed in the Civilian Labor Force

Notes: Vertical gray lines indicate recessions, as determined by the National Bureau of Economic Research. Data smoothed by locally estimated regression. The household-resident population excludes people living in group quarters, including prisons, dormitories, and military barracks.

Source: Author's calculations from Flood et al. 2015.

DISCUSSION

Young Americans' employment outcomes during and after the Great Recession reflected their youth, their gender, their race, their credentials, and, of course, the hard times. Each factor mattered, but education stood out as the key. College graduates had less unemployment and better jobs than other 22- to 24-years-olds. People with some college did better than high school graduates. Young people who had no credentials, disadvantaged in good times, were even more affected by the Great Recession than others.

The question remains whether the differences by education arose because what happens in educational institutions really enhances labor market success or because young people select how much education to pursue. That is, those who expect to benefit from education keep going while those who see no advantage to it leave school without credentials. Observational studies like this one can verify that differences are worth figuring out, but they lack information that might separate a real effect from self-selection. Studies that were carefully designed to remove the self-selection effects repeatedly obtained estimates of the effect of education *larger* than comparable estimates from observational studies (see Hout 2012 for a review). Most of the studies I am referring to analyze annual incomes, so it is hard to say if the educational payoff comes in the form of fuller employment, higher wages, or a combination of the two. The first studies used natural experiments and instrumental variables that focused on earning a high school diploma (Card 1999); more recent studies have looked at entering college or earning a degree (Hout 2012). A number of mechanisms for producing these surprising findings are under consideration, including "underplacement" (Bowen, Chingos, and McPherson 2009)—a tendency for first-generation students to weight features such as distance from home more highly than graduation potential when given a choice between colleges. Scholars have not yet reached consensus on why estimates adjusted for selection are higher rather than lower, but the finding itself appears to be robust.

For individuals, the implication of these findings is clear: pursue as much education as you can. At the very least, more education makes young people more attractive to employers. The preponderance of evidence indicates that they are likely to be more productive. With some caveats, the findings also imply that federal and state governments should help students, schools, colleges, and universities make bigger investments in secondary and higher education.

Recommending more investment in education is easy. Getting specific about what government should do in education is much harder. Reduce the cost of tuition seems like a straightforward enough recommendation. The Obama administration had a version of that, working through community colleges. Governors, candidates for governor, and at least one presidential candidate in 2016 touted free college tuition in their speeches. In Wisconsin and North Carolina the governors capped tuition even as they cut subsidies. Overall states support public higher education much less than they did 10 years ago (Eaton et al. 2017). But there is next to no evidence that tuition is the problem. Enrollments continued to rise as tuition soared over the last 20 years; applications for admission rose even faster than enrollments.

Academic drift, in high school and college, is probably a more serious impediment to academic progress and productivity (Arum and Roksa 2011; Armstrong and Hamilton 2013). Accountability based in broad indicators could potentially reduce drift, but the wrong measures can do more harm than good (Sullivan et al. 2012). If the measure is the graduation rate, faculty might make courses easier to reach a target. Community colleges are a portal for entry for those most likely to drop out of 4-year colleges. They are also far more affordable. Students who enter higher education through community colleges face an uphill struggle though. Their graduation rates are significantly lower than graduation rates among students with comparable high school grades and test scores who start college at a 4-year institution (Voss, Hout, and George 2017). That gap is half as big as it was 30 years ago, but it is still very important (Voss, Hout, and George 2017).

Secondary education offers few positive models of successful reform. The nation has been "reforming" high schools for at least 40 years. Accountability has yielded more anxiety than results. No Child Left Behind raised scores on the tests that were mandated to implement the law but did not improve scores on other tests, leading to charges of "teaching to the test" (Hout and Elliott 2010). Easy battles—if there were any—have been won. Communities of all kinds resist change (Sánchez-Jankowski 2008, chap. 11).

And suppose we got "college for all"—degrees, not just enrollment. Could the labor force take the infusion? In a list of social problems, real and imagined, too many college graduates would rank as a good one to have. But the United States is nowhere near a college-for-all labor force. By my calculation, 37 percent of the current civilian labor force has a college degree or higher.[4] Those with a college degree are far more likely than those with less education to be employed, have sufficient hours, and work in an occupation that pays most workers above the median.[5]

The dignity of livable wages fuels the nostalgia in everything from *Mad Men* to the Trump campaign. Values and reputation depend on working on the job and at home, maintaining the property and property values (Kefalas 2003). When work disappears, the moral order can flip (Sherman 2009). The after-work beer stops being a release and becomes a crutch and a threat to the family. The drinking man's reputation sinks from a sign of liveliness and fun to a barrier and handicap when seeking the next job.

Rising inequality in the United States has raised the economic stakes in good times and bad. While more jobs fall short of a living wage, jobs at the high end offer affluence. This trend started a generation ago. The first wave were young people displaced in the recession of 1974.[6] They have gone through their entire working lives with a "scar" of unemployment (Gangl 2006). The 18- to 24-year-olds in 1974 are 59–65 years old now, at or near retirement age. In 2014, 39 percent of the men and 50 percent of the women from that cohort were not in the labor force. The persistent hammer of inequality has affected their whole working lives. Today's 18- to 24-year-olds face similar struggles unless wages equalize.

NOTES

1. "US Business Cycle Expansions and Contractions," National Bureau of Economic Research, http://www.nber.org/cycles.html. Published 20 September 2010.

2. That is, the slope for the previous smoothed values in the regression model was estimated to be 1.078 with a standard error of 0.001.

3. The slopes for the interaction effects of smoothed values by race were –0.178 for blacks, –0.170 for Hispanics, and –0.195 for others; their standard errors were 0.003, 0.002, and 0.004, respectively.

4. Based on the 2014 annual socioeconomic supplement to the CPS (Flood et al. 2015), restricting the sample to persons 25–80 years old who were in the labor force at the time of the survey.

5. See Hout (2012) for similar calculations from before the Great Recession.

6. The National Bureau of Economic Research dates for that recession are November 1973 through March 1975.

REFERENCES

Armstrong, Elizabeth A., and Laura T. Hamilton. *Paying for the Party: How College Maintains Inequality*. Cambridge, MA: Harvard University Press, 2013.

Arum, Richard, and Josipa Roksa. *Academically Adrift*. Chicago: University of Chicago Press, 2011.

Bowen, William G., Matthew M. Chingos, and Michael S. McPherson. *Crossing the Finish Line: Completing College at America's Public Universities*. Princeton, NJ: Princeton University Press, 2009.

Card, David. "The Causal Effect of Education on Earnings." In *Handbook of Labor Economics*, vol. 3, part A, edited by Orley C. Ashenfelter and David Card, 1801–1963. Amsterdam: Elsevier, 1999.

Cleveland, William S. *The Elements of Graphing Data*. Summit, NJ: Hobart Press, 1994.

Eaton, Charlie, Sheisha Kulkarni, Robert Birgeneau, Henry E. Brady, and Michael Hout. "Affording the Dream: Student Debt and State Need-Based Grant Aid for

Public University Students." Working Paper 4.17, Center for the Study of Higher Education, Berkeley, CA, 2017.

Flood, Sarah, Miriam King, Steven Ruggles, and J. Robert Warren. "Integrated Public Use Microdata Series, Current Population Survey." Version 4.0. Minneapolis: University of Minnesota, 2015. https://www.ipums.org/doi/D030. V4.0.shtml.

Freeman, Richard B., and Harry J. Holzer, eds. 1986. *The Black Youth Employment Crisis*. Chicago: University of Chicago Press.

Gangl, Markus. "Scar Effects of Unemployment: An Assessment of Institutional Complementarities." *American Sociological Review* 71 (2006): 986–1013.

Hout, Michael. "Social and Economic Returns to Higher Education in the United States." *Annual Review of Sociology* 38 (2012): 379–400.

Hout, Michael, and Erin Cumberworth. "Labor Markets." Special issue, *Pathways* (2015): 10–15. http://web.stanford.edu/group/scspi/sotu/SOTU_2015.pdf.

Hout, Michael, and Stuart Elliot, eds. *Incentives and Test-Based Accountability in Education*. Washington, DC: National Academies Press, 2010.

Kefalas, Maria. *Working-Class Heroes: Protecting Home, Community, and Nation in a Chicago Neighborhood*. Berkeley: University of California Press, 2003.

Pettit, Becky. *Invisible Men: Mass Incarceration and the Myth of Black Progress*. New York: Russell Sage Foundation, 2012.

Sánchez-Jankowski, Martín. *Cracks in the Pavement*. Berkeley: University of California Press, 2008.

Sherman, Jennifer. *Those Who Work, Those Who Don't: Poverty, Morality, and Family in Rural America*. Minneapolis: University of Minnesota Press, 2009.

Sullivan, Theresa A., Christopher Mackie, William F. Massy, and Esha Sinha, eds. *Improving Measurement of Productivity in Higher Education*. Washington, DC: National Academies Press, 2012.

Voss, Kim, Michael Hout, and Kristin George. "College Dropout in the United States, 1980–2010: Persistent Problems and Inequalities." Working paper, Department of Sociology, University of California, Berkeley, 2017.

Western, Bruce, and Katherine Beckett. "How Unregulated Is the U.S. Labor Market? The Penal System as a Labor Market Institution." *American Journal of Sociology* 104 (1999): 1030–60.

2

Precarious Work and Young Workers in the United States

Arne L. Kalleberg

Young people in the United States are facing great challenges in the labor market today. Finding jobs that meet their needs, values, and expectations is difficult, even for those who have college degrees. The most commonly studied aspect of this problem, youth unemployment, is a significant hurdle. But perhaps a larger challenge is to enhance the *quality* of jobs that young people have. The jobs generally available to young workers are often low-wage, do not lead to career opportunities, and frequently result in workers being underemployed or overqualified. These challenges have contributed to career stagnation and problems for young workers as they seek to develop a career narrative that would help guide their futures.

The difficulties that youth are now experiencing with regard to low-quality jobs reflect the broader rise in polarized and precarious work in the United States and in a number of other industrial countries. There has been a growing polarization of jobs into good, well-paying, and high-quality jobs and bad, low-wage, relatively dead-end jobs. In addition, there has been a general increase in the uncertainty and insecurity associated with all jobs, most notably temporary and involuntary part-time work but also jobs that were formerly relatively permanent and part of job ladders that facilitated wage growth and training opportunities. Young people have borne the brunt of this expansion of low-quality and precarious work.

This chapter provides an overview of how the growth of precarious work and the polarization of the US labor market have produced major problems for the employment experiences of young workers (generally defined as those aged 16–24). It is divided into three parts: (1) a brief summary of the emergence of precarious work in the past three decades and how this has resulted in greater uncertainty of employment, as well as the polarization of the labor market into good and bad jobs; (2) a discussion of recent trends in the quantity and quality of jobs that are available to young

workers in the United States and how they impact youth according to social factors such as class and race; and (3) a discussion of possible policies
that might alleviate the employment difficulties facing young workers in
the United States.

THE CHANGING LANDSCAPE OF WORK

The growth of precarious work characterizes all advanced post-industrial societies. By "precarious work" I refer to the *uncertainty, instability, and insecurity of work* in which *employees bear the risks* of work (as opposed to businesses
or the government) and *receive limited social benefits and statutory entitlements*
(e.g., Kalleberg 2011). Examples of precarious work include "nonstandard
employment relations" such as temporary and contract work in the formal
economy. Such nonstandard employment relations represent a shift from
the normative forms of employment during the three decades after World
War II, which were embodied in the notion of a "standard employment relationship" that featured open-ended contracts and the exchange of security
and training for commitment and loyalty.

The rise of precarious work was rooted in employers' strategies to reduce their costs and increase their workforce flexibility in response to
growing competitive pressures associated with the internationalization of
the economy and rapid technological changes. Macrostructural changes
in political, social, and economic institutions and structures constitute
the basic drivers that have shaped the organization of work in the United
States since the mid-1970s and thereby largely account for the growth of
polarized and precarious employment systems during this period. Forces
such as the globalization of production, technological change, and the
continued rise of the service sector—combined with political decisions
to deregulate markets and to reduce enforcement of market standards—
weakened unions and the collective power of workers and strengthened
the control of employers, who consequently had relatively free rein to
restructure employment relations. These changes represent long-term
structural transformations in employment relations rather than being
simply reflections of short-term business cycles. These social, economic,
and political forces have affected all high-income countries; but the relatively weak labor market institutions and welfare protections characteristic of the United States heightened their impacts on employment
systems in this country.

These macrostructural changes continue to affect the nature of work in
the present. Their effects were exacerbated by the Great Recession (December
2007–June 2009), which created the greatest economic upheaval in the

United States since the Great Depression of the 1930s. The economic dislocations associated with the Great Recession have undoubtedly interacted with and intensified several preexisting trends in the US economy, some of which may have been masked by the dot.com and housing bubbles. Thus, some important consequences often associated with the Great Recession may well have their roots in the events beginning in the United States in the mid-1970s discussed above.

The transformation of work—coupled with the Great Recession—has had a profound and disproportionate impact on young workers entering the labor market in recent years. Young workers are particularly vulnerable to adverse labor market conditions, and the Great Recession further reduced the employment and career opportunities for young workers in the United States as well as in those European countries whose economies were relatively weak.

YOUNG WORKERS AND THE QUANTITY AND QUALITY OF WORK

A prominent indicator of young workers' difficulties in the labor market has been the sharp increase in their unemployment rates since the Great Recession. Another, equally if not more severe, problem faced by young workers today is the relatively low quality of the jobs, that they are able to get. I discuss several of these concerns in this section, including youth unemployment; exclusion of young workers from the labor market and from education and training opportunities; inability to find jobs that utilize their education, training, and skills (i.e., underemployment or overeducation); and inability to obtain jobs that provide them with an opportunity to get a foothold in a career that would lead to progressively better jobs and thus be able to construct career narratives.

Youth Unemployment

Young workers have relatively high unemployment rates compared to other age groups. They generally lack the experience that employers are increasingly demanding given employers' reluctance to provide on-the-job training (Cappelli 2012). Youth also do not have the networks that more experienced workers have and, hence, are not aware of many job opportunities that are available or what kinds of work best suit them. Employers also have information problems as they cannot easily assess the productivity potential and trainability of the young applicants and so must rely on very imperfect signals such as education or race and ethnicity, which disadvantages particular subgroups of young people (Gebel 2015).

Figure 2.1 shows the trend in the percent unemployed for youth aged 15–24 from 1985 to 2013 for the United States and several other advanced post-industrial countries (based on data from the Organisation for Economic Co-operation and Development [OECD]).

Youth unemployment rose sharply in the United States and many other advanced countries during the Great Recession, increasing in the United States from 12.8 percent in 2008 to 18.4 percent in 2010, before falling to 15.6 percent in 2013. These figures are about twice as large as those for the rest of the US labor force and are considerably higher for black workers than non-Hispanic whites. In addition to having trouble finding jobs, young workers were more likely to have lost their jobs as they are often the first to be let go during layoffs. Those who are looking for a job for the first time, in particular, are likely to experience the full brunt of reduced wages and job opportunities. Moreover, there are large "scarring" effects of unemployment on earnings as the earnings for the average worker typically double over the first 10 years in the labor market due to productive job mobility and increasing experience. Studies based on past recessions in the United States show that beginning to work in a recession leads to reductions in earnings that last for at least 10 years (Kahn 2010; Kalleberg and von Wachter 2017).

These percentages for youth unemployment in the United States are fairly similar to the OECD average for the period shown in Figure 2.1, slightly lower than those for the United Kingdom, much lower than those for Spain, but quite a bit higher than the rates for Denmark, Germany, and Japan.

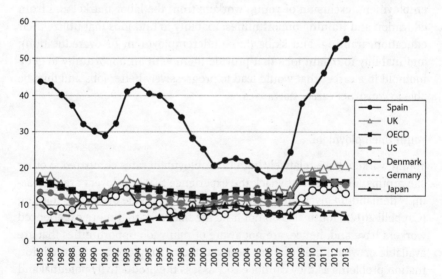

Figure 2.1 Percent Youth Unemployment (Ages 15–24), 1985–2013

Source: Organisation for Economic Co-operation and Development. https:// data.oecd.org/ unemp/youth-unemployment-rate.htm

Perhaps more striking than the percentage unemployed is the length of time young workers have been unemployed. In 2011, 30 percent of unemployed young workers (age 16–24) in the United States were jobless for more than 6 months compared with 7.3 percent in 2000 and 11.9 percent in 2007. In all cases, though, the percent of long-term unemployment among young workers was smaller than the percentages in other age groups, which is perhaps a reflection of the low quality of jobs that young workers are willing (or forced) to take (Mishel et al. 2012, table 5.7).

These overall unemployment figures underestimate somewhat the employment difficulties faced by young workers. The overall unemployment rate masks the very high rates of joblessness among racial minorities, those who have given up looking for a job, and those who are underemployed. Moreover, a considerable number of 20-year-olds are stuck in unpaid internships, and more than 10 million Americans under 25 cannot find full-time work (Steinberg 2013). Hence, they are unable to pay down their student loans and are often forced to move back with their parents.

Besides lower earnings, workers entering the labor market during a recession are more likely to have worse jobs and occupations and to experience lasting reductions in health and a change in attitudes. Bell and Blanchflower (2011), for example, show that there are negative effects on both wages and happiness from early childhood unemployment until at least age 50. In addition, Giuliano and Spilimbergo (2014) found that entering the labor market during a recessionary period during the formative years led affected individuals to believe that success in life depends more on luck than on effort, to support more government redistribution, and to be less confident in public institutions. The high long-term unemployment rates for younger workers, moreover, are likely to have lasting impacts on their earning power, opportunities for upward mobility, and difficulties in family formation, leading to concerns about a "lost generation" (e.g., Coy 2009).

Youth unemployment rates, however, provide only a partial picture of the difficulties young people in these countries have in obtaining a foothold in the labor market. Young people who cannot find jobs might decide not to continue to search for them but rather choose to stay in school or otherwise pursue training opportunities that delay their entry into the labor market until such time as they perceive that their chances of finding a suitable job have improved. The decision to forgo labor force entry might also reflect young peoples' decision to wait until a "good" job comes along rather than to take a job that they regard as a "bad" one. This is especially likely if parents are willing to subsidize their children living at home for an extended period of time, and there is little stigma attached to such arrangements.

Participation Rates

In addition to having difficulty finding jobs, young workers often find themselves excluded from both jobs and educational and training opportunities. The employment-to-population ratio (the ratio of employed workers in a particular age group to the population of that age) for those 16–19 and 20–24 years old has declined since the 1970s, while it has increased for workers aged 25–54 years, according to the Bureau of Labor Statistics (2015). This decline for young workers is concentrated among men, showing increases for women.[1]

A broader indicator of participation of young people in productive economic activity as well as a measure of the degree of exclusion of youth from the labor market and other major societal institutions is the NEET measure (i.e., persons who are not in employment, education, and training). According to OECD data (Organisation for Economic Co-operation and Development 2014), about 15 percent of youth in the United States were NEETs in 2012.[2] This includes 5.7 percent who are unemployed and 9.3 percent who are classified as inactive (which includes people who either are discouraged or do not desire to work for various reasons). The proportion of NEET young workers in the United States in 2012 was relatively high (the OECD average for 2012 was 12.6 percent), and the increase in NEETs from 2008 to 2012 in the United States was the highest among non–European Union nations in the OECD and was relatively high compared to other rich industrial countries (Fanjul 2014; Shah 2014). The NEET rates are especially high for young black adults, who were twice as likely as non-Hispanic whites to be in this category. Further, this trend appears to predate the recession as young Americans aged 20–24 were also less likely to be in school or jobs than older Americans in the late 1990s (Shah 2014).

NEETs are the most marginalized group of young people. Being detached or disconnected from both school and work is likely to harm both their current and future career prospects as they do not have the opportunity to develop their human capital at a very critical time in their lives. The relatively high NEET rate in the United States reflects in part the results of the economic downturn associated with the Great Recession as well as the relatively fewer (compared to Europe) educational and training opportunities available in the United States, which are due in part to the big cuts in state and local government education budgets in recent years (Gumbel 2012). Moreover, the United States has no real vocational training system, unlike most other industrial countries.

Youth Underemployment/Overqualification

The considerable increase in educational attainment of young Americans, coupled with the decline in middle-level jobs that has accompanied the polarization of the occupational structure, has led to a growing mismatch between young workers' educational attainments and the skill requirements of their jobs. This phenomenon has been called "overeducation" (e.g., Freeman 1976), "underemployment," "underutilization," "overqualification," and "mal-employment" (Kalleberg 2007; Fogg and Harrington 2011) and is most often applied to college graduates who work in "non-college-level" jobs. While this is not a new occurrence (for example, it was also fairly widespread in the United States in the early 1970s, during the Great Depression, as well as in other historical periods), it has re-emerged as a major concern of young workers today due largely to the tremendous increase in education coupled with the decline in middle-level jobs.

Figure 2.2, which is based on the analyses of data from the 2000, 2007, and 2010 Current Population Surveys (CPSs) by Fogg and Harrington (2011), shows that there was a sharp increase in the percentage of college graduates who worked in "non-college-level" jobs (i.e., jobs that do not require a college education to perform them) after the Great Recession: the overall proportion of college-educated workers who were overqualified increased from 25 percent in 2000 to 28 percent in 2010, with about half of the increase occurring between 2007 and 2010. The biggest increase in "mal-employment" occurred among the youngest college graduates (20–24), which grew from 29.8 percent in 2000 to 39.1 percent in 2010. More generally, James (2011) reports that 29 percent of 18- to 24-year-olds (compared to 16 percent of 25- to 34-year-olds) are underemployed, and these rates are much higher for African American and Latino youths.

Uncertainty about job outcomes is a barrier to enrollment in postsecondary education and contributes to the lack of alignment between

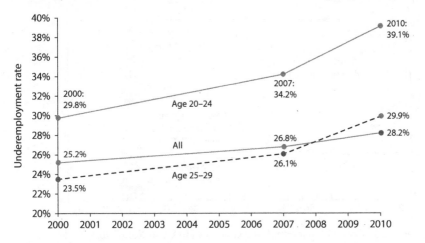

Figure 2.2 Underemployment of College Graduates, by Age, 2000–2010

Source: Mishel et al. 2012, figure 4AK, which is based on Fogg and Harrington 2011, table 1.

education and jobs that are available, according to a December 2013 survey by the Board of Governors of the Federal Reserve System (2014). This uncertainty has contributed to the fact that only 42 percent of young (aged 18–30) working survey respondents had a job that is closely related to their field of study. In this survey, 28 percent of working respondents said they were overqualified for their jobs, with persons who had an associate's or a bachelor's degree being the most likely to say that they were overqualified. In addition, the Pew Research Center (2012) reports that only 30 percent of young workers (here, aged 18–34) regard their current job as a "career" compared to 52 percent of workers aged 35 and older.

The results of a recent study by the New York Federal Reserve shed light on the quality of jobs obtained by college graduates (Abel, Deitz, and Su 2014; see also Thompson 2015). Using data from the census and CPS along with the O*Net, the authors found that the share of recent college graduates (aged 22–27 with a bachelor's degree or higher) who are employed in good non-college jobs (paying an average wage of $45,000 in 2012) has been declining since the recession of the early 2000s (and, more generally, since the early 1990s), while the share of recent college graduates in low-wage jobs (average wage below $25,000 in 2012) has been growing.[3] (See Figure 2.3). This study underscores that the major problem for young college graduates is perhaps not so much finding a job at all but rather obtaining one that utilizes their skills and abilities and pays fairly well.

The job prospects for young college graduates continue to be challenging: "Underemployment (the share of college grads in jobs that

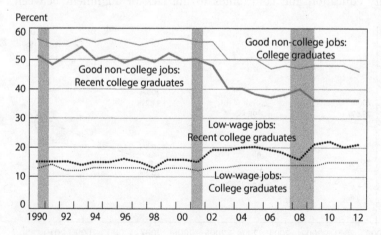

Figure 2.3 Share of Underemployed Graduates in Good Non-College and Low-Wage Jobs

Source: Abel, Deitz, and Su 2014.

historically do not require a college degree) is high. The quality of these first jobs is getting worse. And, for these reasons, wages are growing slowly, if at all" (Thompson 2015).

These challenges are illustrated by the Bureau of Labor Statistics' (2015, table 6) projections of the 15 occupations with the most job growth from 2014 to 2024. Only four of these typically require a bachelor's degree for entry (registered nurses; general and operations managers; accountants and auditors; and software developers, applications). Two others require only a postsecondary nondegree award (nursing assistants and medical assistants), one requires a high school diploma or equivalent (customer service representatives), while the rest require no formal educational credential at all (personal care aides, home health aides, food preparation and serving workers, retail salespersons, restaurant cooks, construction laborers, janitors and cleaners, and laborers). Assuming the continued pressure on youth to obtain higher educational credentials, the prospects for continued overqualification loom fairly large.

Youth in Nonstandard Work Arrangements

Young people have also had considerable difficulty in recent years in obtaining stable, full-time jobs that provide them with opportunities to receive training and promotions to better-paying jobs. For example, only 29 percent of young workers (defined as those aged 18–30) held a single, full-time job for the previous year, according to the 2013 study by the Board of Governors of the Federal Reserve System (2014). Workers aged 26–30 were more likely to have held a job for more than 2 years (66 percent) than younger workers. Moreover, Millennials (aged 18–34) change jobs more than other age groups, though this may be due alternatively to age, the business cycle, or generational differences (Allison and Mugglestone 2015). In addition, 39 percent said that they were dissatisfied with their jobs because of a lack of career advancement; workers with higher levels of education were more likely to characterize themselves as being in a career rather than just having a job.

Young workers (aged 16–24) are much more likely to work part-time than the other demographic groups, as shown in Figure 2.4, which is based on CPS data (and adjusted for the CPS's 1994 survey redesign).

The incidence of part-time work among young workers has been increasing considerably since the 1970s. Part-time work among young workers (and single men and women with less than a high school degree) tended to rise during recessions and grew sharply in the Great Recession. There are, of course, many reasons for the relatively high incidence of part-time work among young workers, notably the fact that some are also going to school.

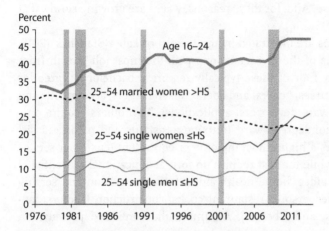

Part-time employment for selected groups

Figure 2.4 Part-Time Employment for Selected Groups

Notes: Percent of total employment for each group; gray bars show National Bureau of Economic Research recession dates.

Source: CPS data from Valletta and Bengali 2013.

But a key factor is also their inability to secure full-time work due to the lack of availability of such jobs for this age group.

Moreover, younger workers are more likely to work in temporary jobs (either as direct-hire temporaries or as agency temporaries) or as contract company workers. This is shown in Figure 2.5, which presents the proportion of temporary and contract workers for two age categories (18–24 and 25–54), based on data from the General Social Surveys in 2002, 2006, 2010, and 2014. Figure 2.5 shows that a higher proportion of workers aged 18–24 than those aged 25–54 worked in temporary or contract jobs, especially right after the Great Recession (in 2010).

Information on the incidence of nonstandard work arrangements among youth is provided by the CPS's February Contingent Worker Supplements (CWS), which collected data on "alternative work arrangements" (defined as consisting of temporary and contract workers, as well as independent contractors and on-call workers [i.e., workers who are called to work when needed by employers, such as substitute teachers]) in 1995, 1997, 1999, 2001, and 2005. The CPS conducted this survey again in 2017. However, Katz and Krueger (2016) conducted the RAND-Princeton Contingent Worker Survey, which included a version of the CWS, as part of the RAND American Life Panel in October and November 2015.

The probability of employed young (aged 16–24) workers being in an alternative work arrangement in 2015 (6.8 percent) was slightly less than

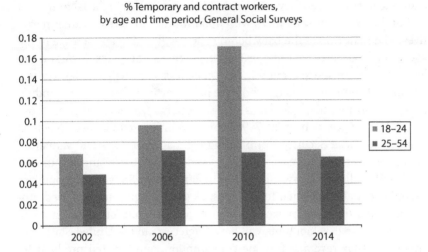

Figure 2.5 Percent of Temporary and Contract Workers, by Age and Time Period
Source: General Social Surveys (2002, 2006, 2010, 2014) (gss.norc.org).

the figure in 2005 (7.1 percent) and about the same as that in 1995 (6.7 percent) (Katz and Krueger 2016). Moreover, the percentages of young workers being in alternative work arrangements were considerably less than those in other age groups. The main reason for this is the relatively low percentage of young workers who were independent contractors, which is the largest type of alternative work arrangement.

The placement of young workers in temporary and contract jobs is a pattern found in most rich post-industrial economies; *The Economist* (2013), for example, estimates that more than a third of young employed workers in these countries on average have temporary jobs. A major reason for this in the United States is that employers are increasingly reluctant to form long-term relationships with younger workers as healthcare benefits become increasingly expensive, preferring rather to hire them as temporary workers (Schrager 2013). Such reluctance to hire young workers on open-ended, relatively permanent contracts is also the case in many countries in Europe where employment protections have made it difficult to fire older workers, thus not opening much space for younger workers to gain a foothold in the labor market (as in Spain and France).

CONFRONTING YOUTH EMPLOYMENT CONCERNS: POLICIES

The difficulties young workers have had in recent years in getting good jobs are likely to persist for at least the near future. Younger workers will continue to struggle as they seek to establish themselves in the labor market and find jobs that provide them with opportunities to develop career narratives. The maturing of the baby boom cohort will lead to an increase in the age of the labor force over the next several decades, especially if workers are less able to retire due to economic circumstances. A growth in older workers will impact younger workers, who have had a particularly hard time finding jobs—not to mention good jobs—in recessionary periods such as those in the Great Recession of 2007–9. Poor economic circumstances (such as inadequate Social Security, diminishing company pensions and vanishing 401[k] savings plans) have led older men and women to take and stay in jobs that would otherwise have gone to younger people. So, young people are more likely to be relegated to bad jobs, as well as being unemployed, underemployed (involuntary part-time), overqualified, and often discouraged workers. These developments will have huge costs to the United States, including lost tax revenue, forgone consumption, and lowered productivity due to the loss of human capital (O'Sullivan, Mugglestone, and Allison 2014), not to mention severe negative consequences for a possibly "lost generation" of young workers and their families.

The United States is not alone among rich industrial countries in having these problems associated with youth unemployment and underemployment. They too are seeking to develop policies that facilitate the integration of young workers into the labor market and enable them to acquire skills that will make them productive and happy workers. I will draw upon some of these lessons from abroad in identifying some of the key policy changes that are needed to address the employment difficulties faced by young workers. Effective policies need to recognize the basic reasons for the work-related problems of young Americans. My discussion has highlighted three main sources of difficulty: the paucity of demand for young workers; inadequate education and training opportunities; and the lack of good jobs for young workers, especially college graduates. I consider each in turn.

First, the Great Recession has exacerbated the higher unemployment rates typically characteristic of young people. In many ways, this is the most straightforward policy issue as it links directly to the ongoing efforts to boost demand and job creation that are being carried out to enhance the recovery from the Great Recession. Policies are also needed to focus specifically on young workers, such as expanding service opportunities (e.g., the Edward M. Kennedy Serve America Act) and implementing summer and year-round jobs programs for youth, especially low-income youth. Policies that invest in broad-based job creation (such as rebuilding infrastructure, enhancing funding to education), while not targeted specifically at youth, would still benefit them as the economy recovers from the Great Recession and the overall unemployment rate drops (Ayres and Dillon 2013).

Second, greater efforts are needed to provide young workers with more opportunities for education and training. Formal education is valuable for providing foundational skills and greater access to education (preschool, K–12, and postsecondary education) is needed for all persons. However, formal education is often not very useful for teaching workers the kinds of specific skills needed to perform particular jobs. Such training was usually provided in the past to workers on the job, but the growth of precarious and nonstandard work has made companies much more reluctant to invest in training since they are unable (or unwilling) to offer workers long-term employment commitments; for example, only 21 percent of young workers in large firms in the United States in 2011 reported receiving any company-provided training during the previous year (*Economist* 2013).

Germany is the model of a country with a well-functioning system of apprenticeship and vocational training and as a result has been fairly successful in keeping youth unemployment low (see Figure 2.1).[4] O'Reilly et al. (2015) identify a variety of additional programs designed to address the problem of youth unemployment, most of them associated with Europe 2020, a 10-year strategy proposed by the European Commission in 2010 to guide the economic advancement of the European Union. These include several "flagship initiatives" designed to enhance the quality of education and training as well as to promote the mobility of workers and the matching of young workers to jobs (see also Newman and Winston 2016).

There are some promising developments in the United States that are designed to strengthen the long-term employment prospects of youth by enhancing education and training opportunities and helping to facilitate the transition from school to work (e.g., Jacobs 2014). Eichhorst et al. (2015) review the literature on vocational training in industrial societies and conclude that vocational education and training are valid alternatives to general education and that apprenticeships are more effective when combined with institutional learning rather than when they are based in schools. Efforts to enhance apprenticeship programs in the United States, such as the American Apprenticeship Grants administered by the Department of Labor, seek to double the number of US apprenticeships by 2020. The current investment is not enough, however; and more federal government investment is needed as well as greater support by state and local governments and private industry (Hanks 2015).

Community colleges are another key source of education and training for youth. In the United States, nearly half of undergraduates (over 10 million students each year) are enrolled in the nation's 1,200 community colleges (Bailey, Smith Jaggars, and Jenkins 2015). Nevertheless, community colleges receive only 20 percent of federal higher education funding (Jacobs 2014). Investing in community colleges and designing curricula that provide "career pathways" represent proven, cost-effective ways to enhance students' labor market success.

The third, and perhaps most vexing, issue is the need to create more high-quality jobs for young workers, especially those who are college graduates. This is a difficult problem as it requires actions by employers, acting singly or in concert with each other and/or in private–public partnerships, to create job ladders by which workers can move from entry-level jobs to higher-level jobs. Creating job ladders is easier in some occupations than others, naturally, since some do not allow much room for advancement; this makes it even more essential that all jobs pay at least a living wage. Career-ladder programs are also more apt to be effective if they are part of a broader strategy to provide enhanced compensation and advancement opportunities for workers (Fitzgerald 2006). It is helpful for career-ladder programs to have a combination of public policy support (regulatory policies, in some cases mandatory ones), employer commitment to career ladders, and tight labor markets if they are to succeed in more than a token fashion. Training and education are needed to help people move from one rung to the next, and financial and other types of support are necessary to enable them to undergo the training. Establishing career ladders also requires that there are higher-level jobs to move to (e.g., nursing aides to licensed practical nurses, bank tellers to loan officers, clerical workers to information technology workers).

There are, of course, many ideological, social, political, and economic obstacles to implementing these kinds of policies in the United States. These include a neoliberal ideology that relies on the market to produce good jobs, an individualistic ethos that eschews collective solutions in favor of personal strategies, lack of confidence and trust in institutions such as the government and big business, political gridlock especially at the federal level, weak labor market institutions, and so on. Nevertheless, we cannot as a nation afford *not* to attempt to overcome these obstacles and to address in a serious way the employment problems associated with youth that I have outlined here.

CONCLUSION

Young people have always had relatively high unemployment rates as they sample the labor market in search of jobs that fit better their interests, preferences, and skills. Their diminished ability to move from this period of searching to find a more stable career path presents a particular challenge in the current age of precarious and polarized work. Young workers are increasingly forced to rely on their own devices to acquire the training and skills that will make them marketable in the rapidly changing structure of jobs and work. While the onus is now more than ever on their shoulders, we cannot assume that individuals are able to address these concerns by themselves; rather, these are public issues that require collective responses. Moreover, the difficulties faced by young workers are not temporary manifestations of economic cycles such as the Great Recession and its aftermath but reflect more basic structural transformations in the nature of employment relations that characterize post-industrial societies more generally. Addressing these issues requires concerted efforts on the part of the government, business, and labor.

NOTES

1. The proportion of the workforce that is 16–24 has declined over time, dropping from about 22 percent in 1970 to just over 12 percent in recent years (Valletta and Bengali 2013).

2. Over 40 percent of 18- to 24-year-olds are currently enrolled in educational institutions (Allison and Mugglestone 2015).

3. Younger workers (18–24) are most likely to work in the relatively low-paying leisure and hospitality or retail and wholesale sectors in every state (Allison and Mugglestone 2015).

4. See Euler (2013) for a discussion of the issues involved in exporting the German system of dual vocational training to other countries.

REFERENCES

Abel, Jaison R., Richard Deitz, and Yagin Su. "Are Recent College Graduates Finding Good Jobs?" *Federal Reserve Bank of New York Current Issues* 20, no. 1 (2014): 1–8.

Allison, Tom, and Konrad Mugglestone. "The Future of Millenial Jobs." (2015) http://younginvincibles.org/wp-content/uploads/2017/04/FUTURE-OF-MILLENNIAL-JOBS-1.20.2015-1.pdf. Accessed May 5, 2018.

Ayres, Sarah, and Molly Dillon. "Middle-Out for Millennials: Creating Jobs for Young People." Center for American Progress, November 4, 2013. https://www.americanprogress.org/issues/economy/reports/2013/11/04/78621/middle-out-for-millennials-2/. Accessed May 5, 2018.

Bailey, Thomas R., Shanna Smith Jaggars, and Davis Jenkins. *Redesigning America's Community Colleges: A Clearer Path to Student Success.* Cambridge, MA: Harvard University Press, 2015.

Bell, David N. F., and David G. Blanchflower. "Youth Unemployment in Europe and the United States." IZA Discussion Paper 5673, Bonn, Germany, 2011.

Board of Governors of the Federal Reserve System. *In the Shadow of the Great Recession: Experiences and Perspectives of Young Workers.* Washington, DC: Federal Reserve System, 2014. https://www.federalreserve.gov/econresdata/2013-experiences-and-perspectives-of-young-workers-201411.pdf. Accessed May 5, 2018.

Bureau of Labor Statistics. "Employment Projections—2014-24." US Department of Labor, 2015. https://www.bls.gov/news.release/archives/ecopro_12082015.htm. Accessed May 5, 2018.

Cappelli, Peter. *Why Good People Can't Get Jobs: The Skills Gap and What Companies Can Do About It.* Philadelphia: Wharton Digital Press, 2012.

Coy, Peter. "The Lost Generation." *BusinessWeek*, October 19, 2009, 33–35.

Economist. "Generation Jobless." April 27, 2013. http://www.economist.com/news/ international/21576657-around-world-almost-300m-15-24-year-olds-are-not-working-what-has-caused. Accessed September 27, 2015.

Eichhorst, Werner, Núria Rodríguez-Planas, Ricarda Schmidl, and Klaus F. Zimmerman. "A Road Map to Vocational Education and Training in Industrialized Countries." *ILR Review* 68, no. 2 (2015): 314–37.

Euler, Dieter. *Germany's Dual Vocational Training System: A Model for Other Countries?* Gütersloh, Germany: Bertelsmann Stiftung, 2013. https://www.bertelsmann-stiftung.de/fileadmin/files/BSt/Publikationen/GrauePublikationen/GP_ Germanys_dual_vocational_training_system.pdf. Accessed May 5, 2018.

Fanjul, Gonzalo. *Children of the Recession: The Impact of the Economic Crisis on Child Well-Being in Rich Countries.* Florence, Italy: United Nations Children's Fund (UNICEF) Office of Research—Innocenti, 2014. http://www.unicef-irc. org/publications/pdf/rc12-eng-web.pdf. Accessed September 27, 2015.

Fitzgerald, Joan. *Moving Up in the New Economy: Career Ladders for U.S. Workers.* Ithaca, NY: Cornell University Press, 2006.

Fogg, Neeta P., and Paul E. Harrington. "Rising Mal-Employment and the Great Recession: The Growing Disconnection Between Recent College Graduates and the College Labor Market." *Continuing Higher Education Review* 75 (2011): 51–65.

Freeman, Richard B. *The Overeducated American.* New York: Academic Press, 1976.

Gebel, Michael. "Labor Market Instability, Labor Market Entry, and Early Career Development." In *Emerging Trends in the Social and Behavioral Sciences*, edited by Robert Scott and Stephen Kosslyn. Wiley Online Library, 2015. https://doi.org/ 10.1002/9781118900772.etrds0198. Accessed May 5, 2018.

Giuliano, Paola, and Antonio Spilimbergo. "Growing Up in a Recession." *Review of Economic Studies* 81, no. 2 (2014): 787–817.

Gumbel, Peter. "Why the U.S. Has a Worse Youth Unemployment Problem than Europe." *Time*, November 5, 2012. http://business.time.com/2012/11/05/why-the-u-s-has-a-worse-youth-employment-problem-than-europe/. Accessed September 27, 2015.

Hanks, Angela. "American Apprenticeship and Beyond." Center for American Progress, September 9, 2015. https://www.americanprogress.org/issues/labor/ news/2015/09/09/120840/american-apprenticeship-and-beyond/. Accessed September 27, 2015.

Jacobs, Elisabeth. "Twelve Ways to Fix the Youth Unemployment Crisis." Governance Studies at Brookings, May 22, 2014. http://www.brookings. edu/research/papers/2014/05/22-youth-unemployment-crisis-workforce-- jacobs. Accessed September 27, 2015.

James, Matt. "Ideas to Get Young Americans Working." Next Generation, November 3, 2011. http://thenextgeneration.org/blog/post/ideas-to-get-young-americans-working. Accessed September 28, 2015.

Kahn, Lisa B. "The Long-Term Consequences of Graduating from College in a Bad Economy." *Labor Economics* 17, no. 2 (2010): 303–16.

Kalleberg, Arne L. *Good Jobs, Bad Jobs: The Rise of Polarized and Precarious Employment Systems in the United States, 1970s–2000s.* American Sociological Association Rose Series in Sociology. New York: Russell Sage Foundation, 2011.

———. *The Mismatched Worker.* New York: W.W. Norton, 2007.

Kalleberg, Arne L., and Till M. von Wachter. "The U.S. Labor Market During and After the Great Recession: Continuities and Transformations." *RSF Journal of the Social Sciences* 3, no. 3 (2017): 1–19.

Katz, Lawrence F., and Alan B. Krueger. "The Rise and Nature of Alternative Work Arrangements in the United States, 1995–2015." Working Paper 22667. National Bureau of Economic Research, Cambridge, MA, 2016. http://www.nber.org/papers/w22667. Accessed October 7, 2016.

Mishel, Lawrence, Josh Bivens, Elise Gould, and Heidi Shierholz. *The State of Working America*, 12th ed. Ithaca, NY: Cornell University Press, 2012.

Newman, Katherine S., and Hella Winston. *Reskilling America: Learning to Labor in the Twenty-First Century.* New York: Metropolitan Books, 2016.

O'Reilly, Jacqueline, Werner Eichhorst, András Gábos, Kari Hadjivassiliou, David Lain, Janine Leschke, Seamus McGuinness, Lucia Mýtna Kureková, Tiziana Nazio, Renate Ortlieb, Helen Russell, and Paola Villa. "Five Characteristics of Youth Unemployment in Europe: Flexibility, Education, Migration, Family Legacies, and EU Policy." *Sage Open* 5, no. 1 (2015): 1–19.

Organisation for Economic Co-operation and Development. "Youth Neither in Employment, Education nor Training (NEETs)." In *Society at a Glance, 2014: OECD Social Indicators.* Paris: OECD Publishing, 2014. http://dx.doi.org/10.1787/soc_glance-2014-14-en. Accessed September 29, 2015.

O'Sullivan, Rory, Konrad Mugglestone, and Tom Allison. "In This Together: The Hidden Cost of Young Adult Unemployment." Young Invincibles, January 2014. http://younginvincibles.org/wp-content/uploads/2014/01/In-This-Together-The-Hidden-Cost-of-Young-Adult-Unemployment.pdf. Accessed September 27, 2015.

Pew Research Center. "Young, Underemployed and Optimistic: Coming of Age, Slowly, in a Tough Economy." Pew Research Center, February 9, 2012. http://www.pewsocialtrends.org/2012/02/09/young-underemployed-and-optimistic. Accessed October 7, 2016.

Schrager, Allison. "Temporary and Part-Time Jobs Are Going to Kill the Global Economy." *Quartz*, May 10, 2013. http://qz.com/83073/temporary-and-part-time-jobs-are-going-to-kill-the-global-economy/. Accessed September 27, 2015.

Shah, Neil. "Among Rich Countries, America's Youth Took the Recession Especially Hard." *Wall Street Journal*, November 4, 2014. http://blogs.wsj.com/economics/2014/11/04/among-rich-countries-americas-youth-took-the-recession-especially-hard/. Accessed September 27, 2015.

Steinberg, Sarah Ayres. "America's 10 Million Unemployed Youth Spell Danger for Future Economic Growth." Center for American Progress, June 5, 2013. https://www.americanprogress.org/issues/economy/report/2013/06/05/65373/americas-10-million-unemployed-youth-spell-danger-for-future-economic-growth/. Accessed September 27, 2015.

Thompson, Derek. "The Economy Is Still Terrible for Young People." *Atlantic*, May 19, 2015. http://www.theatlantic.com/business/archive/2015/05/the-new-normal-for-young-workers/393560/. Accessed September 27, 2015.

Valletta, Rob, and Leila Bengali. "What's Behind the Increase in Part-Time Work?" *Federal Reserve Bank of San Francisco Economic Letter*, August 26, 2013. http://www.frbsf.org/economic-research/publications/economic-letter/2013/august/part-time-work-employment-increase-recession/. Accessed September 28, 2015.

Part II

PRIVILEGE AND DISADVANTAGE IN THE YOUTH LABOR MARKET

3

Take This Job and Love It?

The Millennial Work Ethic and the Politics of Getting Back to Work

*Jamie K. McCallum**

"You see this chair?" asks my personal tour guide at Facebook
   headquarters, pointing to a stray simple chair on their company's
   sprawling Menlo Park campus. "This is Mark's favorite chair because
   it's great for work *and* relaxing, so we bought a few hundred of them
   and put them everywhere." "This restaurant," she continues, "is
   Mark's favorite Mexican joint in Palo Alto, so he had them build one
   in here so we don't have to leave campus to eat there. Lots of people
   eat lots of meals here because we provide it free."
"Mark?" I ask.
"Zuckerberg," she says, half rolling her eyes. "This is Facebook."
The tour continues inside, where the office doors are labeled Sun
   Microsystems. Sun Microsystems was a Silicon Valley giant that drifted
   toward obscurity over a number of years and was eventually acquired by
   Oracle in 2009.
"I thought this was Facebook," I say.
I am then informed that Facebook headquarters is located in the old
   Sun building, and though it has largely completed an overhaul of the
   vestiges of the old, the doors were left as an enduring motivational
   symbol for Facebook employees. "Mark thought it would be a good
   idea to leave these doors on here, as a reminder of what happens
   when you don't work hard enough. You die. Your competitors kill
   you," she stated flatly.
"Who are Facebook's competitors," I ask?
"We don't have any competitors," she said. "But you never know."

* The author thanks Adriana Ortiz-Burnham, Sophie Vaughan, Daniel Schneider, and Ari
Grant-Sasson for their research assistance.

It is hard to argue with uncertainty in these uncertain times, but most data suggest that young coders and engineers at Facebook are not lacking in motivation. Nor are many young workers anywhere in the United States for that matter. A large body of research analyzes the structural transformation of the conditions of work for the Millennial generation including increased precarity, unstable scheduling, stagnated wages, and the rise of internships. But comparatively little scholarly attention has been paid to their work *ethic*. What there is, however, is a barrage of popular polemics characterizing young workers as lazy, slothful, indolent, and entitled.

My research suggests the opposite. Workers, especially young workers, have been socialized toward the work ethic in a way that impresses on them the importance of finding the inherent value of work, nearly regardless of the task, and of being committed to it, nearly regardless of the conditions. The popular myth of the lazy Millennial is unsupported by facts, figures, and ethnographic data. Below I examine the persistence of the myth of the lazy Millennial by evaluating the work ethic of young workers. I pay special attention to two industries that employ many young people, the technology sector of California and retail workers in major chain stores.

Below I critique the popular portrayal of Millennials as lazy. Next, I discuss post-2008 economic challenges and the divergent industrial contexts of Silicon Valley and formula retail stores to show why young workers endorse the work ethic as fervently as they do—even though slated, as a generation, to benefit less economically from their work than their predecessor generations. While much research focuses on the development or "rise" of the work ethic, as it corresponds to other historical phenomena, my research focuses on debates around its decline.

The findings are based on an in-depth assessment of policy-oriented white papers and scholarly research on youth unemployment, values, and work habits. In addition, I completed interviews with young coders, engineers, and marketers at major California-based technology firms (Facebook, Twitter, Dropbox, Apple, and Google, among others) and formula retail stores in Burlington, New York City, and San Francisco (Macy's, H&M, Banana Republic, Nike, and Uniqlo, among others). Finally, I consulted young worker advocacy groups such as the Retail Action Project in New York City and Young Workers United in San Francisco. I conclude by discussing policy proposals to alleviate the youth unemployment crisis.

A POOR WORK ETHIC IS NOT THE CAUSE OF YOUTH UNEMPLOYMENT

A dominant popular narrative argues that the Millennial generation is unemployable on the basis of its members' individual failings. For example, the *Boston Globe* lambasts unemployed youth as "trophy kids" and as "an amiable, tech-savvy, yet minimally employable crop of Americans who will ultimately need more subsidies than a dairy farmer" (Graham 2013). A prominent workplace consultant argues "millennials are not willing to make work the central focus of their lives as Baby Boomers have." A CBS poll asks what we can do to save the "narcissistic praise-hounds now taking over the office," suffering the impacts of "the coddling virus" and "safety diapers" compliments of their parents (Safer 2007). To critics of Millennial culture these millions of young people out of work are damning evidence of the decadence that eschews work in favor of the cushy entitlements their boomer parents worked hard for.

Nearly sixty percent of chief financial officers surveyed by Duke's School of Business say they are not targeting Millennials in their hiring process, in part because they are perceived as disloyal and have poor work skills (Phillips and Owens 2014). In fact, managing the allegedly odd work habits of Millennials seems at times even to be an issue of national security. Wikileaks cables show that the global security consultant Stratfor circulated information via email on how best to handle irksome young workers: "If your managers handle millennials the same way their bosses handled them [boomers, Xers], they'll fail. This new generation requires a new approach if you want to manage them better, make them more productive, and retain them longer than your competitors" (Wikileaks 2013). But these interrelated positions of laziness, uniqueness, and increased managerial burden do not hold up to scrutiny.

The Millennial generation is the only one in the country who does not cite "work ethic" as one of its "principal claims to distinctiveness," according to a Pew Research Center study (2010). Only 5 percent of respondents claimed a "work ethic" defined their generation, the same amount who also listed "clothes" as significant. Although reports such as this have added fuel to the claim that they are lazy and concerned mostly with cheap thrills, they are technically correct. Their commitments to work do not distinguish them from their predecessor generations.

Numerous popular press articles have discussed generational differences in work ethic, with some articles concluding that baby boomers endorse higher levels of work ethic than Millennials (Marikar 2013). Twenge et al. (2010), who are often cited in the press, characterize young workers as those who epitomize the "combination of not wanting to work hard but still wanting more money and status" (1134). Yet this characterization falsely defines an emphasis on leisure as sloth, a definition absent from the survey questions administered by the study: quite the contrary, the study defined this value as work–life balance and vacation time. Furthermore, according to their own results, it is the Generation X cohort that displays the greatest value placed on leisure (Twenge et al. 2010, 1135). Smola and Sutton concur that, in regard to work values, "As we have so often assumed, differences exist among the generations" (2002, 381).

However, in their recent article, Costanza and Finkelstein argue that "there is little solid empirical evidence supporting the existence of generationally based differences" (2015, 321). Older evidence supports this conclusion as well. At least one study concludes that Millennials are more committed to the work ethic than both of their generation predecessor groups, finding that Millennials demonstrated statistically higher valuations of "work for work's sake" and the "virtues of work" (Jobe 2014). Kowske, Rasch, and Wiley (2010) determined that, despite much popular focus about "job-hopping," Millennials exhibited a lower turnover retention rate than Generation Xers, with only a slightly higher rate of actual job turnover. This indicated that, despite employment structures that may cause higher turnover, " 'job-hopping' is not a generational trait" (Kowske et al. 2010, 275). The most comprehensive study to date has been done by Zabel et al. (2016), who analyzed 77 published studies that measured the work ethic and included "age" as a variable in order to develop a list of 105 distinct metrics of a "work ethic." The analysis found no differences in the work ethic of Millennials from boomers or Gen Xers.

The idea of a work ethic is difficult, though not impossible, to quantify. Most recent quantitative research finds that Millennials are not lazy, nor are their high rates of unemployment evidence of a cultural defect. Rather, they are not working because the economy is not either. To elucidate, in the first volume of *Capital*, Marx (1887) suggests capitalism demands more young workers relative to adults as it expands and transforms; this is especially the case during crisis moments.[1] However, contemporary dynamics seem to contradict this assessment as nations everywhere are being forced to extend their retirement ages so as to accommodate older workers. In the United States, according to the Bureau of Labor Statistics, the unemployment rate among people aged 16–24 is 9.6 percent, more than twice the unemployment rate for those of all ages. There are also nearly 1 million "missing" young workers who are neither employed nor actively seeking work and are thus not counted in the unemployment rate because job opportunities remain so scarce. Even without these additional workers, the number of young adults currently employed (54.8 percent) is the lowest percentage since 1948 (Mendelson 2013).

Some have argued that this is normal. Youth unemployment is typically higher than the national average, according to this view, in good times and bad; supposedly, this trend persists over time because young workers are relatively new to the labor market, often looking for their first or second job, and may be passed over in hiring decisions due to lack of experience. But, on the other hand, one can argue that the 2008 economic crisis exacerbated a preexisting problem. Currently, high rates of youth unemployment inordinately deprive millions of young workers of the opportunity to advance through hard work. For those lucky enough to find work, these same structures ensure that they work for wages that have only barely risen since their parents had their first jobs. The loose labor market has also elevated the risk of trying to get a better job or asking for higher wages since the Great Recession devastated the job market for young people, diminishing both the quality and the number of employment choices available (Davis and Kimball 2015).

One of the primary explanations for high rates of youth unemployment, then, is also the most straightforward: there are simply not enough jobs. Young people face a deficit of over 4 million jobs. Then, too, jobs that do exist are increasingly low-wage, low-skill jobs with few opportunities for mobility; they are far from a launch pad into a career. Moreover, the timing could not be worse. Millennials entered college precisely at the moment tuition was skyrocketing, endowments were falling, and interest on student loans was climbing. According to *Forbes*, the average college graduate at present is burdened by a debt of $27,253 in student loans (Touryalai 2013). The high cost of education exacerbates the problem because it keeps young workers from "sheltering in school" (Shierholz 2011), thus expanding the pool of so-called NEET (not in employment, education, or training) youth at precisely the moment there are so few jobs (Organisation for Economic Co-operation and Development 2017). Thus, the popular image of the Millennial worker as an overeducated barista is more of a fiction as 60 percent of this generation does not hold a bachelor's degree (Thompson 2015).

If they are not sheltering in school, some Millennial workers—the richer ones—do seem to be sheltering at home. Much has been made about the group returning to their parents' homes well after college is over; a higher percentage cohabitate with mom and dad than since 1880 (i.e., before shredded wheat was invented) (Fry 2016). But Robert E. Hall's testimony before the US Senate Committee on Finance indicates that there is a deep class element embedded in the exit of Millennials from the workforce. His findings show that rich teenagers are twice as likely to leave the labor force than poorer ones (Hall 2015). As Joel Stein (2013) has observed, "In fact, a lot of what counts as typical millennial behavior is how rich kids have always behaved."

In *Capital in the Twenty-First Century* Piketty (2014) suggested precisely this—that returns on capital, growing faster than the economy as a whole, would lead wealthy children to exit the labor force because they lacked an incentive to work for income. Thus, if there is any credence to the notion that Millennials are entitled and lazy, it has to be qualified that this is an example of dependence not on the state but rather on rich parents. In other words, it is not a middle- or working-class phenomenon but an elite one. Critics who suggest that "many young adults don't seem to be in much of a hurry to leave their parents' warm, comfortable nests" (Tuttle 2012) may actually be somewhat correct when talking about wealthy, jobless youth.

Consequently, the allegations of narcissism and laziness against young employees appear to be more of an attack on the cultural integrity of a vulnerable segment of the working class than a piece of social analysis. That the work ethic is not to blame for the youth unemployment crisis, though, is not to say it does not matter: it is vitally important. But the popular myth that it is in decline is false—thanks, at least in part, to Millennials.

A DECLINING WORK ETHIC?

Young workers are the latest scapegoats for what seems to be a national obsession with a decline in the work ethic overall. A recent Bloomberg poll, taken as one example of many similar polls, finds that 72 percent of Americans feel the United States "isn't as great as it once was" (McCormick 2015). One of the main byproducts of this decline has been anxiety about the disappearing work ethic. More people thought "our own lagging work ethic" (27 percent) was a greater harbinger of American peril than the Islamic State (26 percent), wealth inequality (25 percent), and competition with China (21 percent)—and Millennial workers are disproportionately the source of this concern (Malanga 2009).

Yet public anxieties about a declining work ethic seem unfounded. If anything, the reverse is true. Americans rank near the bottom of any kind of work–life balance scheme, at 29 out of 36 countries, according to the Organisation for Economic Co-operation and Development (Doerer 2015). This means Americans are working so hard that they sacrifice time with their families and do not take enough vacation even when earned. When compared with Europeans, Americans get less time off, less family leave, and fewer sick days. This evidence accords with reports from sociologists as well. Juliet Schor's the *Overworked American* (1991), Jill Andresky Fraser's *The White-Collar Sweatshop* (2001), and Arlie Hochschild's *The Time Bind: When Work Becomes Home and Home Becomes Work* (1997) all chronicle a growing tendency for the hours and intensity of work to increase that has been occurring steadily since the 1980s. One might be inclined to think this reversal of history would draw public condemnation, but it has strangely been just the opposite.

Studies routinely show that the American workweek is expanding as wages and standards are stagnating or declining. This trend has existed during the exact same time that the elite invocation to "do what you love" became the "unofficial work mantra of our time" among young people (Tokumitsu 2014). The directive to love your job has become so intense that the National Labor Relations Board had to recently rule against it.[2]

The alleged need to "take this job and love it" has had important consequences, often pushing young workers toward a dire and fruitless search for meaning at work. The *Harvard Business Review* recently published a guide to finding meaning in boring, monotonous, low-paying jobs (Hansen and Keltner 2012). The business consultant Jessica Amortegui proposes that young people can easily access the rewards derived from meaningful work, as if it were an espresso shot: "If you consider yourself part of the 70 percent of disengaged employees in America, what could a boost of meaning at work do for you?" (2014). Strange as it sounds, it appears to be working. A recent *Fast Company* poll shows that young Americans tend to be more enamored by their jobs than in the previous decade, even though their jobs have become objectively worse (Bellis 2015). Stairs et al. (2006) suggest that Millennial employees are significantly more focused than earlier generations on finding work that allows them to make a meaningful social contribution regardless of the pay.

For many Millennials, that search has led them to work for free, for multiple employers at once, in what they see as a necessary path to a meaningful job. A recent National Association of Colleges and Employers (2015) report shows that, from the mid-1980s to the mid-2000s, the share of college graduates participating in at least one internship rose eight times. Yet, while internships are still popular, they have faded as a pathway to a paying job. A 2013 report on students who held unpaid internships shows that they are almost no more likely to get a job offer (37 percent) than those who have no internship at all (35 percent). But *Forbes* writes "millennials' high hopes and desire for meaningful work drive them to seek out these internships over other options" (Howe 2014). The winners in this equation are employers who attract lots of young workers.

Finally, young workers tend to believe in the necessity of hard work more than any other group of people in recent history. The General Social Survey, which began polling Americans on general values in 1973, has almost every year asked respondents how people "get ahead" in American society. Is it through "hard work," "luck," or some combination of the two? As Figure 3.1 shows, from 1973 to 2016 there was an 18 percent increase in the number of workers 25 years old or younger who favor the "hard work" explanation over others. It also shows that today's young workers seem to believe more in the greater necessity of work than other age cohorts.

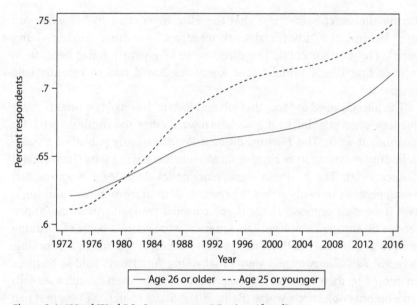

Figure 3.1 "Hard Work" Is Important to "Getting Ahead"

Source: Author's calculations from the 1973 cumulative file of the General Social Survey data set (weighted estimates from lowess).

SILICON VALLEY AND FORMULA RETAIL

The palatial offices on Sandpoint Road in Silicon Valley and the sales floor of a chain retail store in Burlington, Vermont, could not be more different places. Yet workers share some of the same concerns about the divisions, or lack thereof, between life and work. The majority of popular critics have either misunderstood or willfully misrepresented the significance of the Millennial demand for what an MTV survey called "a life–work smoothie" (Shore 2012). By insisting on blurring the lines between life and work even further, they are often in search of a more transcendental reason to work and, by extension, reason to live. The unintended consequence of that endless search is to further the same policies and cultural norms that have been in effect for decades. Arlie Hochschild's *The Time Bind: When Work Becomes Home and Home Becomes Work* (1997) illuminates this crisscrossing of worlds that were previously thought to be separate. Her findings are that large chunks of men and women, even those with children, often prefer the peace and creativity of the workplace to the chaos and stress of the home. The home is not, as Lasch (1995) famously put it, a "haven in a heartless world."

Popular discussions of life–work balance (for example, Slaughter 2015), often promoted by boomers and aging Xers, seek to reinstate more rigid boundaries between the home and the job site. Yet those same people, when occupying their positions as captains of industry, often preach a different gospel, with implications for the younger generation's orientation to a work ethic. When she got the job in 2012, Yahoo chief executive officer Marissa Mayer announced she would work through her maternity leave. To make sure no one thought she was kidding, she built a nursery next to the office right after she ended the telecommuting option for Yahoo employees. Facebook chief operating officer Sheryl Sandberg, author of the neoliberal feminist manifesto *Lean In: Women, Work, and the Will to Lead* (2013), gloated about pumping breast milk while on conference calls and returning to work after the kids were tucked into bed. Apple's leader, Steve Jobs, was often considered one of the main proponents of marrying the work ethic and deep emotional commitment. In his graduation speech at Stanford in 2005 Jobs said, "Your work is going to fill a large part of your life. . . . And the only way to do great work is to love what you do."

Given this environment, it is unsurprising to find a strong culture of overwork present in the technology sector. "Look at our bosses," said one young Twitter coder at her first job since graduating from Stanford. "They practically kill themselves with work. So . . . yes, of course there's pressure to keep up. There's this environment that keeps everybody going. You're always on." And, as a female employee at Dropbox told me, "People say that the work environment here is so that people will want to stay all day, as if that's a bad thing." Facebook's leave policy is called Recharge. Its stated mission is to encourage workers to take time off to recover from a hectic work schedule so that they can prepare to go back to work. "It's like your phone," one employee says, "It dies a lot from overuse, so you have to recharge it. So you can kill it again."

One recent MTV study (Hillhouse 2012) shows that about half of young workers would "rather have no job than a job they hate," listing "loving what I do" over salaries and big bonuses in order of importance. Approximately 90 percent said the workplace should be social and fun, with the vast majority (83 percent) "looking for a job where my creativity is valued." Miya Tokumitsu (2014) argues that the do-what-you-love dictum has functioned as a political battering ram: "Why should workers assemble and assert their class interests if there's no such thing as work?"

In the 1960s, the management theorist Burkhard Sievers (1994) declared that theories of motivation are "surrogates for meaning." In other words, since work had lost its inherent meaning for the worker in the late twentieth century, companies must compel them to work by dangling all kinds of carrots. On the one hand, then, Millennials receive messages that work should be fun and exciting (i.e., they should *want* to do it). On the other, they are ridiculed as juvenile when their employers entice them to work with infantilizing sliding boards, ball pits, and free food. The Valley has recently become a haven of skilled labor for young workers again, and it is exactly these kinds of perks—the ability to enjoy being at work—that is bringing them there.

But different factors motivate low-wage retail workers. A leaked email at Urban Outfitters asked its salaried employees to volunteer their weekends as a "team building activity" where you get to "experience our fulfillment operations first hand" (Sargent 2015). Hard to pass up, some people might say in jest. However, for a working population socialized to accept unpaid internships, long hours, and few prospects, companies advertise these "opportunities" without irony or shame.

Of the top 20 industries employing young people, more work in retail than in any other category (AFL-CIO 2013), with 20 percent of US workers under the age of 25 employed in this sector. On average, they make low pay—about $22,500 per year for a full-time employee—and erratic on-call schedules are increasingly the industry standard. By and large, though, the young workers in this industry want more hours. During a meeting of the Retail Action Project (RAP) in midtown Manhattan, about 20 young workers circle up to discuss their jobs and ways to improve them through collective action. RAP, an offshoot of the retail workers' union, has joined forces with the Center for Popular Democracy (CPD), the umbrella organization of this growing movement. "The problem is not that we don't want to work," one young retail worker said. "The main problem for everyone I know is that . . . there doesn't seem to be enough work for those of us who want it." Her anecdotal understanding relays a larger truth. Across the country, the number of retail employers who are considered "involuntarily" part-time expanded from 644,000 in 2006 to 1.5 million in 2010 (Luce and Fujita 2012). While the desire for more hours exists across the board of low-wage workers, the interest of young people in the 18–24 age bracket has increased the most (Buffie 2016).

Another person I interviewed confirms this fact. "I work hard just to prove them wrong," said a 21-year-old retail worker on 34th Street in Manhattan, visibly annoyed and tired. When she says "them," she gestures toward the store, indicating managers. On a 10-minute break from H&M, where she has been hired, laid off, and then rehired in 1 year alone, she barely has time to make the arrangements to get to her next job at the Guess store on Broadway that same day. She said she resents the popular conception of her generation as lazy and entitled. "They got us runnin'," she said.

But too often the *fact* of high youth unemployment has been used to further a cultural explanation about lazy Millennials. As one H&M worker said at the RAP meeting, "They always say we're too lazy for this, too slow for that. . . . Yo, give us a job. I mean a decent job where I actually have hours. I'll show you how to work hard."

PERCEPTIONS OF THE YOUTH WORK ETHIC IMPACT POLICY PROPOSALS

Workers in different classes, status hierarchies, industries, and geographical locations are ideologically committed to working hard or need to do it to survive. Either way, laziness rarely intervenes. Yet, it is common for policymakers to act on the opposite assumption. For example, in 2015, while vying to be president, Jeb Bush proclaimed that "people need to work longer hours," a remark that reportedly bothered young voters most (Smith 2015). But his is only the latest conservative order for "lazy youth" to get to work. While on the road to his own losing bid for the Republican Party's nomination for president 4 years earlier, Newt Gingrich went off script at a press conference with a plan to replace unionized janitors with schoolchildren, calling child labor laws "truly stupid." He was explicit that the plan was intended to indoctrinate poor youth into a world of work, which, even by his own admission, was not worth it in economic terms. "Get any job that teaches you to show up on Monday," he said, adding, "any job that teaches you to stay all day even if you're fighting with your girlfriend . . . the whole process of making work worthwhile is central."

Other conservatives took him seriously. Congressman Jack Kingston, who ran for the Republican nomination to fill a Georgia Senate seat, followed suit and suggested that students receiving free or subsidized school lunches be required to perform janitorial work in exchange for welfare benefits their parents receive. Finally, in 2012, Rick Santorum derided then-president Obama's plan to make college more accessible by calling him "a snob" to great applause. He then went on to say that "not everyone is gifted" and that some people, especially those who plan on making a living working with their hands, should be able to do so without feeling the shame of the snide liberal establishment (Jacobson 2012).

However, the reality is that young people want to work, and work hard. What policy alternatives might usefully help to grow the number and quality of job opportunities? There are a number of policy proposals directed at solving an expensive and "leaky" school-to-jobs pipeline. For example, Elizabeth Warren—noting that from 2013 to 2014 over 1 million young borrowers have fallen behind on their skyrocketing loan repayments—has proposed legislation that calls for student loans to carry the same low interest rates that beginning borrowers at big banks enjoy (Warren 2015). By contrast, Secretary of Education Betsy DeVos has proposed doing the opposite by punishing those very same borrowers and subjecting them to major fines for defaults. This allowance was seen as so counterproductive that even the loan companies that stood to benefit rebuked the change as overly punitive (Nasiripour 2017).

But the private sector has its own solution to the huge debt carried by many college students: don't go to college. Mission U, the brainchild of a young tech executive, Adam Braun, is an online job-training institute for high school graduates that connects students with companies—for instance, Lyft, Warby Parker, and Spotify have already signed on—in need of talent with highly specialized skills (Clifford 2017). Braun says the idea arose because although rich parents allowed him to graduate debt-free from Brown, his wife was not so lucky. Rather than fix the particular problem, he devised a profitable way for students to avoid it altogether. And he is not alone. Other specialized schools, such as Alamo Academy in Texas, are partnering with companies to train high school students for lucrative careers in aerospace, healthcare, and tech before college. (See also Chapter 9.)

The European context offers other possibilities. Areas in the United States with high concentrations of European manufacturers have a greater track record of collaborating with middle and high schools to train young workers around their plants through apprenticeships and other direct placement plans. This could reflect a growing familiarity with Europe's "youth guarantee," which the European Union argues "should ensure that all young people up to the age of 25 receive a good quality offer of employment, continued education, an apprenticeship or a traineeship within 4 months of leaving formal education or becoming unemployed" (Wyman 2015).

While education scholars argue that 4-year college students are not learning all that much (Arum and Roksa 2011), management experts suggest that they are not job-ready either. They tout the European model that sends large percentages of young adults to apprenticeship programs; these programs are also pathways to well-paying jobs. For these reasons, the Brookings Institute and a host of other think tanks believe that schools should refocus their efforts on generating greater connections between students and the job market through internships and other mechanisms that introduce workers to the job market sooner (Skarda 2014).

One way to do this would be to revive a manufacturing base, a process that has been at least partially underway in some places for the last decade. Yet, rather than malign workers as unskilled or unmotivated, employers will need to adopt a series of commitments to promote jobs and youth employment. For example, training programs will need to be considered an investment, not a negative mark on the balance sheet. Additionally, manufacturing jobs will need to be viewed as secure, not subject to capital flight and deindustrialization. The popular nostalgia for manufacturing is not a longing for the factory floor so much as for a stable middle-class life once provided by high-wage union labor.

Another way to accomplish this goal would be to increase federal support for AmeriCorps programs. AmeriCorps offers year-long paid positions for young people in public service at nongovernmental organizations, churches, schools, and other sites. With over half a million AmeriCorps applicants looking for about 80,000 spots each year, demand far outstrips supply and the program would have no problem finding willing participants (Jacobs 2014).

The impetus to expand education and apprenticeship programs is based on a questionable premise (i.e., allegedly, a woeful lack of skills among young workers). The idea of a "mismatched worker" (Kalleberg 2007)—that one's skills are poorly matched to the available jobs in which employers can make a profit—has been a powerful argument in favor of greater public investment in job training since the early 1980s (Gardner et al. 1983). But the idea that the problem of youth unemployment lies primarily in the knowledge base of the labor force is an open question. For example, a 2012 nationwide survey by the Manpower agency confirms that many employers feel that workers lack both hard and soft skills needed for entry-level work. However, as *The Atlantic* points out, the percentage of firms that listed "lack of available applicants" as a reason for their hiring woes was virtually identical to those that listed applicants who are "looking for more pay than is offered," a reminder that "the labor market is a market" (Kiviat 2012). What looks like a skills mismatch from one angle, then, appears like what Kalleberg (2007) calls a "pay mismatch" from another.

Another factor complicating the notion of a skills gap is the employer preference for foreign flexible laborers. Why not, for example, regulate the size and character of the legal migrant youth labor force? For instance, approximately 155,000 young workers come to the United States every summer on a summer work travel visa; they staff restaurants, amusement parks, and other low-level service industries. Originally founded as a diplomatic mission to bring young people to the United States to experience American culture, the numbers of tourist workers exploded after the 2008 financial crash just as domestic youth unemployment began to increase as well (Bowman, forthcoming). Amendments by Bernie Sanders and others to restrict the program, or otherwise amend it, have failed and are often fought by employer lobbies that see the stream of reliable cheap labor as beneficial. The good news is that the latest research suggests that a skills gap does not really exist and that most manufacturing employers have almost no problem filling spots with qualified candidates (Weaver and Osterman 2016). Why, then, do employers routinely suggest the opposite? Regardless of its validity, the idea that a jobs problem lies in an unskilled workforce is a powerful ideological boost to the work ethic.

One interesting recent strategy is not just to increase jobs for youth but to mitigate the worst effects of the growth of bad jobs and precarious employment with a different kind of safety net. The idea is a portable benefits system in which workers are able to accrue benefits and maintain them when they leave a job (Appleby 2017). Such a system has the dual purpose of preventing employers' avoidance of paying benefits by hiring part-time workers and thus encouraging the growth of more stable employment. As conceived by Steven Hill (2015), it is exactly the kind of policy instrument that can succeed at the state or local level. In San Francisco, the heart of the youth-dominated gig economy where precarious jobs are the only ones on offer, a law already mandates that employers either provide health insurance or supply dedicated healthcare from an account employees can access. A more robust portable benefits system would simply expand these existing policies, as well as try to scale them up to states.

Many Millennial workers have shown support for more movement-oriented solutions. Take, for example, the campaigns to reform working conditions called the Fair Workweek Initiative (FWI), led primarily by young workers of color. They have introduced legislation in several major American cities to constrain the power of employers to make erratic schedules the new norm in formula retail stores.

The FWI grew quickly since 2012 due to frustration with new employment practices that treated workers like "just-in-time" parts on an assembly line. New software technologies allowed companies to schedule workers in smaller and smaller increments because the software would apply multiple variables to determine the appropriate amount of hours needed to run a given retail store. Jamba Juice, for example, uses software that predicts the necessary daily hours of employment based on sales in previous years, the neighborhood's economic profile, the time of day, demographics, and the weather. The result is that an increasing number of retail workers are hired as on-call employees, sometimes only working 2- or 3-hour shifts in the middle of the day. The other result is an inordinate preference for young workers—namely, those without children, spouses, or other obligations that would mitigate their availability.

The FWI seeks to end these practices by forcing employers to inform workers of their schedules in advance. "These new technologies are great. They could be used to schedule workers far in advance, so they can plan their lives and childcare and get to other appointments," said one advocate of Jobs With Justice (JWJ) in San Francisco, who added, "The problem is that the technologies aren't used in that way." JWJ helped to establish the first Retail Workers' Bill of Rights in the city of San Francisco that includes a host of reforms of the way workers are treated. The city has even established an independent board of advocates to monitor the agreement and respond to violations. It is too early to tell how useful this system will be, but the CPD is interested in expanding on this victory. It also has no illusions about the relevance of a policy instrument in an industry the size of retail. "The policy stuff is important," explains one CPD staffer. "But the point is to build a movement of workers that can use the policy and defend it if need be. But without the movement it's pretty weak."

A "movement of workers" sounds very much like a union, and Millennials tend to approve of unions as well. A Pew Research survey found that a majority of Millennial voters, regardless of party affiliation, viewed labor unions favorably (Bruenig 2015). Since unions tend to raise the wages of those at the bottom of the labor market first, young workers stand to benefit from a revived labor movement.

CONCLUSION

Blaming a failing work ethic for a structural problem echoes a revised "culture of poverty" argument, analogously mistaking cause for effect. Combined with popular assessments of undergraduates and young workers as coddled, overprotected, and emotionally volatile, an image has emerged of an ideal–typical Millennial: unstable, unskilled, and unmotivated (Lukianoff and Haidt 2015).

Yet hard evidence points to a different conclusion. Data suggest that young workers are not substantially different from workers in previous generations in their outlook toward work. When they are different, though, it is often in ways that defy both media and business consultant stereotypes about the Millennial workforce. But by one measure, at least, Millennials *are* unique: they tend to believe that hard work is more important than boomers do. An increasing percentage of General Social Survey respondents—from 65 percent in 1973 to 70 percent in 2014—have responded that hard work is a more important factor than luck in getting ahead, signaling an increased perception that people who make it big do so because they overcame obstacles in their life. Significantly, however, 74 percent of respondents who are 18–25 thought that hard work mattered the most compared to 71 percent of those aged 60–65.

The work ethic is an important dimension of classical social theory, but it is far less discussed than the state of work in general. Here, the work ethic is considered an ideological bulwark to the dominant class's economic preferences, the latter tending to inform political interests and policy debates as well. The policy overview presented in this chapter suggests a variety of

ways to ameliorate the poor conditions in which young workers find themselves. They involve job training programs, partnerships with educational
institutions, union- and movement-based solutions, and new kinds of social safety net programs. Moreover, it seems that Millennial workers often
know better than their elected representatives what kinds of reforms are
useful to them. Millennial voters disproportionately lean Democratic and
are showing up to vote, increasing their numbers at the national presidential polls by almost 10 percentage points since 2000. This is significant
since Democratic candidates tend to support legislation that is more favorable to young workers. So while the political and economic context is
unsupportive of them at the moment, it will be their penchant to engage in
movements and push for policy for better work—not their work ethic—that
will make a different kind of economy for young workers.

NOTES

1. Cited in an unpublished manuscript edited by McCallum, Mayer, and
Moorti.
2. The board's decision argued that T-Mobile was unable to enforce a level
of happiness at its job sites. To comply, T-Mobile had to remove any rule that
could prevent workers from saying negative things about the company and
its products, services, customers, or other employees and any rule that might
prevent employees from arguing with co-workers, subordinates, or supervisors.
See https://www.nlrb.gov/case/28-CA-106758.

REFERENCES

AFL-CIO. "The Young Population and Workforce." AFL-CIO Department for
    Professional Employees, June 2013. http://dpeaflcio.org/wp-content/uploads/
    The-Young-Population-and-Workforce1.pdf. Accessed October 11, 2015.
Amortegui, Jessica. "Why Finding Meaning at Work Is More Important Than Feeling
    Happy." *Fast Company*, June 26, 2014. https://www.fastcompany.com/3032126/
    how-to-find-meaning-during-your-pursuit-of-happiness-at-work. Accessed July 1,
    2017.
Appleby, Julie. "What If You Could Take It With You? Health Insurance, That
    Is." National Public Radio, February 28, 2017. http://www.npr.org/sections/
    health-shots/2017/02/28/517720563/what-if-you-could-take-it-with-you-health-
    insurance-that-is. Accessed July 1, 2017.
Arum, Richard, and Josipa Roksa. *Academically Adrift*. Chicago: University of
    Chicago Press, 2011.
Bellis, Rich. "The Unlikely Reasons Why We're More Satisfied at Work." *Fast
    Company*, September 16, 2015. https://www.fastcompany.com/3051044/

the-future-of-work/the-counterintuitive-reasons-why-were-more-satisfied-at-work. Accessed October 23, 2017.

Bowman, Catherine. "The Rise of the J-1 Summer Work Travel Program and Its Rhetorical Links U.S. Youth Unemployment," forthcoming.

Bruenig, Elizabeth. "Even Conservative Millennials Support Unions." *New Republic*, May 1, 2015. https://newrepublic.com/article/121688/pew-releases-new-labor-survey millennials-supports-unions. Accessed August 1, 2017.

Buffie, Nick. "The Rise of Involuntary Part-Time Employment—By Race, Gender, Age, Industry, and Occupation." Center for Economic and Policy Research, August 10, 2016. http://cepr.net/blogs/cepr-blog/the-rise-of-involuntary-part-time-employment-by-race-gender-age-industry-and-occupation. Accessed October 23, 2017.

Clifford, Catherine. "Start-up Partners with Lyft, Spotify to Help Young People Skip College and Land High-Paying Jobs." CNBC, March 21, 2017. http://www.cnbc.com/2017/03/21/start-up-partners-with-lyft-spotify-to-help-young-people-skip-college.html. Accessed October 23, 2017.

Costanza, David, and Lisa Finkelstein. "Generationally Based Differences in the Workplace: Is There a *There* There?" *Industrial and Organizational Psychology* 8, no. 3 (2015): 308–23.

Davis, Alyssa, and Will Kimball. "Millennials Aren't Lazy: Millennials Aren't Working Because the Economy Isn't Either." Economic Policy Institute, May 28, 2015. http://www.epi.org/blog/millennials-arent-lazy-millennials-arent-working-because-the-economy-isnt-either/. Accessed October 23, 2017.

Doerer, Kristen. "U.S. Has a Lousy Work–Life Balance." *PBS News Hour*, July 3, 2015. https://www.pbs.org/newshour/economy/u-s-lousy-work-life-balance. Accessed October 23, 2017.

Fraser, Jill Andresky. *White-Collar Sweatshop: The Deterioration of Work and Its Rewards in Corporate America*. New York, NY: Norton, 2001.

Fry, Richard. "For First Time in Modern Era, Living With Parents Edges Out Other Living Arrangements for 18- to 34-Year-Olds." Pew Research Center, May 24, 2016. http://www.pewsocialtrends.org/2016/05/24/for-first-time-in-modern-era-living-with-parents-edges-out-other-living-arrangements-for-18-to-34-year-olds/. Accessed July 1, 2017.

Gardner, David. A Nation at Risk: The Imperative for Education Reform. Department of Education April, 1983. https://files.eric.ed.gov/fulltext/ED226006.pdf. Accessed May 9, 2018.

Graham, Jennifer. "A Generation of Idle Trophy Kids." *Boston Globe*, November 4, 2013. https://www.bostonglobe.com/opinion/2013/11/04/idle-millennials-are-victims-their-parents-success/2rWDFWXQHo290FqUpz0HOO/story.html. Accessed October 23, 2017.

Hall, Robert E. "Testimony Before the U.S. Senate Committee on Finance." US Senate, January 22, 2015. http://www.finance.senate.gov/imo/media/doc/Hall%20testimony.pdf. Accessed October 23, 2017.

Hansen, Morten, and Dacher Keltner. "Finding Meaning at Work, Even When Your Job Is Dull." *Harvard Business Review*, December 20, 2012. https://hbr.org/2012/12/finding-meaning-at-work-even-w. Accessed October 23, 2017.

Hill, Steven. *New Economy, New Social Contract*. New America, August 2015. https://na-production.s3.amazonaws.com/documents/New_Economy_Social_Contract.pdf. Accessed October 23, 2017.

Hillhouse, Alison. "Consuer Insights: MTV's 'No Collar Workers.'" Blog.Viacom, October 4, 2012. http://blog.viacom.com/2012/10/consumer-insights-mtvs-no-collar-workers/. Accessed October 23, 2017.

Hochschild, Arlie Russell. *The Time Bind: When Work Becomes Home and Home Becomes Work*. New York, NY: Metropolitan Books, 1997.

Howe, Neil. "The Unhappy Rise of the Millennial Intern." *Forbes*, April 22, 2014. http://www.forbes.com/sites/realspin/2014/04/22/the-unhappy-rise-of-the-millennial-intern/#5f79a8115b73. Accessed October 23, 2017.

Jacobs, Elisabeth. "Twelve Ways to Fix the Youth Unemployment Crisis." Governance Studies at Brookings, May 2014. https://www.brookings.edu/wp-content/uploads/2016/06/Brookings_JacobsUnemployment_To-Print.pdf. Accessed August 1, 2017.

Jacobson, Louis. "Rick Santorum Calls Barack Obama a 'Snob' for Wanting 'Everybody in America to Go to College.'" Politifact, February 27, 2012. http://www.politifact.com/truth-o-meter/statements/2012/feb/27/rick-santorum/rick-santorum-calls-barack-obama-snob-wanting-ever/. Accessed August 1, 2017.

Jobe, L. L. "Generational Differences in Work Ethic Among 3 Generations of Registered Nurses." *Journal of Nursing Administration* 44, no. 5 (2014): 303–308.

Jobs, Steve. "You've Got to Find What You Love." Stanford News, June 14, 2005. http://news.stanford.edu/2005/06/14/jobs-061505/. Accessed October 23, 2017.

Kalleberg, Arne. *The Mismatched Worker*. New York: W.W. Norton, 2007.

Kiviat, Barbara. "The Big Jobs Myth: American Workers Aren't Ready for American Jobs." *Atlantic*, July 25, 2012. https://www.theatlantic.com/business/archive/2012/07/the-big-jobs-myth-american-workers-arent-ready-for-american-jobs/260169/. Accessed October 23, 2017.

Kowske, Brenda, Rena Rasch, and Jack Wiley. "Millennials' (Lack of) Attitude Problem: An Empirical Examination of Generational Effects on Work Attitudes." *Journal of Business Psychology* 25, no. 2 (2010): 265–79.

Lasch, Christopher. *Haven in a Heartless World: The Family Besieged*. New York: W.W. Norton, 1995.

Luce, Stephanie, and Naoki Fujita. *Discounted Jobs: How Retailers Sell Workers Short*. New York: Retail Action Project, 2012.

Lukianoff, Greg, and Jonathan Haidt. "The Coddling of the American Mind." *Atlantic*, September 2015. http://www.theatlantic.com/magazine/archive/2015/09/the-coddling-of-the-american-mind/399356/. Accessed October 23, 2017.

Malanga, Steven. "What Ever Happened to Work Ethic?" *City Journal*, September 2009. http://www.city-journal.org/html/whatever-happened-work-ethic-13209.html. Accessed October 23, 2017.

Marikar, Sheila. "For Millennials, a Generational Divide." *New York Times*, December 20, 2013. http://www.nytimes.com/2013/12/22/fashion/Millenials-Millennials-Generation-Y.html. Accessed October 23, 2017.

Marx, Karl. *Das Kapital*. Moscow: Progress Publishers, 1887.

McCormick, John. "Most Agree with Trump on America's Lost Greatness, Bloomberg Poll Finds." Bloomberg, September 24, 2015. http://www.bloomberg.

com/politics/articles/2015-09-24/most-agree-with-trump-on-america-s-lost-greatness-bloomberg-poll-finds. Accessed October 23, 2017.

Mendelson, Maeona. "The Millennial Generation: Receiving a Fair Exchange?" *Journal of Intergenerational Relationships* 11, no. 3 (2013): 324–28. http://www.tandfonline.com/doi/abs/10.1080/15350770.2013.810056. Accessed October 23, 2017.

Nasiripour, Shahien. "Trump's Student Loan Default Penalty Has an Unlikely Foe." Bloomberg, March 29, 2017. https://www.bloomberg.com/news/articles/2017-03-29/trump-s-student-loan-default-penalty-has-an-unlikely-foe. Accessed October 23, 2017.

National Association of Colleges and Employers. "Percentage of Students with Internship Experience Climbs." National Association of Colleges and Employers, 2015. http://www.naceweb.org/s10072015/internship-co-op-student-survey.aspx. Accessed October 23, 2017.

Organisation for Economic Co-operation and Development. "Youth Not in Employment, Education or Training (NEET)." OECD Data, 2017. https://data.oecd.org/youthinac/youth-not-in-employment-education-or-training-neet.htm. Accessed October 23, 2017.

Pew Research Center. "Millennials: Confident. Connected. Open to Change." February 4, 2010. http://www.pewsocialtrends.org/2010/02/24/millennials-confident-connected-open-to-change/. Accessed October 23, 2017.

Phillips, Gregory, and David W. Owens. "CFO Survey: Few Companies Making Special Effort to Attract Millennials or Achieve Board Diversity Targets." *CFO Magazine*, 2014. https://www.cfosurvey.org/2014q4/press-release.pdf. Accessed October 11, 2016.

Piketty, Thomas, and Arthur Goldhammer. *Capital in the Twenty-first Century*. Cambridge, MA: The Belknap Press of Harvard University Press, 2014.

Safer, Morley. "The 'Millennials' Are Coming." *CBS News, 60 Minutes*, November 8, 2007. http://www.cbsnews.com/news/the-millennials-are-coming/. Accessed October 22, 2017.

Sandberg, Sheryl. *Lean In: Women, Work, and the Will to Lead*. With Neil Scovell. New York: Alfred A. Knopf, 2013.

Sargent, Jordan. "Urban Outfitters' Fall Strategy: Asking Employees to Work for Free." Gawker, October 7, 2015. http://gawker.com/urban-outfitters-fall-strategy-asking-employees-to-wor-1735228986. Accessed July 1, 2017.

Schor, Juliet. *The Overworked American: The Unexpected Decline of Leisure*. New York, NY: Basic Books, 1991.

Shierholz, Heidi. "Are More Young People 'Sheltering in School' Now Than Ever Before?" Economic Policy Institute, April 20, 2011. http://www.epi.org/publication/snapshot-2011-young-workers/. Accessed October 23, 2017.

Shore, Nick. "Turning on the 'No-Collar' Workforce." *Media Daily News*, March 15, 2012. http://www.mediapost.com/publications/article/170109/turning-on-the-no-collar-workforce.html. Accessed July 12, 2017.

Sievers, Burkhard. *Work, Death, and Life Itself: Essays on Management and Organization*. Berlin: Walter de Gruyter, 1994.

Skarda, Erin. "Ask the Experts: How Can We Solve the Young Adult Unemployment Crisis?" Nation Swell, June 18, 2014. http://nationswell.com/ask-experts-can-solve-young-adult-unemployment-crisis/. Accessed August 1, 2017.

Slaughter, Anne-Marie. *Unfinished Business: Women Men Work Family*. New York: Random House, 2015.

Smith, Candace. "Jeb Bush: People Need to Work Longer Hours." *ABC News*, July 8, 2015. http://abcnews.go.com/Politics/jeb-bush-people-work-longer-hours/story?id=32313997. Accessed October 23, 2017.

Smola, Karen Wey, and Charlotte D. Sutton. "Generational Differences: Revisiting Generational Work Values for the New Millennium." *Journal of Organizational Behavior* 23 (2002): 363–82.

Stairs, Martin, Martin Galpin, Nicky Page, and Alex Linley. "Retention on a Knife Edge: The Role of Employee Engagement in Talent Management." *Selection & Development Review* 22, no. 5 (2006): 19–23.

Stein, Joel. "Millennials: The Me Me Me Generation." *Time*, May 20, 2013. http://time.com/247/millennials-the-me-me-me-generation/. Accessed October 23, 2017.

Thompson, Derek. "The Economy Is Still Terrible for Young People." *Atlantic*, May 19, 2015. https://www.theatlantic.com/business/archive/2015/05/the-new-normal-for-young-workers/393560/. Accessed October 23, 2017.

Tokumitsu, Miya. "In the Name of Love." *Jacobin*, January 12, 2014. https://www.jacobinmag.com/2014/01/in-the-name-of-love/. Accessed July 12, 2017.

Touryalai, Hannah. "College Costs Slow Down, but Aid Falls and Average Student's Debt Hits $27k." *Forbes*, October 23, 2013. http://www.forbes.com/sites/halahtouryalai/2013/10/23/college-costs-slow-down-but-aid-falls-and-average-students-debt-hits-27k/#540f7dc91506. Accessed May 9, 2018.

Tuttle, Brad. "Being 30 and Living with Your Parents Isn't Lame—It's Awesome." *Time*, March 20, 2012. http://business.time.com/2012/03/20/being-30-and-living-with-your-parents-isnt-lame-its-awesome/. Accessed July 10, 2016.

Twenge, Jean, Stacy Campbell, Brian Hoffman, and Charles Lance. "Generational Differences in Work Values: Leisure and Extrinsic Values Increasing, Social and Intrinsic Values Decreasing." *Journal of Management* 36 (2010): 1117–42.

Warren, Elizabeth. "Warren, Courtney Introduce Bank on Students Emergency Loan Refinancing Act to Tackle Student Debt." March 18, 2015. https://www.warren.senate.gov/newsroom/press-releases/warren-courtney-introduce-bank-on-students-emergency-loan-refinancing-act-to-tackle-student-debt. Accessed July 1, 2017.

Weaver, Andrew, and Paul Osterman. "Skill Demands and Mismatch in U.S. Manufacturing." *ILR Review* 70, no. 2 (2016): 275–307. http://journals.sagepub.com/doi/abs/10.1177/0019793916660067. Accessed October 30, 2017.

Wikileaks. "Xers, Yers & Millennials: How to Maximize Their Productivity and Keep Them Focused on Results." The Global Intelligence Files, November 15, 2013. https://wikileaks.org/gifiles/docs/39/395147_xers-yers-and-millennials-how-to-maximize-their-productivity.html. Accessed October, 23, 2017.

Wyman, Nicholas. "Here's How We Fix the Youth Unemployment Problem." CNBC, February 5, 2015. https://www.cnbc.com/2015/02/05/heres-how-we-fix-the-youth-unemployment-problem-commentary.html. Accessed October 23, 2017.

Zabel, Keith L., Benjamin B. J. Biermeier-Hanson, Boris B. Baltes, Becky J. Early, and Agnieszka Shepard. "Generational Differences in Work Ethic: Fact or Fiction?" *Journal of Business and Psychology* 32, no. 3 (2017): 301–15. https://doi.org/10.1007/s10869-016-9466-5. Accessed October 30, 2017.

4

Real Jobs and Redshirting

Job-Seeking Strategies for College-Educated Youth

Patrick J. Carr and Maria J. Kefalas

INTRODUCTION

In 2010, just 2 years after the Great Recession rolled over the United States like an economic tidal wave, we began interviewing young 20-somethings who had grown up and attended three high schools just outside of Philadelphia. Many of these young people had finished or were just finishing their college degrees at the time we spoke with them, and all of them were dealing with an economy that had been utterly transformed for their generation. The Great Recession occurred over 19 months, from December 2007 until June 2009; and as unemployment rose in the United States and other countries severely hit by the crisis, joblessness rates for young people, generally considered those in the 16–24 age group, far outpaced the national average. At one point in 2009 the unemployment rate for young people in the United States stood at almost 17 percent, more than double the national average (see Bell and Blanchflower 2011). But it is not simply having a job that is important. As Sarah Steinberg (2013) points out, it is the loss in earnings over a lifetime that is a major consequence of delayed entry into the labor force, or being underemployed. In other words, doing a job below your skill level or working part-time when you want to work full-time is a debilitating problem. As a result, the young men and women we spoke with were trying to launch their careers when it was hard to even get their first step on the ladder.

Though conditions were tough for everyone, we found in our study of 20-somethings that not everyone experienced the same degree of economic pain. Specifically, those who were from what we call "elite" backgrounds had an easier time getting jobs even during the recession and were additionally insulated from the worst effects of the downturn by having little or no educational debt. The working- and middle-class

young people had a much more difficult time both in securing employment and in dealing with debt. Below we describe the study, illustrate the
educational and employment experiences of the three groups of young
people, and outline the different pathways that they are on. We conclude
with policy recommendations aimed at ensuring better access to what our
respondents call "real" jobs.

THE STUDY

Between 2010 and 2011, we interviewed 106 young adults who went to
three high schools in Pennsylvania: Upper Darby High School in Upper
Darby, an inner-ring suburb of Philadelphia; Haverford High School in
Havertown, PA, a few miles northwest of Upper Darby; and Lower Merion
and Harriton High Schools in Lower Merion Township, located to the west
of Philadelphia on the Main Line. We chose these high schools because they
have student bodies that broadly correspond to the working class (Upper
Darby), the middle class (Havertown), and the upper middle class (Lower
Merion and Harriton). Each school is not exclusively comprised of working-,
middle-, and upper middle-class students; but each school has a significant
pool to draw upon. We define "working class" as when a respondent did
not have at least one parent with a B.A. and one parent with a professional
or managerial job: 42 interviews with young people from this background
were completed. We defined "middle class" as when a respondent had at
least one parent with a B.A. and at least one with a professional or managerial job: here, we completed 23 interviews. Finally, "upper middle class"
was defined as when a respondent had at least one parent with a graduate/
professional degree or at least one parent with B.A. and a high-level professional, managerial, or entrepreneurial job: 41 interviews were conducted in
this category (see also Tevington 2017).

The research team worked with each of the high schools to generate
a sample from the ranks of their graduates. At times, this consisted of a
small number of contacts from which a snowball sample was generated to
find more contacts. The team also used high school yearbooks to generate
names and contacted former students directly. The research team conducted
interviews in locations of a respondent's choosing, often in public spaces
like restaurants or coffee shops, although some interviews were conducted
in the home of the respondent or at Saint Joseph's University. Interviews
ranged from 1 hour to 3 hours in length; most were between 1.5 and 2 hours
long. The interviews were semi-structured in nature, with questions probing
respondents on their experiences of education, their employment histories,
their family background, and their hopes and dreams for the future (among

other topics). Each respondent received a $40 honorarium for the interview. With the respondents' permission, the interviews were digitally recorded and then transcribed verbatim, and researchers performed spot-checking of interview transcripts. Interviewers wrote up ethnographic field notes after each interview, and interview transcripts were coded using the qualitative data analysis software program Atlas.ti. The coding scheme was developed inductively after reading through the entire sample of interview transcripts for patterns and themes.

In this chapter, we chart the employment experiences of those in the sample who attended and finished college. We also focus on the strategies respondents utilized to secure employment after graduation and what has helped and hindered them in their efforts.

MONSTER VERSUS MENTOR: DIFFERENT STRATEGIES FOR GETTING A "REAL" JOB

What is a "real job"? For the young people we interviewed, a real job was not in retail. It wasn't one that paid a low hourly wage, and it wasn't one that you broke your back doing. A real job almost always needs to be full-time and provide benefits, though benefits can be negotiated in some tougher fields such as in the arts or non-profit sector. A real job needs to be related to your major or what you want to do, and it should earn decent money. Starting at entry level is okay if there is an expectation for moving up. A real job fosters commitment to the company that hires you or to the mission that company espouses.

Jason, from Upper Darby, was 22 when we interviewed him in March 2011. He had dropped out of a prestigious private college after a year and had had a stint in community college that he never finished. Jason was working full-time in a retail management position and reflected that he did not feel fully an adult because he didn't have a "real career." When we asked him to explain what a real career was, he told us,

> A real career I guess [is] something with long-term pay, you know just some-thing that makes you happy, something that isn't *just a job*. Something that you can go to every day and be happy about it. (emphasis added)

Given what young people we interviewed said about real jobs, how did they go about landing one, especially in the aftermath of the Great Recession? Our data illustrate that they pursued two broad paths: one involved applying for anything they could, and the other entailed using mentors, connections, and contacts to land a position. The first approach is scattershot, whereas the second approach is more targeted.

Kenny was 22 when we interviewed him in November 2010. He had graduated from Haverford High School in 2006, and when we spoke he was not long out of college. Like many of his contemporaries, Kenny was taking his first tentative steps in the world of work. In the 6 months since he graduated from Penn State University, Kenny told us that he had applied "to everything, CareerBuilder and Monster, just everything that came up, I would just throw my resume on and expect to hear back. And like I said, I didn't hear back from anywhere." While he figured out how to get his career on track, Kenny worked a number of part-time jobs, notably in a restaurant where he was making "a hundred bucks a night." Though he was qualified for a career in human resources, his experience of not even receiving rejections letters from the scores of applications he sent out and the fact that he was making money albeit in food service meant that he "didn't really care if [he] got a job" in his field. Then Kenny's neighbor asked him if he wanted a job:

> I was applying to HR positions mainly. So when [my neighbor] said, "Do you wanna a job?" I was thinking he was gonna give me an HR position within [the insurance company]. But he said it's in claims. And I was so, just kinda like—get me a job, I wanna start making money, I'm bored just sittin' around all day, so I just—I jumped on it, you know.

Kenny parlayed his contact into a solid entry-level white-collar job; after a few months in, he was content to have established a first foothold in the working world. What is notable about his experience is the fact that he started by applying to jobs and posting his résumé on line, but after not getting any response, he landed a job through a network contact. Part of Kenny's story is quite typical for many of the middle- and working-class respondents in that many describe sending out hundreds of applications in some cases and hearing nothing back. Certainly some of this would have been due to the sluggish labor market. From June through September 2010, the US economy shed an average of 73,000 jobs per month before the economy embarked on a period of sustained job growth, adding jobs every month since then. However, what is notable from our respondents is how many of them, especially those from working- and middle-class backgrounds, are speculative jobseekers who employ the scattershot approach to the search for employment. Kenny starts off that way and ends up drawing on the ties he has to land his first "decent" job.

Many others were not as fortunate as Kenny, though, and were more like Eddie. Eddie was from Upper Darby, and was 9 months post-college graduation when we interviewed him in February 2011. At that time, 22-year-old Eddie was cobbling together a number of part-time jobs at an after-school program and stocking shelves at Petco. For Eddie, there are no magic networks that can help him find a job, and he is in a holding pattern, trying to add another job that would take him close to working 60 hours a week. Claire was 23 years old and 7 months out of college when we interviewed her in December 2010. She was juggling four part-time jobs and trying to "figure out what I really wanna do later." Claire concedes that "coming out of college I really didn't know what I wanted to do." She underscores that the summer after graduation she drifted back into a summer camp job she had done for "six or seven summers" and, when the season ended, she struggled to figure things out:

> Once the summer ended I really didn't have anything and I was thinking about what I would want to do, where I'd wanna apply and I just literally was clueless. I had no idea, it scared me thinking about doing that, trying to apply for jobs and figure my life out. So slowly opportunities, like part-time jobs, just slowly started coming out. Like beginning of September, I got this opportunity to work at the gym, so I took that. And pretty soon after that, I got the opportunity to do like just filing work for my friend's mom and then babysitting came up. And then I kinda got into my mind that that—this is okay for now, like the part-time jobs, living at home, like, you know, for a little bit, it's okay.

The experiences of Claire, Eddie, and Kenny illustrate how ill prepared many young people are to get their first jobs. Some employ the Monster.com approach and apply wildly to anything for which they feel qualified, usually with little or no feedback, while others cobble together a number of part-time jobs that are enough to make ends meet. The abiding theme here is the lack of a plan. Many respondents say they leave college with only a vague idea of what they want to do, and while this was certainly compounded by the timing of their graduation in the teeth of the Great Recession, it is not clear that their lack of a plan would have been any different in a thriving economy.

If Kenny and Claire's experiences were marked by a lack of planning— and, it should be added, by a lack of mentoring—then Gwen's experience provides an interesting contrast. Gwen graduated from Lower Merion High School in 2006 and attended college in Pittsburgh. Like many of her peers, Gwen admits that she "started to panic" 6 months before graduation because she did not know what she wanted to do with her life and career. She thought about applying for City Year but rethought that plan. She returned home after graduation and got a job that she thought would gain her experience in different aspects of business only to find that she had been tricked into taking a face-to-face sales job. Gwen started applying for jobs online with no success and then signed up with an employment agency, where she worked as a temp in offices, often being let go with no notice when the need for her services dried up. Gwen was spinning her wheels, not unlike

Eddie and many others; but in the midst of her travails her mother stepped in. Gwen explains,

> My mom was like, "well I have this friend from work who used a career coun-
> selor and I think it would be a great idea if you did it." So I put it off for a while,
> I really didn't want to go. Anyway, then it came like November [laughs] and
> I was still unemployed so I was like OK, maybe I'll give her a shot. It ended up
> being like a great experience. I loved it! I really did enjoy it and my mom's like
> "well I told you so, you should've done it like 5 months ago." But I did that and
> then at the end of that, you kind of go through this process of like, personality
> assessment, a career assessment, an interests assessment, kind of all coupled
> together and by the end, you kind of figure out what your motivation is, where
> you'd be happiest in the career and what environment would play well to that.

Though the sessions with a career counselor did not lead immediately to a job, Gwen says that her approach to job hunting changed dramatically. Whereas she used to apply online, now she says she has "started over and, clearly, networking is how you get everything these days." Gwen has been in touch with a family friend who is "a bigwig HR person"; this friend has helped her with contacts that she sees as a prelude to getting a job. While Gwen was content to take anything just out of college, she is "holding out a little bit" for a good job that will launch her career now that she has "fig-ured out that path." What is interesting about Gwen's story is not that her networking approach is novel: it is not. Scholars going back to Granovetter (1973) have demonstrated the so-called strength of weak ties, and even Kenny's example underscored this.

The difference here is the resources that Gwen was able to call upon when she hit a brick wall in her search for a good job. Her mother pays the tab for career counseling, costing about $150 per session. Also, Gwen enlists a family friend who is big in HR. And, most important of all, she says that now she has figured things out and has the luxury of waiting until the right job comes along. We call this process "redshirting," which is meant to be an employment equivalent of a college athlete who is able to sit out a season because of injury and not lose eligibility. Redshirting for our elite students means that they can shelter from the economic storm because they have the means to do so. Moreover, with the help they can procure through mentoring and contacts, they will be well placed to succeed when the economy brightens.

We will return to the theme of redshirting later in this chapter. For now, we re-emphasize that our respondents describe the process of getting their first real job in one of two main ways—either a monster.com way or by using contacts and/or mentors—which breaks down mostly along the lines of so-cial class groupings. Specifically, working- and middle-class respondents are more likely to employ a scattershot approach to landing a job, which more often than not results in failure or in securing a low-end job. Elite respondents are more likely to use a targeted approach and to be able to utilize connections or mentors to gain a foothold in the world of work.

Respondents' experiences trying to land a first real job reveal factors that help and hinder them. We turn now to respondents' descriptions of what helped them as they emerged from higher education.

MAJORS MATTER

For many of the young people we interviewed, choosing a major in college was done primarily because of their interest in the field of study. Some had one eye on what a major could furnish for their future career, but many others did not look that far ahead. What you study in college is increasingly important, and this was especially true for the young people we interviewed who were navigating the choppy waters after the Great Recession. A recent report from the Georgetown Center for Labor and the Workforce on the economic value of college majors points out the economic differences in outcomes for college graduates with different majors. In particular, the authors illustrate how students in so-called STEM (science, technology, engineering, and math) majors earn significantly more over their lifetime than those in social work, education, or the arts (Carnevale et al. 2016). The difference is more pronounced for minority youth, and even though black youth are going to college in greater numbers than ever, they are opting for majors that will "lead to low-paying jobs, setting up many for future debt and underemployment." Another study, this time of the University of Texas (UT) higher education system, finds that "The choice of major is the most important factor in determining UT system graduates' wages even after controlling for other . . . graduate characteristics such as test scores, institutional selectivity, demographic characteristics, and family income" (Carnevale et al. 2017). Choice of major even outweighs institutional selectivity, meaning that if a person attends an open-access college and graduates in a high-paying major like architecture, she or he could earn more than someone who gets into a selective school and chooses a low-paying major.

The young people we spoke to elaborated on good and bad experiences with choosing majors and on the important implications this had for their entry into the job market following college. For instance, Heather is a 22-year-old first-generation college student from a middle-class family in Haverford. She is close with her immediate and extended family, all of whom live within a few blocks of each other. During her senior year of high school, Heather and one of her cousins were torn between several colleges, ultimately choosing to attend Syracuse University.

Savvy to the realities of the job market, Heather majored in nursing, knowing about the ongoing shortage of qualified candidates in the field and that she could expect to make good money while working flexible hours. When she was a junior in college, Heather applied to and accepted an "externship" at the Children's Hospital of Philadelphia (CHOP). Falling in love with her experience there, Heather was determined to seek permanent employment with the hospital and possibly stay there indefinitely. Between the end of her externship and her graduation, Heather took care to keep her "name" out there at CHOP by working the occasional weekend shift as an aide. This strategy did the trick: she was eventually offered full-time work upon her graduation.

For Heather, there is no doubt that her college degree—and, in particular, her major—made all the difference in the world. She told us,

> I think nursing is definitely a degree that helps you once you get your job, especially if you're in the hospital setting or like patient care. Just anything from how to deal with people to skills. I mean, I know a lot of my friends were like, business majors, and like, some of their jobs like they're starting at like, you know anyone could start at. One of my friends graduated with a psych degree and she's subbing, so I feel like my degree has definitely helped me.

For every young person like Heather who is practical about a course of study, there are those who eschew STEM majors, preferring to focus on what excites them intellectually. Mary was 25 when we interviewed her. She grew up in affluent Lower Merion, the daughter of a carpenter and a nurse. Mary excelled at school; her parents expected her to continue her studies, and there was never any doubt she would attend college. She explained, "in this community, going to college is the bare minimum requirement that you need to do. I mean, I even feel inadequate that I don't have more than a college degree where I live." In her senior year of high school, Mary applied early to a private college and was accepted. However, she was unhappy there and soon transferred, eventually graduating from a prestigious private university near her home on Philadelphia's Main Line.

With a sigh, Mary recounts how she chose her major, saying, "I don't know who but someone in my life said, 'just choose the classes that are most interesting to you. Like freshman year, just choose whatever you think is cool and then really the end of sophomore year . . . the classes you took the most of, that'll sorta indicate to you what your major should be.'" Mary followed this strategy and pursued her love of languages, majoring in Spanish.

After graduation, Mary spent 2 years abroad in Spain, working as an English teacher. Returning stateside, she had tremendous difficulty in the job market. She explained,

> So like the first few months the jobs I was applying to were mostly just teaching jobs and then like any job that had Spanish in it. Administrative

assistant needs Spanish, that's what I was applying to. Anything that would maybe let me use Spanish, I would do that. . . . I have no standards now. I mean, I tried to get a job back at Starbucks . . . and they wouldn't take me. Trader Joe's wouldn't take me.

In retrospect, Mary laments her decision to major in Spanish. She continues to love the language. But this passion alone cannot pay the bills. She says, "the way the world is right now, like, yes, I really wish that I had been an education major with Spanish so that I could have been a certified teacher right now. . . . I definitely wish I had done that."

The contrast between Heather and Mary could not be starker. Heather is already thinking about her major before she goes to college and chooses something that she knows will be in demand, while Mary is given some bad advice that she follows, to her detriment. Part of the reason for the divergent approaches could be due to the guidance that each receives, and part of it is no doubt due to Mary not thinking through what a major means beyond the classes she is taking in college.

We are not saying that there is a direct relationship between majors and jobs, but it was clear from the experiences of the young adults we spoke to that in a difficult labor market the type of qualification they had acquired mattered a great deal. There is an established argument that majors matter less than we think they do (for instance, Selingo 2013; Stahl 2015), and articles are quick to recount four, six, or even 10 reasons why majors don't matter. Employers often say that, aside from positions requiring a technical skill, majors don't matter as much as critical thinking, communication, and problem-solving skills (see Korn 2013). But what is not in doubt is that young people are increasingly choosing a major that they believe will help them land a job. LaVelle, Silverstone, and Smith (2015) report a survey of college grads that illustrates that 82 percent consulted the job market before choosing a major in 2015, up from 69 percent in 2013. As 22-year-old Molly, who had graduated college and was unemployed when we interviewed her, told us,

A lot of times it just feels like I'm never gonna be able to find a job. It just feels like I have been like completely shut out. I mean, sometimes I think, why didn't I major in business? Why didn't I major in chemistry? It's scary, because the longer I'm sitting at home applying for jobs and not hearing back, it wears you down. It's kind of like, is there any point in trying?

The choice of major seems to matter to the young people we interviewed, especially as a way to prepare for what has become an extremely uncertain job market. However, what someone studied as an undergraduate was not the only thing that could help. As Kenny's experience showed, having connections that you can activate to land a job was also crucial for these young people.

CONNECTIONS COUNT

Alex was 22 when we interviewed him in November 2010. A 2006 graduate of Haverford High School, Alex attended a state school in Pennsylvania and majored in sports management. He was preparing for a career in his field and took an internship at a Division 3 college in his senior year. With the help of his internship supervisor, he began looking for jobs months before graduation. Alex sent out résumés and email applications to scores of jobs and did not hear back. After receiving no emails, he "kind of got discouraged"; while he continued his search for work during the summer after graduation, things came to a head in August. Alex decided he would take up a neighbor on an offer she had made to help him get a job. Although Alex was not qualified for the position in logistics that he ended up taking, he believed his obtaining the position was because his friend's father is "the vice president" of the company. He speculates that he would not have "gotten hired based on having no experience or not even knowing what the word logistics meant before my job interview" if he didn't know the guy who was interviewing him. In the end, landing his first job boiled down to the strength of his contacts. He reflects that his friend told him that she would "get [him] an interview, we probably can get you a job."

The flip side of being able to call on connections is not having them in the first place, something that many of the working- and middle-class respondents lamented. Kate was 22 when we interviewed her in February 2011. She graduated from Upper Darby High School in 2006, and though she was intent on studying art, a house fire that destroyed all of her work also destroyed her confidence: she ended up with a degree in advertising from a local public university. Kate has loan payments of over $24,000 that she has had to defer and only a waitressing job to make ends meet; at the time we spoke with her, this was barely enough to cover gas money. She had applied for hundreds of jobs since graduating and had heard nothing back from any of them. Kate feels locked out from the real job market, and she is acutely aware that her lack of contacts hinders her progress. She told us,

> I think I've always thought that some places are corrupt and you'll always get a job because of "It's my cousin's friend's daughter" . . . that's how people are getting jobs now. And I think that the recession made that even more apparent because it's not—it's not really how good you are at something, it's who you know.

Kate's preferred field of creative advertising was one that shed jobs during and after the recession, making it especially difficult for her to find a position. But if she could have called on connections like Alex or Kenny, she might well have secured employment.

By and large, our respondents found it difficult to secure a real job or even get a toehold on the way to one. Those who fared best had chosen majors that helped them in a tight labor market, and they had connections they could use to get a start. For many of the young people who came of age during and after the Great Recession, though, the prospect of underemployment loomed large.

GETTING A JOB OR BUILDING A CAREER? THE UNDEREMPLOYMENT TRAP

Who gets good jobs when they enter the labor market? The prevailing wisdom is that those with a college degree will fare better than those with a high school diploma or less education. The foundation of the *college for all* clarion call has seen participation in degree-granting institutions increase significantly, rising from 25.7 percent of all 18- to 24-year-olds in 1970 to 40.5 percent in 2015 (Digest of Education Statistics 2016). The assumption has been that the credential earned beyond high school will make a difference in the type of job or career you secure after graduation. And as participation in higher education has increased, so has educational attainment. In 1960, 7.7 percent of the population over the age of 25 had graduated from college or another higher education institution. By 2015, the rate had increased dramatically to 32.5 percent of the US population over 25, a more than 4-fold increase (Statista 2017).

Certainly, the available lifetime data illustrate what is commonly called a "college earnings premium," namely, that having an advanced degree or even some college with a degree translates into higher earnings compared with having a high school diploma or less (see Greenstone and Looney 2013). Estimates of the amount of the premium vary as, for instance, the Federal Reserve Bank of New York estimates the difference in lifetime earnings between a college graduate and a high school graduate to be about $1 million. Even though returns on a college degree have dipped in the wake of the Great Recession, the rate of return on investment is estimated at 15 percent overall (Schwartz 2015). Thus, while the college degree premium has flattened in recent years, it is still substantial (Valletta 2016).

But what happens if someone finishes a degree and finds that she or he is overqualified for many of the jobs available? The phenomenon of so-called underemployment, whereby, for example, a college graduate takes an entry-level job that she or he would have been qualified for without the degree, is hardly new (see Abel, Deitz, and Su 2014). Indeed, a certain amount of underemployment has always been assumed as part and parcel of career paths: it's not where one starts in terms of employment but where one ends up. Yet, some scholars suspect that the Great Recession has caused a rising number of recent college graduates to suffer this fate (Fogg and Harrington 2011). Certainly, among the young adults we interviewed, there was ample evidence of underemployment as they set out on their working lives.

Alison from Havertown was 23 when we interviewed her in November 2010. She graduated with a degree in education and spent months afterward trying to find a full-time position; this was something she was finding hard to accomplish. Alison told us that she feels "prepared" for the tough economy but wishes "there were more jobs." Alison had been on lots of interviews, and though she has been rejected from all of the full-time positions she applied for, she was sanguine about the process. She expressed feeling satisfied that "it's not me, I've done everything I can . . . there's just someone who has more experience, that's what it comes down to." So Alison took a number of part-time positions. She is a substitute teacher for a local school system and a grading assistant at a high school and works some hours at an early learning center. She is prepared to "sub for another year, and go back" to school if she doesn't land a permanent position. To all intents and purposes, Alison is underemployed, but, as Abel, Deitz, and Su (2014) point out, her story is familiar and common to the path that many teachers take in starting their careers. Other young people we spoke with, who were also trying to get a start in teaching, told a similar story to Alison's.

Abe's story is one that perhaps is more telling when it comes to underemployment and, given his circumstances, more portentous. Abe was 22 when we interviewed him in November 2010 and had graduated with a business degree from a small college in upstate New York 6 months prior to our conversation. Abe admits to not being a great student in high school or college, and the driving force for him was getting as far away from his dysfunctional family as he could. He applied to colleges based on location and chose one where he received no scholarship money. Abe traveled as much as he could while in college, spending most of 2 years abroad, but returned home soon after graduation in the hope that he could find a full-time job in the Philadelphia region and move out on his own. However, Abe has had to compete with graduates with similar and, in some cases, better degrees, in a saturated market. Though Abe wants a job that he "can enjoy going to," all he has to show for 6 months of job hunting is a $7.15 an hour position at a movie theater concession stand; this is a job that does not require even a high school diploma, never mind a bachelor's degree. Sizable college debt looms for Abe, and he has already deferred payments. He is frustrated and will accept anything that gives him some financial autonomy, remarking "I just wanna have a job I can enjoy and I don't care what the money is, I just need the money." Abe's road to a full-time job that befits his qualification will be a difficult one, and he knows it. Reflecting on whether he is on the pathway to adulthood, he says, "I'm not quite on it, like I'm on the highway and I haven't reached that exit yet type of thing."

Many of the young people we spoke with, especially from working- or middle-class backgrounds, were underemployed. While we concede that there is always a certain amount of underemployment that goes with taking those first steps after college, these young people sensed that something was different. For instance, many respondents who pursued elementary education in college were fearful they would not get their "turn" as easily as previous cohorts of teachers: opportunities were contracting, and more senior educators were postponing retirement. Moreover, many were similar to Abe in being unable to get a job reflecting their level of education and no longer marking time until their slot opened up. Abel, Deitz, and Su (2014) note that for the group of college graduates entering the labor market in 2009–11, the underemployment rate was 56 percent; while this drops over time, it reflects the effect of the Great Recession on this cadre of young people. More telling, say Abel, Deitz, and Su (2014), is the quality of jobs that the underemployed occupy. The authors measure job quality in two ways. First, they examine the proportion of underemployed college graduates in what they call "good non-college jobs" and in "low-wage jobs." Examples of good non-college jobs are electricians, dental hygienists, and mechanics; definable by not requiring a bachelor's degree, these jobs have paid $45,000 a year or better since 2012 and are skill- and career-oriented. Examples of low-wage jobs are bartenders, cashiers, and food service workers; these pay $25,000 or less. In 1995, over 50 percent of recent college graduates who were underemployed held good non-college jobs as opposed to about 16 percent who held low-wage jobs. The share of the underemployed recent college graduates in good non-college jobs dropped to 36 percent by 2009, while over 20 percent were in low-wage jobs. Consequently, the trend seems to be that there are fewer good non-college jobs for recent graduates, and this was precisely the case for the young people we interviewed.

Abel, Deitz, and Su (2014) also measure job quality in terms of the extent to which the underemployed are working part-time, or less than 35 hours per week. They find that the share of underemployed recent college graduates working part-time rose from 15 percent in 2000 to 23 percent in 2011. The authors conclude that the "downward trend in the quality of jobs for underemployed recent college graduates compounds the increase in the level of the group's underemployment over the past decade" (6). While it is unclear whether underemployment or having a low-wage job will be transitory or more permanent for our respondents, much more certain is that many who find themselves in this position feel desperate to escape it.

REDSHIRTING THE RECESSION

In our interviews with working- and middle-class young people who were cobbling together a slew of part-time jobs or who were stuck in a low-wage position for which they were clearly overqualified, one theme repeatedly emerges—anxiety about their futures (Tevington 2017). These young people faced an economy that had gone through its largest contraction in decades and feared they would be the generation who would not surpass their parents as they scrambled to secure a foothold in a faltering job market. Many young people had student loan debt that would have to be paid back and were beginning to doubt that they could ease their way into adulthood. But for some of our respondents, the ravages of the recession did not matter as much: these were young people who were relatively sheltered from the worst effects of the downturn and could afford to "redshirt."

Sean was 25 when we interviewed him in May 2011. A 2006 graduate of Harriton High School, he was living with his parents and working part-time as a bartender. Sean graduated from college with a degree in finance; after graduation, he took some time off instead of looking for a job in his field. His parents paid for college, so Sean has no student loans to pay back; and while he earns less than $15,000 a year at his part-time job, he doesn't want for anything. Sean was able to assess his options as the recession raged and decided he would go to law school. It was not that Sean had always dreamed of a career as a lawyer: rather, this path could provide a shelter from the economic realities outside. In short, the resources that Sean could access allowed him to wait out the storm. As he recounted to us,

> I don't think I would be very competitive [if I was looking for a job now]. Do I think I would have options? Absolutely, but I am not interested in a job that you can get with a bachelor's in finance right now. [Interviewer: Why?] For the same reason sitting in a cubicle sucks. It would just suck. I'll probably end up being an attorney for a while. I will most likely practice for a few years out of law school. Commercial litigation perhaps, I'm so open to let the wind take me where it goes. I'm not picky, I don't live to work. I work to live, I want it to be interesting, I won't settle for things, just for the money you know.

Sean's cavalier attitude is in stark contrast to many of our respondents who were struggling with gaining a foothold in the world of work regardless of whether they were underemployed or not. He can afford to dabble in finance and law because he has the resources to do so.

This particular type of redshirting was rare among our respondents, but there was another more common form that centered around the issue of college debt. Half of our elite respondents had no college debt at all, while our working-class respondents had the highest average debt. This simple fact meant that many elite respondents could afford to wait a little for a job that might advance them in their careers, while the middle- and working-class young people we interviewed were often compelled to take a job because the first repayments of their loans were due. Being shielded from debt is a huge advantage when starting in the world of work after college, and as shown below, some of our respondents had a very difficult time coping with the debt they accrued when financing their educations.

COLLEGE DEBT

Valerie was 22 when we spoke with her and was originally from Haverford. When considering her post–high school plans, she explained, "College was always expected, we didn't have a choice. If I said I didn't wanna go to college, [my dad]'d be like, 'Whatever, you're going anyway.'" For their part, Valerie's parents contributed as much as they could to the tuition at the state college Valerie attended. Beyond this, Valerie was responsible for the remainder of her tuition as well as room and board. As a result, she accumulated approximately $50,000 in student loan debt by the time of her graduation.

Initially, Valerie planned to follow her "dream" to major in marine biology in college. During her junior year, though, Valerie began to give this route some second thoughts—not because her passion had altered but because she was concerned about her job prospects. As she explained, "And I'm doing teaching now, and one of the chief reasons I'm doing teaching is for job security and good benefits, I wanna have a job. Like I said, 'cause both my parents are laid off." But since Valerie thought she was too far along into her bachelor's degree to switch majors, she was compelled to attend graduate school after leaving college.

Pressing financial concerns interfered with Valerie's long-term plans. Knowing the debt that awaited her, Valerie grudgingly moved back in with her father, brother, and father's fiancée after college. She also enrolled in a teaching certificate program at a local college—a program that necessitated her taking out and paying for even more loans. Meanwhile, she took a part-time job at Old Navy to help defray some of her costs. Even though Valerie has a bachelor's degree, she is making roughly $8 an hour, which she considers a humbling experience. She comments bitterly, "I have a degree. And I'm doing the same thing as sixteen-year-olds."

Valerie was on her own when it came to choosing colleges to attend and, more importantly, when it came to taking out loans to pay for her living expenses; her parents had covered most of her tuition costs, not including room and board. Because neither of her parents had to deal with educational loans in their own time, they offered her no guidance. Valerie paints a poignant picture of sitting at the computer desk, sobbing uncontrollably out of frustration and confusion, with her father reminding her that she was on her own with this task. Four years later, Valerie has nothing but venom for the government and the banks that lent her this money. Her interest rates are variable—and too high. She is unable to consolidate her loans, and she "knows" that this debt will hinder her future. For Valerie, there is no opportunity to redshirt. She has to take a job for which she is overqualified so that she can pay her recently laid-off father the $100 monthly rent.

If Valerie's tale is instructive about the perils of student loans and the need for young people to be counseled properly in their decisions, then Dustin's is the cautionary tale. Dustin was 22 when we interviewed him in February of 2011; he was living with his parents after graduating from college 9 months earlier. His parents, Mark and Paula, had no education beyond high school but wanted Dustin and his younger brother to go to college and do many of the things they could not achieve themselves. At 51, Mark had worked for 33 years removing asbestos in oil refineries, as his father had done before him in Philadelphia. Paula worked part-time in a small shop that specialized in Lladro, Wedgewood, and other fine crystal and glassware. Together, they had earned enough to own their own home on a neat, tree-lined street next door to Mark's parents. There were always two cars in the garage and enough presents under the tree at Christmas. When Mark's father died, Mark used the small inheritance to build a small extension off the back of the house and outfit the new family room with a 60-inch flat-screen TV. In their eyes, they had made it.

Mark and Paula had high hopes for Dustin; he was, as they said, the smart one in the family. Having themselves grown up in an era of hands-off parenting and at a time when the college race was unheard of, they encouraged Dustin to aim for college; having not gone themselves, though, they had no idea what that process would entail. Like many in the middle class, Dustin's parents had absorbed the importance of a degree for long-term security but had missed an important part of that message: standing out in the college application process means starting the race early and using every advantage to make your child shine. "We were naive," Paula told us, "We were just happy he got in and we figured our job was done. Now we know better."

Elite parents know how this game is played, and they make sure that they enroll their children in a set of enriching activities that look good to college admissions offices. They make sure their kids prep endlessly for the SAT and ACT tests. They hire tutors when their children lag in a subject and bring in private consultants to assemble the most impressive college applications. They are concerned about the rankings and prestige and know the importance of a brand name when it comes time to land a job. Finally, and perhaps most important presently, they have the means to offset the financial burden that college brings along. Dustin's family heard the message: college is the path to success. But they did not realize how the game was played or how costly not playing it strategically could be.

Over lunch at a diner, Dustin talks about his college debt, all $100,000 of it. How he got into that position is the story of far too many families in the middle class and threatens the steady upward mobility that his father and grandfather enjoyed. Mark was able to raise his family into the middle class on hard work alone. Dustin may not be able to attain that same status, for a variety of reasons, some of which are personal and others systemic.

College for Dustin, and many of those we interviewed, was a place to get away from home and party, to have some fun. Plus, he said, "every job you think of, you need a college degree." His high school had left that impression. The school newspaper regularly reported the destinations of recent graduates and the college acceptance rates. It spent much less time discussing the jobs of those in the first tier, the voc-tech students who, as Dustin put it, were the "kids who don't do very well and this gives them something to do after high school." Despite the fact that Dustin did not do well in high school—he managed Cs and Ds by just "phoning it in"—he was never encouraged to take a path other than that through a 4-year college.

Dustin's troubles started before he set foot on campus. His college search was done almost on a whim, beginning extremely late in the application cycle. He began searching for a college to attend in July after graduating from high school. Dustin gathered the pamphlets he had collected at a college fair and haphazardly chose two that he thought he could get into with his low grades, which were also far from home. He ultimately chose a private school in upstate New York that cost $24,000 a year for tuition and $13,000 a year for room and board, which had neither financial aid nor scholarships. He chose the bank for his student loan based on the brochure the college handed out.

Four years later, he graduated with a B.A. in sports management. His internship was a distant memory as he had opted to do it in his sophomore year. Moreover, his job-search networks were minimal as he was the first in his family to go to college. Currently, Dustin delivers pizzas for Domino's, working for $7.25 an hour when he is in the store and $5.25 when he is delivering. He gets to keep part of the delivery charge and tips, but he pays for his own gas. If he works until 4 a.m., he can clear $60–$70 in tips in a night. He works 3 nights a week delivering pizzas. His second part-time job is as a checkout cashier at Kohl's, scrambling to hit his target of 10 emails and three credit card applications from customers every day, all for $7.50 an hour.

Making matters worse, Dustin will soon owe $1,000 a month on his private college loans by his estimation—not counting the federal loans, payments on which amount to about what he takes home in pay each month. He also revealed that he is pinning his hopes on a bank teller position, one of the 200 jobs he had applied for since graduation. The job would pay about $25,000 a year, a salary that would allow him to start paying back the student loan and perhaps move out of his parents' home.

The debt weighs on Dustin. He is hoping for another 6-month grace period where he will only pay on the interest in order to save up a little bit more money. Then he hopes to consolidate and extend the loan out a few more years so that the payments might be cut in half. He applies for every job he can find, although he has landed nothing yet.

His parents, no strangers to financial strain, say they are happy to have him home. "We don't mind doing this until he can get on his feet," his mother tells us. "We raised him to be independent, but it's just not possible yet. I worry for him with that debt. That's the mortgage on a fixer-upper around here. How can he move out with that?" As we sat talking, Dustin flipped through the mail. A letter from the bank where he had applied for the teller position was in the batch. He didn't need to open it. He knew it was a computer-generated rejection letter from a corporate office.

We know about the overall negative effect of increasing amounts of college debt. Having debt delays young adults from settling down and purchasing homes, and it has a negative overall effect on the economy. But there are also subtle ways in which college debt dampens economic growth. For instance, Busteed (2015) finds that student loan debt damages entrepreneurship, and he finds that "among those who graduated between 2006 and 2015, 63 percent left college with some amount of student loan debt. Of those 19 percent say they have delayed starting a business because of their loan debt. That percentage rises to 25 percent for graduates who left with more than $25,000 in student loan debt." This equates to about 2 million graduates saying that they have delayed starting a business because of the debt they have accrued.

Many of the young people in our study were, in Sara Goldrick-Rab's (2016) words, "paying the price" for their pursuit of the American dream, especially at a time when they were starting their full-time working lives. The stories of student debt and the ease with which they slid into it all seemed to come from a single font—namely, young people were making decisions without guidance and, in many cases, not reflecting on the consequences of borrowing such large sums of money. That this happens so routinely is not news, yet it remains shocking that for so many middle- and working-class people, the costs of college leave little choice but to rack up debt that severely hinders their progress as they enter adulthood—whether or not they end up with a degree.

WHAT CAN HELP?

The conversations we had with this group of young adults demonstrate that many struggle after college. They struggle to land a "real job," many grapple with student loan debt, and a large number of young people become discouraged about their futures. It is true that the timing of our study meant that this group of young people was contending with an economy in its worst downturn in decades, but we think that the travails they spoke of are not limited to such precarious times. The cost of college and the increase in student debt predate the Great Recession, as does the phenomenon of underemployment. The Great Recession merely threw these things into starker relief. Given the problems that assailed many of the working- and middle-class young adults we interviewed, what can be done to ensure that more of them achieve at the level of their elite counterparts?

The first thing that must happen for many young people is that they need to plan, and this process cannot start when they are finishing up their degrees. Planning has to start early, and for it to have any chance of success young people and their families need access to information to enable more informed decisions about the paths they should take. The common thread in the stories of many of the young adults we spoke with, some of whom were struggling and others floundering, was that they had made decisions with little or no help, counsel, or information about their options or about the possible ramifications of their actions. To be sure, plans will change and people will adapt to circumstances, but not having a plan seems to invite calamity.

Several concrete measures, though, could help young people plan as they navigate their way through school and begin the process of landing a "real" job. The first area where improvement can be made, relatively easily, is providing timely information to young people as well as their parents, guardians, and mentors about the choices they will face. Simply put, many young people are led to believe that getting into college and getting a degree is the end game. But there is much more to the picture, as the experiences of our respondents illustrated. Many young people blindly choose a college or a major without researching how this will help them once they leave college. Others accrue more debt than they can handle. A few of our respondents were fortunate enough to receive the advice they needed to make strategic decisions that would help them choose a major that they could parlay into usable skills and ease their transition to the world of work, and some figured this out on their own. However, many others were not as fortunate and ended up regretting their choices of college and major. The planning for college should start before junior or senior year of high school, especially for those young people who are the first in their families to go to college. Crucial in this process is having current information on colleges, the majors they have, and where their graduates end up after their education. Perhaps the most important component of this pre-college planning is in the area of how to pay for college. The lack of oversight of banks that engage in predatory lending is hardly likely to change anytime soon, so it is imperative that young people and their families know how to go about navigating financial aid and college loans in such a way as to not end up strangled by debt.

Parents and guardians are central to the planning process. More than simply exhorting parents, guardians, and mentors to become involved, we believe that parents have to be made aware of what their children need in terms of preparation, support, and encouragement. Not everyone can bankroll their kids or has crucial connections that can lead to employment opportunities. However, it is vitally important for parents to be actively involved in the decisions that their children make before, during, and after college. Moreover, it is crucial that we give parents the information that they will need to best prepare their children, regardless of the resources available to them.

In the planning process educational institutions also play a vital role. High schools do a good job of ensuring that many students go to college, but more should be done to help those not versed in the intricacies of the process. To be sure, a portion of the blame lies with third-level institutions and how education is packaged as a commodity, that is, as an experience to be purchased rather than a crucial investment. But the main deficit lies long before the glossy brochures arrive in high school juniors' mailboxes. Many high schools pay little or no attention to the connection between education and work. Instead, the game is to get as many young people into higher education as possible with little or no regard to where they go or what they study. This has become the norm in many high schools, and perhaps the increase in the number of students going on to further education explains how resources are not available to do much else. A recent exception to this trend can be found at the newly renovated Bensalem High School, located just outside of Philadelphia in southeastern Pennsylvania. Bensalem High School has redesigned its curriculum, adapting the career academy model that "will allow high schoolers to focus on fields such as health care, science and technology, business, or arts and communications" (Bocella 2017, B1). The aim here for this predominant working- and middle-class school is to improve college and career chances by fusing academics and careers. The career academies are one way to stimulate planning and show students the range of possibilities in terms of education and work beyond high school.

In helping young people plan for their future, educators have a duty to train and mentor them far in advance of a simple "college-for-all" message that implies that merely getting accepted means that you have won the game. Young people should know what options they have, not just the 4-year degrees but associate's degrees and professional certificates. Educators should let young people know about growth areas in skills and jobs; especially while at college, young people should be informed by education professionals exactly what they can do with their courses of study beyond that it "will get you a job." Young people are investing far too heavily in education to be making choices that are not fully informed, and it is the duty of high schools, universities, and colleges to be open and frank about the connections between education and jobs. Beyond mere transparency, educators need to do more to cultivate opportunities for young people in terms of internships, job shadowing, and work experience that allow young people to try a field before committing to it and to gain invaluable experience while doing so. Educators, especially those in upper administration and leadership positions, also have a primary duty to ensure that the runaway costs of higher education are reined in and do not disproportionately affect those least able to absorb the costs.

We believe that if these steps are taken, many more young people will have the opportunity to get an education that prepares them for a real job and does not saddle them with excessive debt in the process. The problems are not insurmountable, but they do require a commitment to helping those who are not well equipped to deal with the modern economy where certain types of education and training are crucial and lead to rewarding real jobs. Ensuring that everyone has access to these pathways should be a priority for our educators and policymakers.

REFERENCES

Abel, Jaison R., Richard Deitz, and Yaqin Su. "Are Recent College Graduates Finding Good Jobs?" *Current Issues in Economics and Finance* 20, no. 1 (2014): 1–9.

Bell, David N., and David Blanchflower. "Young People and the Great Recession." IZF Discussion Paper 5674. Institute for the Study of Labor, Berlin, Germany, 2011.

Bocella, Kathy. "Bucks School's Makeover Aims to Give Students a Head Start on Careers." *Philadelphia Inquirer*, August 11, 2017.

Busteed, Brandon. "Student Loan Debt: Major Barrier to Entrepreneurship." *Gallup Business Journal*, October 14, 2015.

Carnevale, Anthony P., Megan Fasules, Stephanie Bond Huie, and David Troutman. *Major Matters Most: The Economic Value of Bachelor's Degrees from the University of Texas System.* Washington, DC: Georgetown University Center for Education and the Workforce, 2017.

Carnevale, Anthony P., Megan Fasules, Andrea Porter, and Jennifer Landis-Santos. *African Americans: College Majors and Earnings.* Washington, DC: Georgetown University Center for Education and the Workforce, 2016.

Digest of Education Statistics. "Table 302.60. Percentage of 18- to 24-Year-Olds Enrolled in Degree-Granting Postsecondary Institutions, by Level of Institution and Sex and Race/Ethnicity of Student: 1970 Through 2015." National Center for Education Statistics, 2016. https://nces.ed.gov/programs/digest/d16/tables/dt16_302.60.asp. Accessed July 7, 2017.

Fogg, Neeta P., and Paul E. Harrington. "Rising Mal-Employment and the Great Recession: The Growing Disconnection Between Recent College Graduates and the College Labor Market." *Continuing Higher Education Review* 75 (2011): 51–65.

Goldrick-Rab, Sara. *Paying the Price: College Costs, Financial Aid, and the Betrayal of the American Dream.* Chicago: University of Chicago Press, 2016.

Granovetter, Mark. "The Strength of Weak Ties." *American Journal of Sociology* 78, no. 6 (1973): 1360–80.

Greenstone, Michael, and Adam Looney. *Is Starting College and Not Finishing Really That Bad?* Washington, DC: Brookings Institution, 2013.

Korn, Melissa. "Your College Major Is a Minor Issue, Employers Say." *Wall Street Journal*, April 10, 2013.

LaVelle, Katherine, Yaarit Silverstone, and David Smith. "Are You the Weakest Link? Strengthening Your Talent Supply Chain." Washington, DC: Accenture, 2015.

Schwartz, Elaine. "Four Charts That Show Why We Should Go to College." *Econlife*, December 9, 2015.

Selingo, Jeff. "Does Your Major Matter? Not Really." *New York Times*, April 29, 2013.

Stahl, Ashley. "Six Reasons Why Your College Major Doesn't Matter." *Forbes*, August 12, 2015.

Statista. "Educational Attainment Distribution in the United States from 1960 to 2015." 2017. https://www.statista.com/statistics/184260/educational-attainment-in-the-us/. Accessed June 25, 2017.

Steinberg, Sarah. *The High Cost of Youth Unemployment.* Washington, DC: Center for American Progress, 2013.

Tevington, Patricia. "Privileged to Worry: Social Class, Cultural Knowledge and Strategies Toward the Future Among Young Adults." *Sociological Quarterly* (2017): 1–30. doi:10.1080/00380253.2017.1389251.

Valletta, Robert. "Recent Flattening in the Higher Education Wage Premium: Polarization, Skill Downgrading, or Both?" Working Paper 22935, National Bureau of Economic Research, Washington, DC, 2016.

5

Part-Time Employment and Aesthetic Labor Among Middle-Class Youth

Yasemin Besen-Cassino

INTRODUCTION

Youth unemployment is one of the most persistent problems of our post-recession economy. According to the Bureau of Labor Statistics (2017), young people, especially 18- to 24-year-old workers, are severely affected by unemployment at rates much higher than the adult population. In 2017, the unemployment rate of 18- to 19-year-olds was 12.8 percent, and that of 20- to 24-year-olds was 7.5 percent; after age 25, the rate of unemployment drops to 3.5 percent (Bureau of Labor Statistics 2017).

Approximately 60 percent of youth are employed but with higher rates of employment for white youth than African American youth (62.3 percent and 56.4 percent, respectively). This chapter explores unemployment of youth in the post-recession United States and focuses on the effects of socioeconomic status and racialization—that is, on how differences in class and race among youth affect chances of finding jobs. I also seek to fill a gap in extant research since analyses of youth unemployment have been, to date, insufficient.

Previous research has explored the effects of the recession, but most studies of unemployment have focused on men's unemployment across age (Hoynes, Miller, and Schaller 2012; Legerski and Cornwall 2010), the effects of unemployment on retirement (Coile and Levine 2011), or the effects of unemployment on housework divisions and work/family balance (Bianchi 2011; Kruegger and Mueller 2012; Young and Schieman 2012). In terms of gender, both academic and popular sources have disproportionately surveyed the effects of the recession on men, referring to the recession as a "mancession" and highlighting the experiences of blue-collar males amid declines in manufacturing jobs. While recent research looks at the effects of unemployment for young people (Bell and Blanchflower 2011; Choudhry, Marelli, and Signorelli 2012), such studies typically do not focus on youth who work in part-time jobs and instead focus on unemployment of young people after the completion of formal education.

In addition, earlier research on youth and part-time jobs occurred in stages with different substantive orientations. First, beginning in the 1970s, studies documented youth labor as an important area of social inquiry that has been historically common (Coleman 1984; Engel, Marsden, and Woodaman 1968; Goldstein and Oldham 1979; Johnson and Bachman 1973; Lewin-Epstein 1981; Ruhm 1997; Shapiro 1979). A second wave of research, undertaken during the 1980s, focused primarily on the advantages of work for young people. Here, scholars contended that working while still in high school helps youth, especially non-college-bound youth, find jobs after they graduate from high school (D'Amico and Baker 1984; Meyer and Wise 1982; Stephenson 1980; Stern and Nakata 1989), reduces school dropout rates (D'Amico and Baker 1984; McNeal 1997), improves school attendance (Marsh 1991; Finch et al. 1991), and leads to better academic performance (D'Amico and Baker 1984).

Following this period of optimistic findings, more pessimistic interpretations of youth employment emerged. Beginning in the late 1980s and early 1990s, scholars inquired into the negative effects of working while still in school. Data tapped for these studies concluded, for example, that working (especially working too many hours) lowered academic success (Marsh 1991; Mortimer and Finch 1986; Steinberg and Dornbusch 1991; Steinberg, Fegley, and Dornbusch 1993), interfered with emotional and psychological development (Greenberger and Steinberg 1986; Mortimer et al. 1994), reduced interaction with family and friends (Greenberger and Steinberg 1986; Finch et al. 1991), increased drug and alcohol use (McMorris and Uggen 2000; Mihalic and Elliot 1997; Steinberg, Fegley, and Dornbusch 1993), and was related to crime (Hansen and Jarvis 2000).

Recent research, of which this chapter is a part, moves the debate away from advantages and disadvantages of working to inequalities that characterize workplace opportunities or lack thereof (Entwisle, Alexander, and Olson 2000). This new wave of research looks at the work experience from the perspective of the main actors—young people themselves—so as to capture varied lived experiences of youth employment and unemployment (Liebel 2004). Most significantly, contemporary research on youth employment looks at race-, ethnicity-, class-, and gender-related inequalities that are faced by young people as they seek work (Entwisle, Alexander, and Olson 2000). Consequently, rather than treating all young workers and all youth jobs as uniform entities, recent studies draw attention to the conditions of employment or unemployment that youth face.

In this vein, I focus on the perspectives of young workers themselves. I also argue that, all told, research to date has provided an incomplete picture of youth unemployment, failing to focus on part-time work, even though most students work at least some time throughout high school. According to the Department of Labor, approximately two-thirds of all youth work while still in school. This means that part-time labor comprises an important part of the US labor force overall and of young people's lives in particular. Also, the omission of youth's part-time work from previous research matters because this affects school-to-work transitions and how easily (or not) young people are able to go to and stay in school.

In order to address this gap, this chapter uses a mixed methods approach—combining qualitative interviews and statistical analyses—to illuminate the role of part-time labor and/or unemployment in young people's lives. For this chapter's purposes, I define youth broadly as 16- to 24-year-olds while, of necessity, focusing on a subset of this overall group, namely, 18- to 24-year-olds. I focus on 18- to 24-year-olds for several reasons. This group experiences particularly high unemployment rates. Also salient is that participants younger than 18 could not be included in my qualitative data because of institutional review board restrictions and ethical considerations. Analogously, the quantitative data used here including secondary data from the Pew Research Center exclude participants younger than 18 years of age. A last consideration was that, even though the minimum age required to work is 16, many places of employment only hire workers over 18 years of age. Important to note, too, is that the definition of work here parallels that of the US Department of Labor insofar as it includes any activity performed outside the home for pay. Unpaid labor, internships, household chores, and agricultural labor were outside the scope of this research; the qualitative data collection on which this chapter is based are part of a larger book project (Besen-Cassino 2014).

To understand the everyday lived experience of work from the perspectives of young people, I undertook participant observations at two branches of a national coffee chain. My ethnography at the coffee shop commenced in 2001 at two different branches of the national chain Coffee Bean, located in middle-class suburbs of a large city on the East Coast. While this ubiquitous national chain has branches across the country, the locations were chosen not only for geographic convenience but also for four substantive reasons. First, young people have identified the chain as a highly desirable place to work. Second, the two branches of Coffee Bean where I conducted participant observation employ young people and a good number of students. Third, Coffee Bean is typical of many service sector jobs at which young people work. Fourth, and finally, I wanted to focus on middle-class suburban youth as opposed to fast-food workers at urban locations, who have

been more frequently studied; the branches of Coffee Bean I researched employ predominantly white suburban young people who work while they are
also full-time students, allowing me to investigate part-time work previously
overlooked in other studies of youth labor.

Fieldwork was undertaken between 2001 and 2004 when I observed
workers at Coffee Bean for 1- to 8-hour shifts; I took detailed field notes
and recorded the tasks performed as well as interactions with co-workers,
customers, and friends. My observations included shifts done in the
morning and at night, at store openings and closings, and on weekdays
and weeknights; research was done at times when supervisors were present
and at times when no supervisor was present on a shift. I was also careful
to include shifts when young workers worked with other young workers, as
well as those during which younger and older workers worked together. In
addition to ethnographic observations aided by key informants, I conducted
40 semi-structured, in-depth interviews with present and former young
workers. These interviews varied in length from 1 to 2 hours, and I followed
up with questions on subsequent occasions with some of the respondents.
Interviews included detailed questions about job market experiences, the
process of finding jobs, and young people's experiences of work (full-time
and part-time) and of unemployment.

Both ethnographic observations and in-depth interviews helped to recon-
struct work experiences from the perspectives of youth and to understand
the social meaning of work and brands from their perspectives. It should
also be noted that, in 2007–08, I conducted a second wave of interviews and
surveys with a wider pool of workers. This time, instead of focusing only on
Coffee Bean baristas, I expanded my study to include students working in all
types of service and retail type jobs. I conducted approximately 50 in-depth
interviews with young full-time college students at one public and one private institution and distributed surveys that asked students about their work
experience, social and political views, consumption habits, and branding. In
2011, in order to document the effects of the recession and unemployment,
I embarked on a third round of data collection with supplemental interviews
and surveys conducted that year. I focused particularly on the effects of the
recession on finding part-time jobs and asked about the job search process,
interviews, and expectations they had about the job market.

The majority of the qualitative data used in this chapter comes from
these periods of data collection meant to prove the social meaning and processes through which young people find jobs. In-depth interviews enabled
insights into the mechanisms through which young people find and keep
jobs. I have coded and analyzed the qualitative data using NVivo and
interpreted these findings in the light of my systematic field notes. Finally,

I supplemented this qualitative research with quantitative analysis of data collected in a December 2011 national random digit dialing telephone survey carried out by the Pew Research Center. The sample for this survey includes an oversample of 18- to 34-year-olds and allowed me to draw on a reasonably sized subsample of 18- to 24-year-old students for this chapter. I analyzed these data to estimate logistic regression models to capture the effects of socioeconomic status and race on finding jobs. Supplementing the qualitative research here and increasing the external validity of the findings, these quantitative data placed individual narratives in a larger context and allowed for generalizing from qualitative data. The key questions I aimed to answer were, first, how do young people find jobs? Second, what are the effects of socioeconomic status and race on finding part-time jobs?

YOUTH, PART-TIME EMPLOYMENT, AND AESTHETIC LABOR

Work has always been a central component of the American labor force and especially of young Americans' lives. As Ellen Greenberger and Laurence Steinberg observe in their landmark book *When Teenagers Work* (1986), young people's part-time work is so ubiquitous that we rarely reflect more deeply on its social and economic role in society. As they argue,

> The large teenage, part-time labor force that staffs the counters of fast-food establishments, waits on customers in retail stores, assembles parts in industrial settings, and cleans motel rooms and office buildings has become such a familiar part of our social landscape that we may fail to note its unique character or to ponder its social significance. (3)

Young people are an integral part of our economy, and work is a central part of their lives. This is so not only economically but socially as well. Recent studies document the social benefits of working for students as a common space to socialize and meet new people (Besen-Cassino 2014), meaning that youth unemployment has serious consequences on both economic and social levels. Moreover, according to the US Department of Labor's *Report on the Youth Labor Force* (Herman 2000), youth employment starts early. The largest category of employment is in retail jobs (45 percent), followed by the service sector (29 percent).

Working while in school is a widespread practice inside and outside of the United States; it is typical for young people to work because of economic need, and the youth labor force tends to be dominated by youth from lower-income families (Besen-Cassino 2014). In the United States, though, a comparatively unique feature of youth labor is that this category is dominated not by youth from lower- but upper-class socioeconomic backgrounds

(Herman 2000; Besen-Cassino 2014). In fact, the higher the socioeconomic background, the more likely young people are to work and to have found work (Herman 2000; Besen-Cassino 2014; see also Sternheimer 2016).

Thus, the socioeconomic composition of the American youth labor force begs further inquiry: Why are youth from higher–economic status backgrounds disproportionately represented and obviously frequently hired? How might class status play a role in getting jobs, and what are the mechanisms through which higher–socioeconomic status young workers end up getting these jobs? Below, I present data that emerge from qualitative and quantitative sources.

Finding the "Right Look": The Requirements of Aesthetic Labor

Until recently, retail and service jobs employing young people (Herman 2000) required little formal education or job skills. As Chris Tilly and Françoise Carré (2011, 298) observe, many employers referred to the pulse test (does the employee have a pulse?) or the mirror test (does the candidate's breath fog up the mirror?) in their hiring decisions. But these jobs, once abundant, are now becoming more difficult to procure: many post-recession studies document that employers are now much more selective in their hiring decisions (Tilly and Carré 2011). In addition to the recent economic recession decreasing the available number of these jobs, many employers have sharply increased their emphases on the importance of self-presentation, soft skills, aesthetic skills, and social/cultural capital in hiring (Gatta 2011; Nickson et al. 2011). This is because retail and service sector employers now believe they are selling not only a simple product or service but a brand experience (Nickson et al. 2011).

As a consequence, workers at particular retail and service sector jobs are expected to embody that brand's essence; they are supposed to look and sound like the brand to provide an appropriately "high-quality" experience for consumers (Besen-Cassino 2014; Gatta 2011; Williams and Connell 2010). While aesthetic labor has thus become a much more central component of service and retail jobs for both men and women than at previous times, women may have even more sharply brand-related expectations (Besen-Cassino and Ocejo 2017) because of the gender-skewed effects of traditionally gendered socialization. Thus, the rise of aesthetic labor standards may disproportionately (but not exclusively) affect women both as potential employees and as consumers.

Exemplifying these changes, consider Jules, a 20-year-old female student at a large state university. She recalls her interview for her first job at a fashionable clothing chain, targeting teenagers and younger consumers:

> During my senior year in high school, I decided to find my first job. Many of
> my friends were working at the mall close to my home. So I decided to find a

job in retail (at the same mall). I applied for a job at Seymour and Smith because I knew people that worked there, and I also liked their clothing. Working
at Seymour and Smith gave one status back in the day. It was cool and the hot-
test place. If you told someone you worked at Seymour and Smith, they held
you to a different standard. . . . Since this was my first job, I had nothing on my
résumé. I still remember being asked, "What is your favorite animal?" There
were no questions like, "How would you like to contribute to our company?"
"Do you see yourself working here in five years?" . . . I had no experience. All
I had was personality and appearance; that's all I brought to the table.

Even though Jules did not have any related retail experience or skills, she
was surprised at how easily she was offered the job at this desirable chain
because of the right "look." Indeed, Mary Gatta's (2011) analysis of high-
end boutiques and clothing stores documents that employers in such stores
emphasize looks-related considerations. In researching high-end boutiques
in an affluent New Jersey town, Gatta found that high-end boutiques were
staffed disproportionately with white and middle-class workers. In many
retail and service sector jobs, the workers are the face of the company; therefore, employers look for workers who "look good and sound right" (Williams
and Connell 2010)—expectations that can clearly have racialized as well as
class-skewed implications.

Jules' experience seems to be more typical than aberrant when it comes
to how retail employers hire. For instance, Jenna, another college student,
recalls being asked at her job interview about her favorite music, consumption habits, and hobbies. She did not find this very strange and believes
employers ought to learn about potential workers' interests to determine if
they are a good match for the brand. This is why, after Jenna later became a
supervisor at the Coffee Bean, she herself began using a similar approach
when recruiting baristas. As Jenna explained, personality and looks are very
important in hiring: "You always want cool people to work here."

Jenna's attitude affected her hiring of Josh, a 19-year-old student who
went to town to shop for a job after he moved into his dorm room. He
walked around the college town looking for places where he himself liked
shopping in order to get a job. After a day of shopping for jobs, he walked
into his favorite chain for a cup of coffee. Jenna, who was the supervisor,
chatted with him about his interests and hobbies and asked him if he
wanted a job. As Josh put it, "I came to get coffee, but got a job with it."
According to Jenna, Josh had the right vibe; he listened to "good music" and
had a stylish haircut. Thus, it was not his coffee-making skills (which, she
felt, could easily be learned) but rather his "vibe" which fit the "look" of the
coffee shop. On the other hand, traditional considerations—his previous
work experience (limited) and job-related skills (also limited)—were much
less relevant to her decision. Overall, with his clothes, his look, and his other
consumption habits, he was right for the Coffee Bean gig.

From this observation—that an overwhelming majority of corporations in the contemporary economy are selling not simply a service but a branded service—comes the concept, now to be defined more precisely, of aesthetic labor. As discussed by Nickson et al.,

> the development of what is termed "aesthetic labour" involves the manner in which employees are expected to embody the product in industries such as service and hospitality. . . . This labour refers to the hiring of people with corporeal capacities and attributes that favorably appeal to customers' senses, which are organizationally mobilized, developed and commodified. As a part of this process of embodiment, employees are expected to demonstrate soft-skills associated with personality and attitude, to "look good" and "sound right." (2011, 69)

While employees can be trained in the actual conduct of the job, it is much harder to train someone to project the desired "right" image to fit a company's branding goals.

Young people I interviewed at the coffee shop agreed that Coffee Bean employees had a look and a personality but one that had become highly correlated with race and income—in other words, with mostly white upper-middle-class young workers. As 19-year-old Matt told me, "They [employees] act like they are classier and upper-class, because they kind of are." According to many of my interviewees, and regardless of the location—suburb or inner-city—the "look" of the brand was overwhelmingly white and affluent.

Clearly not all young people have the same advantages: as aesthetic labor and style become an increasingly common components in hiring, race and socioeconomic class also become major determinants of being able to achieve the "right" look and "vibe." Note, too, that employees thereby become central actors responsible for marketing and projecting a lifestyle. Indeed, as Nickson and colleagues have observed, students are often deemed to be "particularly attractive to retail employers due to their flexibility, cheapness and highly developed soft skills" (2011, 68). Complicating the picture, though, is a major question: how do students afford to project a style that, according to David Wright, entails physical attractiveness, a particular style of dress, and types of physical comportment that taken together "contribute to the production of the retail space as meaningful and aesthetically pleasing to the customer" (2005, 305)?

It seems that, in fact, many retailers desire that employees wear the clothes they are selling. A good way to ensure that this happens is to recruit workers from existing customers; if this happens, then the clothing requirement is not just a top-down policy that all employees must follow but a demand about which employees are likely to be enthused. By recruiting from existing customers, corporations also ensure that the employees not only look like the brand but are knowledgeable about the product. Take, for example, the case of Sophia. Sophia recalls management recruiting from existing shoppers at a stylish clothing store where she worked. One teenager had come into the store many times and had spent around $2,000. As a result, this young person was asked if she wanted to work at the store and was offered a job on the spot; she was obviously a devoted and knowledgeable customer-soon-to-turn-employee. By extension, not surprisingly, young people offered jobs in this way tended to be relatively affluent in class terms.

Many young employees are under pressure to consume brand products not only to obtain but to keep their jobs. For instance, Lynne Pettinger's ethnography of London retailers shows that "the ability to present a fashionable appearance is one of the skills needed by sales assistants in many stores" (2005, 468). Jules, too, recalls that wearing company clothes was both required and socially expected: it was not just company policy but the culture at the store that constantly reminded her to keep up with the products. As she recalls, employees would frequently talk about the new season's clothes and new fashions. At the end of her employment, ironically, she had accumulated so much debt that keeping up with the "look" of the company rivaled her student loans. While many corporations offered discounts, they were often too small to help with constantly renewing consumption of new items and lines, leading to accumulation of debt in vicious cycles that can affect even affluent youth.

Many young people who come from lower-socioeconomic backgrounds face difficulties in finding jobs. Mason, a 21-year-old social science major who lives in a low-income town with a large proportion of African American residents, related how he had encountered problems locating a part-time job. Though he invested time in searching, he had the impression that he did not have the "right" look or address to be hired at many retail stores. Like Mason, many young people need local jobs to stay in school, contribute to their families, and/or help with their own expenses. Yet, as the post-recession economy has shifted, they often find themselves left outside the job force and going through long bouts of unemployment that sometimes force them to interrupt their educations or settle for fast-food jobs.

Despite apparent racial and socioeconomic inequalities in hiring, many young people do not notice structural barriers impeding their employment. When I asked young employees to describe a typical Coffee Bean employee, they answered as follows: "They are tree-hugging hippies who play their acoustic guitars" (Noah, 21-year-old male student) and they "are classy hippies who listen to the Grateful Dead and memorize the script to *Rent* and the *Rocky Horror Picture Show*" (Eric, 20-year-old male student). Other responses included that the typical Coffee Bean employee is "Liberal, artsy, upper to middle class with earrings and tattoos, drives a green car, hates the war, loves the trees" (Mike, 20-year-old male student) or that a characteristic employee is "Someone who reads books for fun" (Francesca, 20-year-old female student). According to another participant, Coffee Bean employees "are informed about different bands and are interested in coffee and music" (Emma, 18-year-old female student).

Note that these replies seem to be describing a similar personality; hardly, too, are answers devoid of allusions to class. Indeed, Aaron, a 21-year-old male student, declares that a typical Coffee Bean employee is "A stuck-up Caucasian teenager, spoiled by parents." While many young people thus acknowledge that young people from higher socioeconomic backgrounds are more likely to work at desirable brand retail stores like Coffee Bean, answers were quite different when I asked for descriptions of a typical fast-food worker. Again, replies involved looks but with quite different aesthetic images: some young people answered that the typical fast-food worker would have "untucked shirts, baggy pants and crooked hat" or would be "overweight" or "pimply." As to why someone would work in a fast-food establishment, answers included because they were "dropouts . . . just trying to pay off his or her expenses" (Dylan, 19); another young participant mentioned "lower-class poverty" and being "black" (Mike, 20).

Overall, these narratives show attitudes that have the effect of working against the hiring of lower–socioeconomic status and nonwhite young workers. These qualitative findings also attest to structural barriers like race and class becoming normalized through stratified cultural demands of aesthetic labor.

Socioeconomic and Racial Inequalities of Aesthetic Labor

While in-depth interviews and personal narratives revealed processes by which young people experience socioeconomic and racial discrimination when looking for jobs, quantitative analysis helps in contextualizing these findings. Drawing on quantitative data also allows for generalizability by externally validating research results.

In particular, data from a December 2011 Pew Research Center survey illustrate the role of socioeconomic status in young people's job searches. Using responses from full- and part-time working students, it was possible to estimate the effect that class and other factors have on students entering the workforce (or not) and on whether they are able to find jobs when doing so. Two key elements here are race and family socioeconomic status, both measured through self-reporting. Income was on a 1–9 scale (mean 4.9, median 5), with higher values representing higher levels of income and race simplified to a non-Hispanic white/nonwhite dichotomy (Table 5.1).

Because of the potential problem arising from some students reporting their own income and others reporting *family* income, this analysis focuses

Table 5.1 Likelihood of Looking for a Job

Income	Live with Parents?	White?	P(Looking for Job)	P(Opt out)	P(Have Job)
Lowest	No	Nonwhite	56%	5%	38%
Lowest	No	White	5%	26%	69%
Lowest	Yes	Nonwhite	31%	32%	37%
Lowest	Yes	White	81%	0%	19%
Median	No	Nonwhite	18%	19%	62%
Median	No	White	18%	13%	68%
Median	Yes	Nonwhite	22%	33%	44%
Median	Yes	White	49%	2%	49%
Highest	No	Nonwhite	3%	37%	60%
Highest	No	White	47%	4%	48%
Highest	Yes	Nonwhite	15%	34%	51%
Highest	Yes	White	3%	85%	12%

Notes: Socioeconomic status and race are important predictors for finding jobs for young people. White, high-socioeconomic status students have a clear advantage; but both median-income students and students of color experience a marked disadvantage.
Source: Pew Research Center (2011).

on students who do not live independently of their families. In other words, I have included only those who report living at home or in a dormitory; I have also controlled for age, gender, part-time student status, and whether or not a student was born in the United States. I sought to check whether similar results based on qualitative analysis—that is, factors leading to employment or unemployment among students seemed to include whether a young person had the right "look" to procure a desirable job—were borne out by quantitative research as well.

While there is no direct measure of "look" in these or most other survey data, race made for a reasonable proxy: retail establishments find themselves in legal jeopardy by overtly defining the look of their brand in racial terms so as to favor white job applicants; it is also reasonable to assume that other potential employers are also more circumspect about putting such terms into writing. To parse out all of the potential effects, multinomial logistic regression was used to predict whether students would be employed, unemployed, or opt out of the labor force entirely. Based on this chapter's qualitative findings, expectations about aesthetic labor predicted that (1) students with the lowest socioeconomic status, and therefore the greatest need for a job, would have the highest unemployment rates; (2) socioeconomic status would have the strongest effect on unemployment rates, meaning that students with the right "look" disproportionately would tend to be white; (3) students with high socioeconomic status, with the least need for jobs, would have the easiest time finding a job if they wanted one and by extension the lowest unemployment rates. Also note that since this analysis does not assume linear effects, hypotheses 1 and 3 are not causally related.

Indeed, the regression results presented in Table 5.2 show strong interaction effects between income, race, and whether or not a student lives at home. Among nonwhite students, higher levels of income lead to modestly higher proportions of working students and to lower rates of unemployment. Nonwhite students at the 25th percentile of income have a 40 percent unemployment rate (the proportion looking for work but not able to find it); at the 75th percentile of income, the unemployment rate is 28 percent. Similarly, 41 percent of nonwhite students at the 25th income percentile were employed compared with 48 percent of those at the 75th percentile (Figure 5.1).

However, among white students, the effects of income are enormous. White students at the 25th percentile of income have a 67 percent unemployment rate. At the 75th percentile, this drops to 31 percent. In the top income category, representing the 95th percentile of income, only 3 percent

Table 5.2 Regression Coefficients for Likelihood of Working

Variable	Coefficient	Standard Error	z	$P > |z|$
Age	−0.040	0.127	−0.310	0.755
Income	−0.402	0.230	−1.750	0.080
Living with parents	−0.766	1.136	−0.670	5.000
Income × living with parents	0.270	0.268	1.010	0.313
White	−3.750	1.414	−2.650	0.008
Income × white	0.725	0.283	2.570	0.010
LIVING with parents × white	5.541	2.374	2.330	0.020
Income × living with parents × white	−0.964	0.435	−2.220	0.027
Sex	−0.500	0.448	−1.110	0.265
Part-time student	0.178	0.538	0.330	0.741
Living in dorm	0.781	0.596	1.310	0.190
Parents help	0.089	0.200	0.440	0.657
US-born	0.201	0.489	0.410	0.681
Live with parents omitted				
Constant	1.645	2.993	0.550	0.583

Number of observations = 163.
Likelihood ratio $\chi^2(26) = 63.86$.
Probability $> \chi^2 = 0.0000$.
Log likelihood $= -135.42379$.
Pseudo $R^2 = 0.1908$.
Source: Pew Research Center (2011).

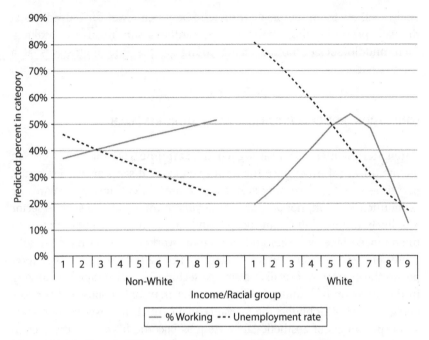

Figure 5.1 Likelihood of Working and Unemployment Rates by Race

Source: Pew Research Center 2011.

of white students are looking for work but unable to find it. Overall, employment rates among wealthier white students do decline a bit relative to middle-income white students, but this relates to a decline in labor force participation rather than an inability to find jobs. Put another way, upper–socioeconomic status whites who want jobs are able to find them.

These results provide support for all three of the hypotheses outlined above and for suspecting the salience of aesthetic labor through the curvilinear relationship between employment rates and income among white students. Higher–socioeconomic status students living at home likely do not need to work, especially when their families are at the 90th or 95th percentiles of income, as evidenced by their lower rates of labor force participation. The low unemployment rate indicates that these individuals are not looking for work but may take it if offered or that they are likely to be able to find a job quickly if they decide to do so.

Finally, these results indicate that socioeconomic status has continuing rather than step effects on the employment prospects of young people. It might be anticipated that only lower-class students are at a disadvantage, but students whose socioeconomic status is in the middle-class range are also relatively worse off than their wealthier counterparts. However, these analyses show the unemployment rate to be much lower for individuals at the 95th percentile than at the 75th percentile; again, relatively speaking, even middle–socioeconomic status young people find themselves at a disadvantage.

CONCLUSION: POLICY IMPLICATIONS AND FUTURE RESEARCH

Karen Sternheimer (2016) has argued that part-time work for youth, once an almost universal experience for young people, is disappearing. For youth, part-time jobs are becoming scarce and more difficult to locate. With the economic recession, not only are employers in the retail and service sector less likely to hire, but young people find themselves in competition with unemployed older workers and immigrant workers, rendering these jobs more competitive than ever before (Sternheimer 2016). Also, as this chapter posits, the character of retail and service sector jobs is also rapidly changing in the direction of brand experiences rather than only goods and services being sold. This highlights the relevance to potential employees of demands and expectations of aesthetic labor. As jobs become fewer and more competitive, class-, race-, and gender-based inequalities appear to be occurring more commonly.

Theoretically it is important to understand that work, as an important economic as well as social component of young people's lives, has lately become more of a privilege than a widespread and extremely standard experience (Sternheimer 2016; see also Besen-Cassino 2014). This is so even though, economically, part-time jobs matter greatly to young people, especially young people from lower–socioeconomic status backgrounds. Part-time work helps low-income youth both with their everyday expenses and daily essentials and with costs relating to schooling; for many low-income youth, part-time jobs may make the difference between being able and not being able to stay in school while contributing to family income and expenses.

As previously discussed and meriting re-emphasis by way of conclusion, part-time work for youth has major social as well as economic benefits. Jobs assist in socializing young people as well as in developing practical job-related skills like punctuality and responsibility (Besen-Cassino 2014). Work also provides a common vocabulary while simultaneously offering social spaces for young people to meet and socialize with other youth with similar interests (Besen-Cassino 2014). Finally, work provides a social arena wherein young people have the opportunity to interact with a diverse group of workers from different racial, ethnic, and class backgrounds. With the rise in youth unemployment and with recently intensifying aesthetic labor requirements, young people do not have the same extent of opportunities for interacting with diverse groups of workers from a range of backgrounds including those who have been socially and economically disadvantaged.

But what are some of the policy implications of these findings about youth and youth employment/unemployment? First, and again, part-time jobs are socially significant for many young people: their value includes, but is not limited to, the economic dimension (Newman 2000). Many young people point to lack of social space in centerless suburbs for socializing and for making new friends and hanging with existing ones away from parental supervision and adult scrutiny. Given increasingly scheduled lives with activities marked by constant parental involvement and adult supervision, many youth seek to socialize with friends away from adult scrutiny. In addition, lack of public transportation or access to cars makes it challenging to access peers.

Malls, shopping centers, and movie theaters have traditionally provided a common space for many teenagers. However, the past few decades have witnessed growing anti-teenage policies in the suburbs. At present, many malls implement parental escort policies; this means that customers under the age of 18 will not be allowed in the mall without a parent or a guardian. In 1996, The Mall of America in Bloomington, Minnesota, became the first to implement a parental escort policy; many other malls, including, for example, the Tri-County Mall in Cincinnati, Ohio, followed suit as they found their sales going up. Other malls, like the Crossgates Mall in Albany, New York, set curfews for teenage shoppers such that no unattended teenagers are allowed to enter after 4:00 p.m. Even more restrictive policies have been implemented at malls like Atlantic Terminal in Brooklyn, New York, which does not allow four or more young people under the age of 21 to congregate (Schaffer 2010). Some movie theaters and other businesses, too, have recently banned or restricted the presence of young people.

Given these evolving policies, especially relevant to suburban youth, work fulfills a major social function for young people to socialize and see their friends even as the contemporary economy is generating more precarity and severe unemployment than in previous periods. For both social and economic reasons, then, it is important to focus social attention on creating alternative spaces for youth to congregate, meet new and old friends, and develop their identities as they are shut out of the workforce.

A second policy implication of this research involves racially and socioeconomically based discriminations that can take place on the basis of address discrimination. Many young people, like Mason and Carter, find potential employers not hiring because of biases they believe are related to the addresses they have written on application forms. This strongly affects youth from towns known to be low-income and/or to have predominantly

African American residents. From this, a clear policy implication emerges about the importance of legislative changes that would prevent employers from inquiring about prospective employees' addresses and acting on racial and class biases when applications are taken.

A third ramification of this chapter's arguments pertains to aesthetic requirements that have become far more common requirements of service jobs even as jobs have become more difficult to obtain. Aesthetic labor requirements are closely related to gender-, race-, and class-related biases and job demands. Yet little, if any, regulation exists when it comes to aesthetic considerations that nonetheless seep into hiring. Although several lawsuits have successfully targeted aesthetic labor, they are the exceptions rather than the norm. For instance, in *Gonzalez v. Abercrombie & Fitch* (03-2817 SI [N.D. Cal] 2003), Eduardo Gonzalez along with other plaintiffs suing Abercrombie & Fitch charged they were not hired despite their strong sales backgrounds and work experience. They argued that, as minority candidates, they were excluded and placed in low-visibility positions; based on stereotypes of race, ethnicity, and gender, the company was said to be biased toward "all-American" and predominantly white "looks" in its hiring practices. As a result of this lawsuit, Abercrombie & Fitch settled and implemented diversity programs. In the second case, *Equal Employment Opportunity Commission v. Abercrombie & Fitch* (575 U.S. ___ 2015), a Muslim woman, Samantha Elauf, sued the same company after being told she could not wear her headscarf at the store. The Supreme Court decided in her favor on the basis of the banned headscarf comprising religious discrimination.

Yet, while these plaintiffs prevailed, much more typical is to find that aesthetic labor requirements are difficult to challenge. In the overwhelming majority of cases, courts have sided with corporations and prejudices related to aesthetic labor bias have been hard to prove. Consequent lack of regulation has enabled many companies to select affluent young laborers with middle-class "presentations of self." In effect, this has meant that aesthetic labor requirements involving biases based on race and socioeconomic status often result in gender, racial, and socioeconomic discriminations that favor upper-class, mostly white, and sometimes female candidates. This has contributed to gender, race, and class stratification among young people at workplaces. As a result, and since youth economically need jobs for survival and/or to stay in school, they often find themselves either without (middle class) jobs altogether or settling for fast-food jobs.

Moreover, lack of regulation of aesthetic labor requirements in the hiring process has also reinforced what sociologist Mary Gatta refers to as "Eliza Doolittle syndrome." While higher–socioeconomic status youth have an easier time finding jobs, aesthetic labor requirements suggest it is their own responsibility to have the right "look" and to spend money on products to achieve that look; American individualism, too, is reinforced as a result. In addition, young people's debt levels as consumers have tended to increase for this reason—paradoxically, given their need for jobs that provide funds for schooling and other expenses.

A policy implication here, then, is that in addition to helping young people find jobs, new policies are needed to regulate the hiring process in retail and service sector jobs. Labor laws and regulations have not caught up with rapid changes in service and retail jobs that have increased their aesthetic labor requirements. Thus, it is important to develop new legislation to protect workers from these hiring practices that are often racially and class discriminatory in effect. Again, aesthetic labor appears to have become one way that corporations contribute to social stratification along racial and economic lines. In addition, aesthetic requirements that force young people to purchase the products they are selling, thereby contributing to young people acquiring large amounts of debt, place lower-income youth especially at disadvantage. This has tended to have asymmetric gender effects on women, who are more likely to find themselves facing demands about their looks. In these respects, too, new policies are needed to regulate corporations' demands and requirements so that young people of diverse and varied social backgrounds can access part-time jobs—and so that both young men and women have equal access to, and equal treatment at, these jobs.

Fourth, and finally, this research has important implications insofar as part-time jobs keep a good number of youth in school. As this chapter shows, work is both socially and economically central to many young people's lives. However, with the recent economic recession, part-time jobs that used to be easy to procure have become exceedingly difficult to find and maintain. These jobs should not be a privilege that elite youth enjoy but rather should be accessible to all youth interested in working. For that purpose, government programs are needed in far greater numbers to help young people find employment across urban, suburban, and rural locations.

Overall, youth unemployment is a crucial social problem to address, and redress, in post-recession America. Since class, race, and gender factors in combination play hefty roles in finding and keeping jobs, new policies and better regulation are required to assist young people in gaining equitable labor market access.

REFERENCES

Bell, David N. F., and David G. Blanchflower. "Young People and the Great Recession." *Oxford Review of Economic Policy* 27, no. 2 (2011): 241–67.

Besen-Cassino, Yasemin. *Consuming Work: Youth Work in America.* Philadelphia: Temple University Press, 2014.

Besen-Cassino, Yasemin, and Richard Ocejo. "Cool for Some: Gendered Experiences of Precarious Work." Presented at the Annual Meeting of the American Sociological Association, Montreal, CA, August 12–15, 2017.

Bianchi, Suzanne M. "Family Change and Time Allocation in American Families." *Annals of the American Academy of Political and Social Science* 638 (2011): 21–44.

Bureau of Labor Statistics. "Labor Force Statistics from the Current Population." 2017. https://www.bls.gov/web/empsit/cpseea10.htm Retrieved May 9, 2018

Choudhry, Misbah Tanveer, Enrico Marelli, and Marcello Signorelli. "Youth Unemployment Rate and Impact of Financial Crises." *International Journal of Manpower* 33, no. 1 (2012): 76–95.

Coile, Courtney C., and Phillip Levine. "The Market Crash and the Mass Layoffs: How the Current Economic Crisis May Affect Retirement." *B.E. Journal of Economic Analysis and Policy* 11, no. 1 (2011): 1–40.

Coleman, James. "The Transition from School to Work." *Research in Social Stratification and Mobility* 3 (1984): 27–59.

D'Amico, Ronald, and Paula Baker. *Pathways to the Future.* Columbus: Center for Human Resource Research, Ohio State University, 1984.

Engel, Mary, Gerald Marsden, and Sylvie Woodaman. "Orientation to Work in Children." *American Journal of Orthopsychiatry* 68 (1968): 137–43.

Entwisle, Doris R., Karl L. Alexander, and Linda Steffel Olson. "Early Work Histories of Urban Youth." *American Sociological Review* 65 (2000): 279–97.

Finch, Michael D., Michael J. Shanahan, Jeylan T. Mortimer, and Seongryeol Ryu. "Work Experience and Control Orientation in Adolescence." *American Sociological Review* 56 (1991): 597–611.

Gatta, Mary. "In the Blink of an Eye: American High End Small Retail Businesses and the Public Workforce System." In *Retail Work*, edited by Irena Grugulis and Odul Bozkurt, 49–67. London: Palgrave Macmillan, 2011.

Goldstein, Bernard, and Jack Oldham. *Children and Work.* New Brunswick, NJ: Transaction, 1979.

Greenberger, Ellen, and Laurence Steinberg. *When Teenagers Work: Psychological and Social Costs of Adolescent Work.* New York: Basic Books, 1986.

Hansen, David M., and Patricia Jarvis. "Adolescent Employment and Psychological Outcomes: A Comparison of Two Employment Contexts." *Youth and Society* 31, no. 4 (2000): 417–36.

Herman, Alexis. *Report on the Youth Labor Force.* Washington, DC: Bureau of Labor Statistics, 2000.

Hoynes, Hilary, Douglas Miller, and Jessamyn Schaller. "Who Suffers During Recessions?" *Journal of Economic Perspectives* 26, no. 3 (2012): 27–48.

Johnson, Jerome, and Jerald G. Bachman. *Transition from High School to Work.* Ann Arbor: Institute of Social Research, University of Michigan, 1973.

Krueger, Alan B., and Andreas Mueller. "Time Use, Emotional Well-Being, and Unemployment: Evidence from Longitudinal Data." *American Economic Review* 102, no. 3 (2012): 594–99.

Legerski, Elizabeth Miklya, and Marie Cornwall. "Working-Class Job Loss, Gender, and the Negotiation of Household Labor." *Gender and Society* 24, no. 4 (2010): 447–74.

Lewin-Epstein, Noah. *Youth Employment During High School*. Chicago: National Center for Education Statistics, 1981.

Liebel, Manfred. *A Will of Their Own: Cross-Cultural Perspectives on Working Children*. London: Routledge, 2004.

Marsh, Herbert W. "Employment During High School: Character Building and Subversion of Academic Goals." *Sociology of Education* 64 (1991): 172–89.

McMorris, Barbara, and Christopher Uggen. "Alcohol and Employment in Transition to Adulthood." *Journal of Health and Social Behavior* 41 (2000): 276–94.

McNeal, Ralph B., Jr. "Are Students Being Pulled Out of High School? The Effects of Adolescent Employment on Dropping Out." *Sociology of Education* 70 (1997): 206–20.

Meyer, Robert H., and David A. Wise. "High School Preparation in Early Labor Force Experience." In *The Youth Labor Market Problem: Its Nature, Causes and Consequences*, edited by Richard B. Freeman and David Wise, 277–348. Chicago: University of Chicago Press, 1982.

Mihalic, Sharon W., and Delbert Elliot. "Short- and Long-Term Consequences of Adolescent Work." *Youth & Society* 28 (1997): 464–98.

Mortimer, Jeylan T., and Michael Finch. "The Development of Self-Esteem in the Early Work Career." *Work and Occupations* 13 (1986): 217-39.

Mortimer, Jeylan T., Michael Finch, Katherine Dennehy, Chaimun Lee, and Timothy Beebe. "Work Experience in Adolescence." *Journal of Vocational Education Research* 19 (1994): 39–70.

Newman, Katherine. *No Shame in My Game: The Working Poor in the Inner City*. New York: Vintage, 2000.

Nickson, Dennis, Scott A. Hurrell, Chris Warhurst, and Johanna Commander. "Labour Supply and Skills Demand in Fashion Retailing." In *Retail Work*, edited by Irena Grugulis and Ödül Bozkurt, 66–87. London: Palgrave Macmillan, 2011.

Pettinger, Lynne. "Gendered Work Meets Gendered Goods: Selling and Service in Clothing Retail" Gender Work and Organization, 12 no. 7 (2005): 460-478.

Ruhm, Christopher. "Is High School Employment Consumption or Investment?" *Journal of Labor Research* 15 (1997): 735–76.

Schaffer, Kayleen. "New Policies Exterminating Teen Mall Rats." *ABC News*, September 23, 2010.

Shapiro, D. "Working Students." In *Pathways to the Future: Preliminary Report on Youth and the Labor Market*, edited by M. E. Borus, 161–67. Columbus: Center for Human Resource Research, Ohio State University, 1979.

Steinberg, Laurence, and Sanford M. Dornbusch. "The Negative Correlates of Part-Time Employment During Adolescence: Replication and Elaboration." *Developmental Psychology* 27 (1991): 304–13.

Steinberg, Laurence, Suzanne Fegley, and Sanford M. Dornbusch. "Negative Impact of Part-Time Work on Adolescent Adjustment: Evidence from a Longitudinal Study." *Developmental Psychology* 29, no. 2 (1993): 171–80.

Stephenson, Stanley P., Jr. "In School Work and Early Post-School Labor Market Dynamics." Working Paper, Department of Economics, Pennsylvania State University, State College, PA, 1980.

Stern, David, and Yoshi-Fumi Nakata. "Characteristics of High-School Students' Paid Jobs, and Employment Experience After Graduation." In *Adolescence and Work*, edited by David Stern and Dorothy Eichorn, 189–211. Hillsdale, NJ: Erlbaum, 1989.

Sternheimer, Karen. "The Privilege of a Summer Job." *Everyday Sociology* (blog). July 21, 2016. http://www.everydaysociologyblog.com/2016/07/the-privilege-of-a-summer-job.html.

Tilly, Chris, and Françoise Carré. "Endnote: Perceptions and Reality." In *Retail Work*, edited by Irena Grugulis and Ödül Bozkurt, 297–306. London: Palgrave Macmillan, 2011.

Williams, Christine, and Catherine Connell. "Looking Good and Sounding Right: Aesthetic Labor and Social Inequality in the Retail Industry." *Work & Occupations* 37, no. 3 (2010): 349–77.

Wright, David. "Commodifying Respectability: Distinctions at Work in the Bookshop." *Journal of Consumer Culture* 5, no. 3 (2005): 295–314.

Young, Marisa, and Scott Schieman. "When Hard Times Take a Toll: The Distressing Consequences of Economic Hardship and Life Events Within the Family–Work Interface." *Journal of Health and Social Behavior* 53, no. 1 (2012): 84–98.

Part III

SOCIOECONOMIC PRECARITY AND YOUTH UNEMPLOYMENT

6

The Children of Low-Status Immigrants
and Youth Unemployment in
the United States and Western Europe

Richard Alba and Nancy Foner

Massive South–North immigration during the last half-century has added substantially to the minority populations of the United States and western European countries, and with it have come additional concerns about youth and jobs. The demographic aspects of this immigration—migrants tend to be young adults and to have higher fertility than the native-majority group—mean that sizable portions of the youth of these societies have grown up in immigrant families. While youth in general face more challenges in the early twenty-first-century labor market than their parents and grandparents did, many of these second-generation youth face a special set of hurdles because of their disadvantaged immigrant origins. At the same time, because of the demographically driven transition to diversity that will occur in North America and western Europe during the next quarter-century, their potential economic contribution is crucial. Our chapter addresses this situation and identifies some of the key disadvantages that they face in education and the labor market.

In examining these issues, our perspective is international, taking in the United States, on one side of the Atlantic, and Britain, France, Germany, and the Netherlands, on the other. These European countries, like the United States, are home to large numbers of immigrants and their children, who represent around a fifth, sometimes more, of each country's population. We focus on a segment of the second generation that is critical to the future of these countries: youth whose parents are low-status immigrants. While immigration streams to the United States and western Europe are diverse and contain many high-skilled immigrants, such as Indians settling in the United States and Great Britain, low-status immigration has been a major component of these streams.

By "low-status immigrants" we refer to migrants from the global South who arrive in wealthy countries with low levels of human capital, particularly educational credentials, and are further disadvantaged by their ethnic, racial, or religious differences from the receiving society mainstreams. In the countries that we examine in this chapter, low-status immigrant groups include Mexicans and Central Americans in the United States, North Africans in France, Turks in Germany and the Netherlands, and Bangladeshis in Great Britain. In some cases, like North Africans in France, they were coming from former colonies of the country they were moving to; in such cases as well as some others (like Mexicans crossing the Rio Grande), they were entering contexts where members of the native-majority population already possessed well-developed negative stereotypes about them.

It is the youths in the low-status groups who challenge most deeply the integration capacities and institutions of the societies where they are growing up, and as we will document, they face a series of disadvantages, not just because of the low human capital in their families and prejudices against them but also because of the ways that mainstream institutions favor those from native majorities. Indeed, a great benefit of looking beyond the United States to western European societies is that a transatlantic comparison calls attention to and brings into sharper focus the role of society-wide institutions, in this case structural features of the educational system, that might otherwise be taken for granted or minimized if we only considered the United States (Alba and Foner 2015).

THE DEMOGRAPHIC CHALLENGE

The United States and western Europe are on the threshold of a demographic transition that will leave them radically changed by the end of the next quarter-century. This transition to diversity—in particular, to working-age populations that have many fewer members of the native majority and many more individuals from immigrant and other minority groups—will be brought about by the synchronization of two huge demographic phenomena. One is the baby boomers, who are aging and in the process of leaving the ages of economic and civic activity; the other is the current child populations that will soon be reaching the ages of school completion and labor-force entry (16–24 years of age).

The baby boom was a universal phenomenon in Western societies that began at the end of World War II. It refers to a spurt in the fertility of native majorities that generally lasted about two decades, although the timing varied across countries (earlier in North America than in war-devastated continental Europe). The baby boom cohorts thus contain larger numbers of the native majority than do younger age groups. In many countries, they were the first to enjoy access to mass higher education, and accordingly their members have been occupying numerous high positions in the economy and civil society. But today they are largely middle-aged and even elderly—in the United States, for example, they are between the ages of 54 and 72 (as of 2018). Over the next quarter of a century, the baby boomers will exit from the ages associated with economic and civic activity.

The child and youth population looks very different throughout North America and western Europe. Consider the children (aged 0–17) of the United States, for example. In 2010, more than 40 percent of them were minorities. Granted, the United States is unusual in having a sizable minority population that is not of immigrant origin; nevertheless, one in four children was growing up in an immigrant household. More than half of these children came from low-status immigrant homes, headed by immigrants from Latin America and the Caribbean. As of 2016, a substantial portion of these children were of working age, between 16 and 24.

The overall minority fractions among children are smaller in European countries, but in some of them, the relatively small size of the child population (relative to working-age adults) makes the issues of the transition equally acute. Consider the Netherlands. It is set to experience a shrinkage of the young-adult population as this population also becomes more diverse. At the end of this century's first decade, the children of immigrants were almost one of every four children, the majority with parents who came from outside Europe, especially from former Dutch colonies (e.g., Surinam) or Morocco and Turkey. These children, particularly those from Muslim groups, are quite disadvantaged in Dutch society.

A question that all the countries we consider will have to face during the coming decades is "who will replace the baby boomers?" The huge group born in the decades following the end of the Second World War has occupied an outsized portion of leadership positions, in the economy and elsewhere, and will soon be leaving them. Nowhere are the numbers of the native majority among youth equal to those in the outgoing baby boom. Inevitably, then, countries on both sides of the Atlantic will depend on the youth coming from immigrant homes, including low-status ones, to make up the shortfall in the majority population.

THE SECOND GENERATION AT SCHOOL

The first institutional sector of the host society that is entered en masse by the children of immigrants, the second generation, is the school system; and their encounter with it is fateful because educational credentials largely determine what strata of the labor market youth can enter.

Our findings on the educational achievements of the children of low-status immigrants reveal some of the barriers they face as they head into adulthood and the labor market. Overall, members of the second generation from low-status immigrant backgrounds begin their adult lives with substantial educational deficits compared to young adults who grew up in native-majority homes. To be sure, these young adults do not represent the entire second generation. Some of its members are the children of high human-capital immigrants, who hold university degrees and pursue highly skilled technical and professional jobs; these children have significant advantages—and often surpass members of the native-majority group in educational attainment (Lee and Zhou 2015). But the educational deficits of the low-status second generation are of obvious concern, especially in light of the demographic transition that will occur during the next quarter-century, which will generate potential opportunities for them to move up. The critical question is whether the young adults from these backgrounds will be prepared to take advantage of these opportunities.

The educational trajectories of students from low-status immigrant families are influenced by a combination of factors. Their immigrant parents generally have very low levels of education by the standards of the receiving society—sometimes even no formal schooling at all, like many Moroccan immigrant mothers in the Netherlands. The immigrant parents' relatively low educational levels, in turn, have a number of consequences, including an inability to provide guidance to their children in important educational decisions and assistance with homework. The children frequently grow up in homes where the immigrant, rather than mainstream, language is used on a daily basis and often enter school behind other children whose mother tongue is the language used there. And they stand out, and sometimes apart, in schools because they are ethnically and sometimes racially and/or religiously different from the native-majority population. This last factor may mean isolation from fellow students who belong to the ethnoracial majority when immigrant-origin and native-majority students attend the same school; it almost certainly implies some degree of distance from teachers.

These accumulated disadvantages mean that most immigrant-origin students need extra attention in the classroom if they are to have a chance to catch up to native-majority peers. The evidence is that they do not usually receive such help—if anything, they typically receive less enriched classroom instruction, although this happens in different ways in different systems. To put matters another way, our analysis demonstrates that no type of educational system has a marked advantage over others when it comes to promoting educational parity between the disadvantaged members of the second generation and the native majority.

School systems vary considerably along a dimension that could be identified as "standardization," or "the degree to which the quality of education meets the same standards nationwide" (Almendinger 1989, 233). France, with its centralized system of school financing and its national curriculum, is the exemplar of a standardized system. The United States, by contrast, gives states considerable power in determining curriculum and employs a financing system dependent on state and local resources that produces large inequalities among schools, inequalities that correspond in a rough manner with the social origins of the students they serve. Another dimension of variation could be described as "stratification," the differential education of students based on presumptions about their abilities and prospects. Germany is the most stratified system among the five countries we consider (with the Netherlands in second place) because students are tracked early in their schooling, in quite fateful ways, into one of three pathways leading to very distinct credentials and adult opportunities. The United States is its opposite in this respect since tracking there is more informal, as students generally attend comprehensive high schools and earn the same diploma at the end.

We can think of school outcomes in terms of skills and credentials. The two are highly correlated, of course; but credentials determine the kind of job that a young person can hope to attain, and skills determine how successful he or she is likely to be at that job. The Program for International Student Assessment (PISA) data, presented in Table 6.1, show us the key academic skills—in literacy and numeracy—that young people have developed by the age of 15. In order to focus on the children of low-status immigrants in these data (where we cannot be sure of immigrant parents'

Table 6.1 Average Scores on Basic-Skills Tests in Reading and Mathematics for Native Students and Those of the Second Generation with Less Educated Parents, by Country

	France	Germany	Great Britain	Netherlands	United States
Reading					
Second generation, parents with little or no secondary education	451	414	470	473	444
Children of native parents	511	529	517	539	511
Difference	60	115	47	66	67
Mathematics					
Second generation, parents with little or no secondary education	457	429	464	488	428
Children of native parents	525	537	514	563	494
Difference	68	108	50	75	66

Note: Scores have been averaged across years.
Source: 2000–2009 PISA studies.

national origins), we limit the immigrant-origin group to children whose parents have not attained final secondary-school credentials. Additionally, all of the children tabulated have been born in the country indicated in the table, to guarantee that their education has been mainly there.

The scores in Table 6.1 show a remarkably consistent picture given the overall variation of average scores on the PISA assessments across and within countries. In terms of literacy, the native students in most of the countries score within a narrow band from 510 to 530; and generally speaking, the low-status second-generation students score on average about 60–70 points less. (We use the term "native" to refer to those born in a country to parents who were also born there.) Two exceptions are the Netherlands, which has relatively high scores for both the native and low-status second-generation groups, and Great Britain, which has a high score for the second-generation group and thus a smaller gap between the two. In general, the gaps are large, given that a difference of about 70 points represents what the PISA researchers view as equivalent to a distinct proficiency level in literacy. In Germany, the second-generation group is the furthest behind, by a margin much larger than in the other countries.

The gaps in mathematics are broadly similar to those for literacy. Again, the native students in several countries exhibit remarkably similar average scores on the assessment, and the gap separating them from second-generation students is generally 60 points or more. This means that on average low-status second-generation students tend to be behind by a proficiency level, estimated for mathematics at about 60 points. The largest gap is found again in Germany, but an equally low score for the second generation appears in the United States.

The US results are noteworthy. Although it has been a cause for concern that overall educational skills there are significantly below those of many European countries, it is often assumed that the United States, because of its long history as an immigration society, provides the children of immigrants with greater opportunities for educational mobility. The PISA results show that this is not the case, at least in terms of the ability of the educational system to close the skills gap between the children of low-status immigrants and the native born.

The native/second generation gap would appear much smaller if we compared the second-generation students to native students whose parents were comparable to immigrant parents in educational terms. But the gap would not disappear, as a number of studies have shown (Buchmann and Parrado 2006; Organisation for Economic Co-operation and Development 2006). Nevertheless, we refrain from making this comparison for two reasons. The first is that the great majority of native students have parents who attained at least the final secondary-school credential and are thus more educated than immigrant parents; in other words, the comparison is unrealistic in terms of the competition immigrant-origin students face in schools and the labor market. The second reason is that the commensurability of parental educations earned in very different educational systems (the Netherlands and Morocco, say) is dubious. Almost all studies show that immigrants tend to be a selective group when compared to those who stay behind in the home country (e.g., Feliciano 2005; Heath and Brinbaum 2014; see in particular Lessard-Phillips, Fleischmann, and van Elsas 2014). This implies that immigrants with low levels of education by the standards of the receiving society (or low occupational positions) may have positive qualities, such as discipline and high aspirations for their children, that are not—or are less—often found among the equivalent group of native parents (Brinbaum and Kieffer 2005; Kao and Tienda 1995; Levels, Dronkers, and Kraaykamp 2008). Native fathers without high school diplomas in the United States, for example, are far more likely than immigrant men to have spent time in prison (Pettit and Western 2004). If our goal is to assess how school systems are faring in equalizing opportunity, then controlling for parental socioeconomic position risks producing unduly rosy results because of the unmeasured positive traits of immigrant homes.

The data on educational credentials, summarized in Table 6.2, which are compiled from a series of post-2000 studies, reveal the extent of second-generation deficits at the moment of departure from school. We have simplified the outcome distribution into a few telling measures. The proportions of immigrant-origin groups advancing to, and earning credentials in, the higher-educational system (or "tertiary" education) indicate the shares of these groups that are likely to be still mainly in school rather than full-time in the labor market in their late teens and early 20s. Obviously, these proportions are also a measure of immigrant-origin students' chances of obtaining middle-class and upper-middle-class jobs. The proportions failing to attain the final secondary-school credential indicate the numbers of these youth who are out of school and possibly at work or seeking work by their late teens. The figures are also a measure of the probability that second generations will wind up, like their parents, at the bottom of the host society's labor market since, without any meaningful educational credential, they are likely to be condemned to the ranks of low-skilled labor. For a standard of comparison, we include data on their same-age counterparts from native families (and from the white native-majority population in the case of the United States).

For the most stratified systems, Germany and the Netherlands, large differences between immigrant- and native-origin young people appear; and they are especially extreme in Germany. At the upper end of the educational distribution, Germany stands out among economically advanced nations for its overall low level of post-secondary attainment. As of 2007–08 about 20 percent of native German men and women were attending an institution of higher education but just 7 percent of the Turkish second generation. Put another way, the chance of a German native obtaining some level of post-secondary education was about three times that of a youth from a Turkish immigrant family.

There are also big differences at the lower end of the educational distribution in Germany. For those in the lowest track, the *Hauptschule*, what matters is whether they obtain an apprenticeship and what its market value is. Those who complete a good apprenticeship are well positioned in the labor market, typically entering highly skilled blue-collar occupations with considerable earning power. There is substantial evidence that some second-generation groups, the Turks especially, are much more concentrated in the *Hauptschulen* than are native Germans and that they are significantly disadvantaged in obtaining an apprenticeship in the first place and gaining a desirable one in the second (Diehl, Friedrich, and Hall 2009). For those who fail to pursue an apprenticeship, jobs involving limited skills at the lowest end of the labor market are typically all that are open. The high percentage of second-generation Turks who leave the school system without a secondary-school credential in Table 6.2, nearly a third, reveals a group with mainly limited economic prospects as adults (Kalter and Granato 2007). Native Germans are only 40 percent as likely to find themselves in this situation.

A similar, if less extreme, picture appears in the Netherlands, where higher percentages of key second-generation groups, Moroccans and Turks, are able to enter post-secondary education (Crul et al. 2013). Still, the native-/immigrant-origin differences at the upper end of the educational system are large, on the order of 2 to 1. It is possible that they are somewhat exaggerated in The Integration of the European Second Generation (TIES) data, which are confined to the two largest cities in the country, a sample no doubt more representative for immigrant groups than for the native population. Yet at the lower end of the educational system, the differences are also large. The disparity in relation to the native Dutch is on the order of 3 to 1, as great as in the German case, with a quarter or more of the Turkish second generation leaving school without a secondary-school credential. However, in the Dutch case, not all non-Western second generations have suffered from such extreme educational disadvantage. The relative success of the Antilleans and Surinamese is notable, as has been shown in other research. The rate of university education for Antilleans is not far behind that of the native Dutch, and the children of the Surinamese occupy an in-between position, doing better than the children of low-wage immigrants of Moroccan and Turkish origins but not as well as Antilleans (Tesser and Dronkers

Table 6.2 Educational Attainment of Selected Second Generations Compared to Native Majorities

	No Secondary Credential	Some Post-Secondary	University Degree
England and Wales (various ages, Youth Cohort Study and Longitudinal Study [see note])			
White British	39.5	—	28.8
Afro-Caribbean	54.4	—	41.7
Pakistani/Bangladeshi	48.4	—	32.0
France (ages 26–35, 2008 *Trajectoires et Origines* survey)			
Males			
Native French	12.5	27.6	23.5
North Africans	27.4	26.4	16.1
Females			
Native French	12.2	30.1	25.7
North Africans	20.5	30.9	16.5
Germany (ages 18–35, Berlin and Frankfurt, 2007–08 TIES data [see note])			
Native Germans	13.2	19.7	
Turks	31.2	6.7	
The Netherlands (ages 18–35, Amsterdam and Rotterdam, 2007–08 TIES data [see note])			
Native Dutch	9.5	62.6	
Moroccans	25.0	29.7	
Turks	29.1	28.7	
United States (ages 26–35, 2005–09 American Community Survey)			
Males			
Anglo natives	8.0	31.4	32.5
US-born Dominicans	14.0	35.5	16.5
US-born Mexicans	20.8	31.8	13.0
Females			
Anglo natives	5.8	33.3	39.8
US-born Dominicans	9.5	39.5	32.8
US-born Mexicans	16.3	36.8	17.9

Notes: The Integration of the European Second Generation (TIES) data (Germany and The Netherlands) include young people who are still in school, and therefore the distinction between university completion and attendance-only is not available. The data for Great Britain are put together from two different, not fully consistent data sets; only the extreme categories are consequently reported.

Sources:

France: calculation for us by Yaël Brinbaum.

Germany: Crul, Schneider, and Lelie (2012).

Great Britain: Waters et al. (2013).

The Netherlands: Crul, Schneider, and Lelie (2012).

United States: calculation for us by Ruby Wang.

2007). Both groups are usually counted among postcolonial migrants, and the immigrant parents possess a greater knowledge of the Dutch language, culture, and educational system than is true of other immigrants. In addition, the Antilleans are Dutch citizens who can move freely between their Caribbean home islands and the European metropole. Still, in other countries, like France, postcolonial status is not associated with school success.

A highly stratified system with early tracking—the German system par excellence—puts children from low-status immigrant homes at a great disadvantage, with little opportunity to demonstrate their academic abilities before their academic fate is decided (Kristen 2008; Heath and Brinbaum 2014). Does later or less systematic tracking make a big difference then? Not necessarily. In France and the United States, where tracking has a much less rigid character, the credentials data also show large native-/immigrant-origin disparities. Nor does it seem to matter much that France is the paragon of a standardized system and the United States, a decentralized one.

Admittedly, in both France and the United States, some second-generation groups—primarily of southern European origin in France and Asian origin in the United States—are doing well, with educational attainment generally at least as high on average as that of the ethnoracial majority. However, the children of large, low-wage immigrant groups are not faring so well. The differences between disadvantaged groups and the native-majority population are pronounced at the lower end of the educational distribution, as shown in Table 6.2. In France, a quarter of North African young men leave school without a culminating secondary-school credential; in the United States, about a fifth of second-generation Mexican young men are in the same boat. The percentages of dropouts are lower in the United States, but Mexicans stand out for their striking difference from those in the native majority. The rate of dropout has verged in the recent past, as shown in the table, on being three times higher for Mexican youth than for their Anglo counterparts, although this disparity has narrowed since 2000 as graduation rates have climbed for all major ethnoracial groups, especially for Hispanics (Murnane 2013).

When it comes to university credentials, such as the B.A. degree in the United States, there are also large differences—more than 2 to 1 between US-born Mexicans and native whites. The differences from national native-white norms are not as large for another generally disadvantaged group, Dominicans, perhaps owing to their proximity to higher educational opportunity in New York City, where a large proportion of Dominicans live and the campuses of the City University of New York make a low-cost college education readily accessible. (Dominicans have been found to be especially dependent on the less prestigious campuses of this system [Kasinitz et al. 2008].) Inequalities among US groups soften somewhat when we consider overall rates of post-secondary education, for substantial percentages of immigrant-origin groups have spent some time in a community or 4-year college. These high rates of entry to the post-secondary system reveal one benefit of open systems like the US one, where entry to the university is not foreclosed by tracking in secondary school (Heath and Brinbaum 2014). Such systems afford working-class and minority students more "second chances." However, their rates of earning post-secondary credentials are generally low. This is especially the case in the United States because of the sharply rising costs of post-secondary education. Inequalities in terms of credentials remain substantial.

Two additional factors complicate the US picture. On the one hand, unlike in continental Europe, the American post-secondary system is highly differentiated internally, with large quality, and social, differences even within the same nominal tier. For example, 4-year undergraduate institutions range from world-renowned, elite private campuses to weakly funded public institutions that accept virtually all who apply. Second-generation students from low-status immigrant origins appear to be concentrated in schools at the lower end of this hierarchy (Kasinitz et al. 2008; Waters et al. 2013). On the other hand, US colleges and universities have used affirmative-action policies to improve access for minority students. While these policies have been disputed, and in some states negated at public institutions by court action or voter-approved referenda, they have had meaningful effects on the upper levels of the higher education system. Their benefits have gone largely to young people from immigrant backgrounds, as opposed to those from long-standing racial minorities (Massey et al. 2007). Nevertheless, as important as affirmative action is in providing opportunity for minority students, it has not counteracted by much the overall, and overwhelming, concentration of young people from disadvantaged immigrant backgrounds in the lower-quality parts of the higher education system.

In France, inequalities in university credentials are moderately lower. Second-generation North Africans acquire university credentials at rates below those of the native French but not by the large gaps evident for Mexicans in the United States. Moreover, acquisition of a vocationally oriented post-secondary diploma is more common in France than in the United States, and there is a smaller gap with the native majority in obtaining this kind of diploma. But, like the United States, France also has a stratified post-secondary system, whose elite tier, the *grandes écoles*, is comprised of schools that are as selective as the American Ivy League and prepare students for top-level careers in government, business, and the sciences. Second-generation North African and other youth with low-status immigrant origins are starkly underrepresented there: for these students, even to attempt

entry into the *grandes écoles* may involve an unacceptable level of risk because it requires 2 years of specialized education beyond the *baccalauréat* at
the end of high school and then passing a competitive entrance examination. Unlike elite schools in the United States, the *grandes écoles* have been
so far unable to create much diversity among entrants through affirmative-
action, or positive-discrimination, policies because these are condemned by
the widely accepted ideology of republicanism. Sciences Po in Paris is the
one exception (Alba et al. 2013).

Britain is the great exception to these patterns. The groups commonly
thought of as the most disadvantaged—Afro-Caribbeans, Bangladeshis, and
Pakistanis—are not far behind native whites. At the upper end of the educational distribution, the Bangladeshi/Pakistani group (the two are merged
here because of sample size) has essentially the same rate of earning university credentials as the native white British group, and Afro-Caribbeans have
pulled ahead. At the other end, the rate for leaving school without a diploma
looks astoundingly high for the white British (40 percent)—although the
rates for Pakistani, Bangladeshi, and Afro-Caribbean youth (around 50 percent) are worse. These figures, however, are misleading in the context of
an international comparison. The British system has an escape hatch for
students who do not like school or want to enter the labor market at the
earliest possible age. At 16, students take the GCSE (General Certificate of
Secondary Examination), and many leave school after passing it. Although
these students do not have a secondary-school *diploma*, they do have a school
credential that is useful in the labor market (Waters et al. 2013). Without
knowing more about the circumstances under which young people leave
school and their labor-market prospects, it is difficult to evaluate whether
passing the GCSE is equivalent to secondary-school graduation in other
systems. It is nonetheless fair to conclude that this educational outcome
is on average more favorable for the white British than for members of minority groups because of the difficulties the latter encounter in the labor
market (Cheung 2014).

There is not a convincing explanation yet for the exceptional parity in
Britain at the upper end of the educational distribution. Tariq Modood (2011)
has suggested that the resources and cohesion of the communities of the
Muslim groups help to explain their educational success in the second generation, and this accords with observations about the role of Asian community institutions in promoting educational achievement in the United
States (Zhou 2009). This argument does not address the Afro-Caribbean
case. However, it is also possible that the British exception is entangled with
the class rigidities that operate among whites, many of whom leave school
at age 16 to enter the labor market; these departures lower the white rate

of university entrance and completion. In addition, some members of the second generation from disadvantaged groups such as the Pakistanis may persist in education in the hope that an additional credential will overcome the difficulties that they anticipate in the labor market.

The British case, however, is not only a story of apparent educational parity in university credentials. At the very top of the British educational system, the native white British group, or at least that slice of it from the right class backgrounds, has a definite edge. The British post-secondary system, like the American one, is internally stratified, with a group of highly prestigious, long-established universities at the apex and a group of new universities, recently upgraded from vocationally oriented polytechnics, at the bottom. Whites who attend university are more likely to go to the most prestigious institutions than are members of many second-generation groups; this is particularly true for Afro-Caribbeans, Bangladeshis, and Pakistanis. Second-generation black Britons are extremely underrepresented at the top of the system, as was revealed by a 2011 controversy over the low rate of black admissions to the University of Oxford (Waters et al. 2013).

This survey of second generations in five countries points to the conclusion that, on average, its members finish their educational careers with substantial deficits compared to their counterparts in the native-majority population. This is not to deny that, by comparison with the generally low education levels of their immigrant parents, they have advanced considerably. But a general pattern is that the second generations from low-status groups leave school without any meaningful credential at relatively high rates. And they enter labor markets where the demand is strong for post-secondary credentials that they generally lack.

The accumulated disadvantages of students who have grown up in low-status immigrant homes are produced in different ways in different educational systems. Germany and the United States, the two systems that arguably reveal the greatest native majority/low-status immigrant disparities, have remarkably different institutional features associated with these inequalities. Nevertheless, an examination of these different features suggests some similar points of leverage to bring about changes to make both systems more welcoming to students from low-status immigrant homes.

The United States could be described as the epitome of an unstandardized system—to invoke the distinction between standardization and stratification introduced earlier. In the United States, the financing system, unusually dependent on local sources such as the property tax, produces large inequalities among schools—for instance, in the credentials and experience of the teaching staff and the educational resources such as computers available to children. Because of the country's high level of ethnoracial and socioeconomic status stratification (Alba and Foner 2015), there is also a rough correspondence between these school disparities and the social origins of the students they serve. Then, in secondary schools, the differences in school-taught skills channel students into different "tracks," though these are defined more informally than in many European systems. As a consequence, students from low-status immigrant families receive on average a lower quality of education than do students from white middle-class ones.

By contrast, in countries like Germany, formal tracking separates students into different instruction streams at an early age—at the end of the fourth year of primary education in most German states—and thereafter they attend different schools that prepare them for quite distinct academic and labor-market destinations. Adding to the difficulties of improving an initially low track placement is that the students on different tracks typically attend different schools (that is, located in different buildings), though they may move from a higher to a lower track. This highly stratified system with an early choice point creates substantial drawbacks for immigrant-origin students (Van de Werfhorst, van Elsas, and Heath 2014). Because of the short period that such systems give these students to adjust to schooling and demonstrate their academic abilities, the systems in effect place a great deal of weight on social origins; and their tracking, owing to such factors as the distinctiveness of the curricula on different tracks, is fateful.

So, even though the German and US education systems are structured in very different ways, they both resolve the division of educational labor—among families, communities, and schools—by emphasizing to an unusual degree the resources of families and communities. They do this in another way that has not yet been mentioned—the relatively brief exposure of students to school, especially during the early years. German schools have an unusually short day; during the primary years, children go home at lunchtime and are expected to complete substantial amounts of homework with the help of a parent or older sibling. The United States has an unusually short school year and lengthy summer vacation. The long summer layoff in the United States has been shown repeatedly to be associated with a regression in learning, especially for poor and minority children (Downey, von Hippel, and Broh 2004; Entwisle and Alexander 1992; Heyns 1979). Thus, one point of leverage for change is to increase the exposure to schooling in both systems. This could be done without demolishing the fundamental structures of these systems that are also implicated in inequalities hampering students from immigrant families—namely, the extreme lack of standardization in the United States and the stratified structure of education in Germany.

THE SECOND GENERATION IN THE LABOR MARKET

The pervasiveness of native-majority/second-generation educational in-equality inevitably raises the question of how the second generations fare in the world of work. Any answers must be regarded as preliminary because their members are still generally quite young, and the research record on their labor-market experiences is not extensive and is truncated, that is, con-centrated on young adults, generally tracking them no farther than the first few years after the end of schooling (e.g., Kasinitz et al. 2008). This said, there are some worrisome patterns.

Britain is a particularly relevant case since the most disadvantaged mi-norities there have done well in educational terms. However, in the labor market, disadvantages persist, especially for Muslims, even though the second generation makes occupational progress compared to the first. The employment and occupational penalties suffered by Bangladeshi and Pakistani immigrants, the two overwhelmingly Muslim groups, are still evident in the second generation, as Sin Yi Cheung has demonstrated for 2010 (Cheung 2014; Heath and Martin 2013). The Bangladeshi and Pakistani second generations show relatively high rates of unemployment as well as high rates of employment by ethnic minority employers (a trait shared by Indians). That large numbers end up working for ethnic minority em-ployers strongly suggests a pronounced disadvantage in the mainstream labor market, which drives some of the second generation into the ethnic economy. At the same time, second-generation Bangladeshis and Pakistanis do appear to be less attached to this part of the economy than the immi-grants are, a sign of some intergenerational progress.

Labor-market disadvantages for the second generation, especially for the two main Muslim groups, Moroccans and Turks, are evident also in the Netherlands. As is generally the case in Europe, a primary manifestation of these disadvantages is in terms of hiring. Compared to native Dutch with the same education levels and demographic characteristics, second-generation Moroccans and Turks are less likely to be employed (and field experiments show immigrant-minority applicants are less likely to be in-vited for job interviews [Andriessen at al. 2012]). When they are employed, they may still not find parity: for example, second-generation Turkish men tend to occupy lower-status jobs than their similarly educated native Dutch counterparts, and Moroccans and Turks are more likely to have temporary, as opposed to permanent, employment contracts (Witteveen and Alba 2018).

The labor-market disadvantages of some second-generation groups seem, if anything, even more salient in France and Germany, despite advances be-yond the position of their immigrant parents. In France, various studies re-veal the problems confronted by the North and sub-Saharan African, as well as Turkish, second generations in the mainstream labor market. Compared to second-generation Mexicans in the United States, for example, members of these French second-generation groups are less likely to have employed relatives who can help them get a foothold in the labor market through a first job. Moreover, they frequently complain of discrimination at the hands of French employers. They also have much higher rates of unemployment—and correspondingly lower rates of employment—than those in the native-majority population. For instance, in 2008, when the rate of unemployment of native-majority men was about 7 percent, the unemployment of North African, sub-Saharan African, and Turkish second-generation men hovered in the 17–21 percent range. When employed, the young men and women in these second-generation groups are unusually likely to hold jobs below their level of qualifications (Alba et al. 2013; Silberman, Alba, and Fournier 2007).

In Germany, too, the second generation makes progress but lags behind the native majority in economic outcomes. This is especially so for the Turkish group, but the children of some other guest-worker migrants are also disadvantaged. In the 1990s, the unemployment rates of second-generation Turkish men and women were almost as high as those of their immigrant parents and more than twice as large as for their native German counterparts. More recent data indicate that the Turkish second generation is overrepresented in the working class, that is, less likely to hold salaried positions, compared to the native German population. Educational inequalities cannot adequately explain this gap in occupational status, which also appears to be associated with inadequacies in German-language proficiency and embeddedness in Turkish social networks (Kalter 2011). These additional explanatory factors can be read in different ways, but we believe that they underscore the barriers the children of Turkish immigrants face in acceptance by, and assimilation to, the German social and cultural context.

The United States is often contrasted with Europe in terms of the availability of employment, but the Great Recession continues to exert an economic toll on the massive Latino second generation. According to the Pew Research Center, 5 years after the onset of the recession, the employment rate of US-born Hispanics remained relatively low and the unemployment rate relatively high (Kochhar 2014). However, even before the recession, when rates of labor-force participation and employment for Mexican American second-generation men were similar to those of native white men, disadvantage was apparent in terms of the quality of employment. Even if members of the second generation generally moved beyond the "immigrant jobs" of their parents, they held jobs that on average were lower in "quality" than those held by third- and later-generation white men. This means in particular that the jobs held by Mexicans were less likely to provide such benefits as retirement plans and health insurance. In addition, the Mexican second generation did not reach parity with third- and later-generation white men in terms of pay. These disadvantages are only partially explicable in terms of educational differences between the groups (Luthra and Waldinger 2010).

In sum, the limited research on the employment and economic prospects of the contemporary second generation is of a piece with what we know about its educational outcomes. The second generation makes substantial advances beyond the immigrant generation. But for the low-status groups—in terms of major groups, we refer here above all to Hispanics in the United States and Muslim groups in Europe—these advances still leave the second generation on average well behind the native-majority group. This is true in education, as we have demonstrated; and when we take the educational disparities into account, it is independently true, it appears, for the world of work and its economic benefits.

CONCLUSION

Everywhere that we have looked we have found unmet challenges with respect to the integration of important immigrant-origin groups. In education, the second generations originating from low-status groups suffer what Heath and Cheung (2007) have called "ethnic penalties." These deficits in relation to the majority population undoubtedly have multiple sources. The children of low-status immigrants grow up in homes with limited socioeconomic resources. Their parents often are not fluent in the mainstream language, have little education (by the standards of the receiving society), and hold jobs in the bottom tiers of the labor market. These factors create large disadvantages for the children in school systems. At the same time, every such system but one (Britain, and the parity achieved there begs for a satisfactory explanation) has features that create high hurdles for students with such disadvantages—such as the low-quality schools created by the highly decentralized US system or the rigid tracking after limited exposure to the mainstream educational culture in Germany. In addition, we have no doubt that many in positions of authority in school systems and workplaces hold prejudices that lead to subtle or occasionally blatant discrimination against these second-generation youth.

Their problems in the educational system are compounded by those they face when they enter the labor market. In general, they are less likely to be employed than native youth with comparable educational attainment, and sometimes, as in France and Germany, these employment penalties are large. When employed, they are often "underemployed," in the sense that they hold jobs that are below their level of qualifications, as assessed by comparison with the jobs that educationally similar native youth obtain.

And in those European studies that have been able to measure the important distinction between contracted, or time-limited, and permanent positions, second-generation youth are less likely than native peers to have obtained secure, permanent employment (see Witteveen and Alba 2018).

In labor markets that are not generating large numbers of "good" jobs, leaving many youth either unemployed or underemployed, the disadvantages of youth from low-status immigrant homes create relative advantages for native youth, who can generally expect to do better than average in the labor market, both because their educational credentials are superior to those of most low-status immigrant-origin youth and because their employment prospects are better than those of their second-generation peers. How much of the labor-market advantages of native youth is due to employer discrimination on their behalf and how much is due to other mechanisms—language or other cultural handicaps of immigrant-background youth, for example—has not been determined. Certainly, there is some employer discrimination, at least in some countries. In France and the Netherlands, for example, audit studies have shown that applicants with Muslim-sounding names are less likely, other things being equal, to be contacted by employers (Andriessen et al. 2012; Valfort 2015). And second-generation youth believe that they are the victims of discrimination (Silberman, Alba, and Fournier 2007; Beauchemin, Hamel, and Simon 2015). However, these demonstrations of discrimination cannot inform us about the other mechanisms that may be involved.

The problem in the longer term may be that the second generations of low-status immigrant background, or at least a very significant proportion of them, are not being prepared to replace the baby boomers, who will leave the workforce and other forms of civil activity during the coming quarter-century. In the societies of the wealthy West, there will not be enough young people from the native-majority population to replace the retiring baby boomers, and the talents of the children of immigrants will be required. Ultimately, this is one of the major challenges involving second-generation youth and jobs for all these societies in the years ahead.

REFERENCES

Alba, Richard, and Nancy Foner. *Strangers No More: Immigration and the Challenges of Integration in North America and Western Europe*. Princeton, NJ: Princeton University Press, 2015.

Alba, Richard, Roxane Silberman, Dalia Abdelhady, Yael Brinbaum, and Amy Lutz. "How Similar Educational Inequalities Are Constructed in Two Different Systems, France and the U.S., and Why They Lead to Disparate Labor-Market Outcomes." In *The Children of Immigrants at School: A Comparative Look at*

Integration in the United States and Europe, edited by Richard Alba and Jennifer Holdaway, 160–203. New York: New York University Press, 2013.

Almendinger, Jutta. "Educational Systems and Labor Market Outcomes." *European Sociological Review* 5 (1989): 231–50.

Andriessen, Iris, Eline Nievers, Jaco Dagevos, and Laila Faulk. "Ethnic Discrimination in the Dutch Labor Market: Its Relationship with Job Characteristics and Multiple Group Membership." *Work and Occupations* 39, no. 3 (2012): 237–69.

Beauchemin, Cris, Christelle Hamel, and Patrick Simon, eds. *Trajectoires et origines: Enquête sur la diversité des populations en France*. Paris: INED, 2015.

Brinbaum, Yaël, and Annick Kieffer. "D'une génération à l'autre, les aspirations éducatives des familles immigrées: Ambition et persévérance." *Éducation & formations* 72 (2005): 53–75.

Buchmann, Claudia, and Emilio Parrado. "Educational Achievement of Immigrant-Origin and Native Students: A Comparative Analysis Informed by Institutional Theory." *International Perspectives on Education and Society* 7 (2006): 335–66.

Cheung, Sin Yi. "Ethno-Religious Minorities and Labour Market Integration: Generational Advancement or Decline?" *Ethnic and Racial Studies* 37 (2014): 140–60.

Crul, Maurice, Jennifer Holdaway, Helga de Valk, Norma Fuentes, and Mayida Zaal. "Educating the Children of Immigrants in Old and New Amsterdam." In *The Children of Immigrants at School: A Comparative Look at Integration in the United States and Western Europe*, edited by Richard Alba and Jennifer Holdaway, 39–83. New York: New York University Press, 2013.

Crul, Maurice, Jens Schneider, and Frans Lelie, eds. *The European Second Generation Compared: Does the Integration Context Matter?* Amsterdam: University of Amsterdam Press, 2012.

Diehl, Claudia, Michael Friedrich, and Anja Hall. "Jugendliche ausländische Herkunft beim Übergang in die Berufsausbildung: Vom Wollen, Können und Dürfen." *Zeitschrift für Soziologie* 38 (2009): 48–67.

Downey, Douglas, Paul von Hippel, and Beckett Broh. "Are Schools the Great Equalizer? Cognitive Inequality During the Summer Months and the School Year." *American Sociological Review* 69 (2004): 613–35.

Entwisle, Doris, and Karl Alexander. "Summer Setback: Race, Poverty, School Composition, and Mathematics Achievement in the First Two Years of School." *American Sociological Review* 57 (1992): 72–84.

Feliciano, Cynthia. "Does Selective Migration Matter? Explaining Ethnic Disparities in Educational Attainment Among Immigrants' Children." *International Migration Review* 39 (2005): 841–71.

Heath, Anthony, and Yaël Brinbaum, eds. *Unequal Attainments: Ethnic Educational Inequalities in Ten Western Countries*. Proceedings of the British Academy 196. Oxford: Oxford University Press for the British Academy, 2014.

Heath, Anthony, and Sin Yi Cheung, eds. *Unequal Chances: Ethnic Minorities in Western Labour Markets*. Proceedings of the British Academy 137. Oxford: Oxford University Press, 2007.

Heath, Anthony, and Jean Martin. "Can Religious Affiliation Explain 'Ethnic' Inequalities in the Labour Market?" *Ethnic and Racial Studies* 36 (2013): 1005–27.

Heyns, Barbara. *Summer Learning and the Effects of Schooling.* New York: Academic Press, 1979.

Kalter, Frank. "The Second Generation in the German Labor Market: Explaining the Turkish Exception." In *The Next Generation: Immigrant Youth in a Comparative Perspective,* edited by Richard Alba and Mary Waters, 166–84. New York: New York University Press, 2011.

Kalter, Frank, and Nadia Granato. "Educational Hurdles on the Way to Structural Assimilation." In *Unequal Chances: Ethnic Minorities in Western Labour Markets,* edited by Anthony Heath and Sin Yi Cheung. Proceedings of the British Academy 137. Oxford: Oxford University Press, 2007.

Kao, Grace, and Marta Tienda. "Optimism and Achievement: The Educational Performance of Immigrant Youth." *Social Science Quarterly* 76 (1995): 1–19.

Kasinitz, Philip, John Mollenkopf, Mary C. Waters, and Jennifer Holdaway. *Inheriting the City: The Children of Immigrants Come of Age.* New York: Russell Sage Foundation; Cambridge, MA: Harvard University Press, 2008.

Kochhar, Rakesh. "Latino Jobs Growth Driven by U.S. Born." Pew Research Center, June 19, 2014. www.pewhispanic.org/2014/06/19/latino-jobs-growth-driven-by-u-s-born/.

Kristen, Cornelia. "Schulische Leistungen von Kindern aus türkischen Familien am Ende der Grundshulzeit: Befunde aus der IGLU-Studie." *Kölner Zeitschrift für Soziologie und Sozialpsychologie* 48 (2008): 230–51.

Lee, Jennifer, and Min Zhou. *The Asian American Achievement Paradox.* New York: Russell Sage Foundation, 2015.

Lessard-Phillips, Laurence, Fenella Fleischmann, and Erika van Elsas. "Ethnic Minorities in Ten Western Countries: Migration Flows, Policies and Institutional Differences." In *Unequal Attainments: Ethnic Educational Inequalities in Ten Western Countries,* edited by Anthony Heath and Yaël Brinbaum. Proceedings of the British Academy 196. Oxford: Oxford University Press, 2014.

Levels, Mark, Jaap Dronkers, and Gerbert Kraaykamp. "Immigrant Children's Educational Achievement in Western Countries: Origin, Destination, and Community Effects on Mathematical Performance." *American Sociological Review* 73 (2008): 835–53.

Luthra, Renee Reichl, and Roger Waldinger. "Into the Mainstream? Labor Market Outcomes of Mexican-Origin Workers." *International Migration Review* 44 (Winter 2010): 830–68.

Massey, Douglas, Margarita Mooney, Kimberly Torres, and Camille Charles. "Black Immigrants and Black Natives Attending Selective Colleges and Universities in the United States." *American Journal of Education* 113 (2007): 243–71.

Modood, Tariq. "Capitals, Ethnic Identity, and Educational Qualifications." In *The Next Generation: Immigrant Youth in Comparative Perspective,* edited by Richard Alba and Mary Waters, 185–206. New York: New York University Press, 2011.

Murnane, Richard. "U.S. High School Graduation Rates." *Journal of Economic Literature* 51 (2013): 370–422.

Organisation for Economic Co-operation and Development. *Where Immigrant Students Succeed—A Comparative Review of Performance and Engagement from PISA 2003.* Paris: Organisation for Economic Co-operation and Development, 2006.

Pettit, Becky, and Bruce Western. "Mass Imprisonment and the Life Course: Race and Class Inequality in U.S. Incarceration." *American Sociological Review* 69 (2004): 151–69.

PISA studies. *Program for International Student Assessment.* Paris: OECD, 2000–2009. http://www.oecd.org/pisa/

Silberman, Roxane, Richard Alba, and Irene Fournier. "Segmented Assimilation in France? Discrimination in the Labor Market Against the Second Generation." *Ethnic and Racial Studies* 30 (2007): 1–27.

Tesser, Paul, and Jaap Dronkers. "Equal Opportunities or Social Closure in the Netherlands." In *Unequal Chances: Ethnic Minorities in Western Labour Markets,* edited by Anthony Heath and Sin Yi Cheung. Proceedings of the British Academy 137. Oxford: Oxford University Press, 2007.

Valfort, Marie Anne. *Discriminations religieuses à l'embauche: Une réalité.* Paris: Institut Montaigne, 2015.

Van de Werfhorst, Herman, Erika van Elsas, and Anthony Heath. "Origin and Destination Effects on the Educational Careers of Second-Generation Minorities." In *Unequal Attainments: Ethnic Educational Inequalities in Ten Western Countries,* edited by Anthony Heath and Yaël Brinbaum. Proceedings of the British Academy 196. Oxford: Oxford University Press, 2014.

Waters, Mary C., Anthony Heath, Van Tran, and Vikki Boliver. "Second-Generation Attainment and Inequality: Primary and Secondary Effects on Educational Outcomes in Britain and the United States." In *The Children of Immigrants at School: A Comparative Look at Integration in the United States and Western Europe,* edited by Richard Alba and Jennifer Holdaway, 129–59. New York: New York University Press, 2013.

Witteven, Dirk, and Richard Alba. "Labor Market Disadvantages of Second Generation Turks and Moroccans in the Netherlands: Before and During the Great Recession." *International Migration* 56 (2018): 97–116.

Zhou, Min. "How Neighbourhoods Matter for Immigrant Children: The Formation of Educational Resources in Chinatown, Koreatown and Pico Union, Los Angeles." *Journal of Ethnic and Migration Studies* 35 (2009): 1153–79.

7

Youth Unemployment and the Illicit Economy

Martín Sánchez-Jankowski

Although the number of employed youth in July 2016 showed an increase from the previous year of 1.9 million, youth unemployment in 2016 remained high at 11.5 percent. Nearly 3 million (2.6 million) youth 16–24 years of age were unemployed. The participation rate within the economy (60 percent) remained roughly the same for this age group compared to the year before, though much lower than the all-time high of 77 percent in 1989. These figures are for the months of June, July, and August, which represent an important financial period for youth because it is during this time that high school and college students tend to actively pursue short-term summer seasonal work (Bureau of Labor Statistics 2016). During other parts of the year, the situation of unemployment/employment is less clear.

One question that has shadowed the youth labor market is whether problems associated with securing employment in the legal economy encourage young people to become involved in the illicit underground economy. Put another way, does unemployment in the "legal" labor market push individuals into the illicit underground economy? If so, what occupations have they assumed, and how long have they worked in them? Why do they continue to work in this economy, and when do they anticipate leaving these jobs? Lastly, if young people do leave, what jobs are they likely to assume in the legal economy?

Scholars interested in these questions have generally gravitated to a structural theoretical approach. Within this theoretical perspective, particularly influential in explaining why individuals who are unemployed would become involved in the illicit underground economy, emphasis has been placed on structural conditions in the current labor market. The general argument of the structural approach is that there is a greater demand for jobs than supply; this is believed to be caused by either a shrinking economy or an economy expanding at a rate slower than the number of individuals seeking employment. For youth, in theory, this means that those sectors of the economy previously providing employment are either no longer operating or operating in another physical location (Harrison and Bluestone 1982; Wilson 1987; Kasarda 1990). This creates a labor market with great demand for jobs and little supply, resulting in youth being unemployed for significant periods of time. Moreover, as time being unemployed increases, so do levels of frustration, forcing some people who are unemployed to seek employment in the illicit market (Sullivan 1989; Bourgois 1995).

The other structural theory that has been used to address the unemployment issue for youth is human capital (Gregg and Manning 1997; Estevão and Tsounta 2011; Scarpetto, Sonnet, and Manfredi 2010). According to this theory, the problem of youth unemployment relates to changing requirements for employment in the labor market. As industries continue to develop technologically, they require workers with increasing levels of human capital; and the youth who have dropped out of high school and/or who have as yet accumulated little human capital find themselves at a significant disadvantage for employment. Thus, a structural mismatch exists among certain sectors of the youth population between the skills demanded by industry for employment and those they have accumulated; this leads to periodic or prolonged unemployment until young people are able to gain those skills (Belfield, Levin, and Rosen 2012). For both of these theories, structural problems cause unemployment among youth and lead youth to abandon the legal labor market for the illegal economy. In essence, they are pushed into the illegal market (Duster 1987). I will address this perspective throughout this chapter by focusing on factors that led youth in the present sample to initially participate in the illicit economy, stay involved, or decide to leave.

THE STUDY DATA

The data for this study come from 84 in-depth interviews of young adults ranging from 18 to 22 years of age living in Los Angeles ($n = 25$), New York ($n = 27$), and Oakland, California ($n = 32$). Because individuals engaged in illegal activity are the subject of the investigation, obtaining a random sample involved structural challenges. The sample of 84 was therefore found by using a snowball strategy, that is, asking young people whom I had met while conducting research on high schools in each area if they knew anyone involved in illegal activity. I had previously done two participant observation research projects on 11 high schools in Los Angeles, Oakland, and New York: the student population of two of these high schools came overwhelmingly from middle-class families; in two other cases, the students came from a mixture of lower- and middle-class families; and in the case of seven high schools, the student population was overwhelmingly lower-class. These projects ran for multiple years—9 years for the first and 3 years for the second—and, over that time period, I came to know a number of the students well.

To pursue the current project, I contacted a number of former and current students I had met and asked for names of individuals who they knew had been, or were currently, involved in illegal activity. More often than not, they provided me with several names. I then proceeded to make contact with these individuals, describing the nature of my research project and the fact that specifics about their activities and names would be kept in strict confidence. If the person who I first contacted was not involved or did not want to talk about his or her previous or present involvement, I would ask for other names and follow up with those people, thus following the snowball sample design. It is well established that a "snowball sample" is not optimal, but given the illegal substantive nature of the present study, a random sample would be impossible.

Once contact was made, I explained that the study involved my conducting an interview that would take anywhere from 45 to 90 minutes depending on the length of an interviewee's answers. In total, I contacted 137 people over a 20-month period, and 84 agreed to interviews. It should be noted that I received names from people who said "they believed" particular individuals were involved in the illicit economy but did not know for sure. In fact, interviewees nearly always responded that they were not involved to my initial inquiry about their involvement with illegal activities. As the conversation continued, however, some of the individuals felt comfortable enough to change their original responses and slowly began to talk about their involvement. I would then tell them that I would like to meet them at a place of their choosing and talk about their experiences; when they agreed, a time and place were arranged. Of the 53 individuals who declined to be interviewed, it is impossible to judge how many declined because they felt the risks outweighed any benefits from cooperating or how many declined because they were in fact not involved in the illicit economy.

The interviews were conducted in a location requested by each of the subjects; no interviews were conducted by telephone, and all were transcribed. There were 65 males and 19 females; 44 people were from lower-income family backgrounds and 40 from middle-income family backgrounds. The interviews were semi-structured, with a number of questions directly asking how and why they became involved, which illegal occupations they had been and/or remained involved with, how long they had or intended to stay, what would encourage them to quit, and how much income on average they made from their activity. There was enough flexibility to allow the respondents to take the conversation in the direction they wanted on any of the topics. Although all the topics were covered for each interview, flexibility allowed each respondent to feel he or she was educating me about the conditions leading up to and during his or her involvement and what ideas he or she had concerning the future (Dexter 2012). None of those interviewed would allow the interview to be tape-recorded, leaving me to record their answers using the Greggs formal shorthand technique I had previously learned. While none of the interviews can be considered verbatim as would be obtained with tape recordings, they are very close to that. Most important, shorthand recorded interviews in no way misrepresented the responders' meanings within their answers.

PARTICIPATING IN THE ILLICIT ECONOMY

Push Factors

Why do youth participate in the illicit economy? From the dominant theoretical perspective, youth become involved because structural conditions have forced them to. However, is their participation due to having no other options, which pushes them into the illegal sector? The youth in this study *all* said that they had decided to participate in illegal activity because they wanted to have "things" they did not currently have. The three "things" they wanted most were money, material possessions, and status. More specifically, all of the youth (100 percent) said they wanted money, 73 percent (61) mentioned they wanted material possessions, and 86 percent (74) wanted to have status. When asked why they did not work in the legal economy to get these things, 81 percent (68) said it was because the jobs available were not attractive to them for a trio of cited reasons. The first was that wages in legal jobs were too low for them to get the material possessions they wanted. These youth all said that if they were to take a job that paid low wages, it would take them too long to buy the things they desired. Take, for example, the comments of a 19-year-old male from a Los Angeles middle-income family as representative:

> Yeah I can get a job as some kind of soda jerk or something, but why would I do that? It would take me forever to get anything that I like so that's just not the way to go, trust me. It's better to do nothing than to do that.

The second reason was that most of the jobs available to them and their peer group were "lower-status" and unacceptable. To the African American youth, these jobs were referred to as "slave jobs." To the white European-origin youth, these jobs were seen as simply "below them." Both the African American and white European-origin youth said that if they were to work at these types of jobs, their status among their peers would be lowered and so too would be their own sense of self-respect (Bourgois 1995). The comment of an 18-year-old African American male from a lower-income family in New York was typical of many responses given by African American interviewees:

> People got to be kidding to tell me to take a job that's got no future to it. You know like you can't live on it, and it may not even be there tomorrow. Hey, maybe my ancestors might have been ok with something like that during Jim Crow, but it ain't Jim Crow no more so ain't too many people I know who's going to do that shit . . . and we deserve better than that given the shit we have had to put up with.

The comment of a 21 year-old white female from a middle-income family in Oakland, California, was also characteristic:

> Well, my folks want me to get some type of work, but I told them that there is not much out there, and they say "there must be some job that pays something that you can do." Since they give me money each month, they think I should take any kind of job, but I am not about to do that just because it would let me know how the other people live. I'm not taking any job that's below me or what I think I'm worth. I'd rather be unemployed than that, but I'm not going to get into an argument with my parents so I just tell them I'm looking.

However, most Latino youth never said that a job was unacceptable because it was a "lower-status" occupation. This is not particularly surprising because 70 percent were immigrants or first-generation immigrants and immigrants generally never complain about the social status of the occupations that they have secured because they are generally happy to be employed. This may be because they are in the country without legal work papers or the need to financially provide for themselves and/or dependents does not give them the flexibility to evaluate how the job is socially conceived. Further, most immigrants or those who are first-generation often compare current jobs with what they would have had to take in their countries of origin. One Puerto Rican youth mentioned not taking a job because it was of lower status, but the Dominican, Central American, and Mexican youth did not. Indeed, for Central American and Mexican youth, a further explanation may have to do with ethnic culture insofar as often value is placed less on job type than on the effort one has put into executing its assigned duties. Consequently, going to work every day and doing one's best in fulfilling a job's requirements are appreciated insofar as demonstrating that an individual has acted honorably.

The third reason given for not working at jobs available in the legal market was that work schedules associated with these jobs were not convenient. Nearly every respondent who expressed this point said that available legal jobs required working after school, nights, or weekends, time periods they considered the best for socializing and which they were not willing to surrender to work. Kindred comments made by both a middle-class white and a lower-class African American youth exemplify this view. The first, from an 18-year-old white middle-class male from Oakland, was typical:

> Getting a job and working is OK, but not if the time you got to work is when everybody's out having fun. All the jobs I've seen so far are during the evening or weekends. So I'm looking for a job that definitely lets me make some money, but doesn't interfere with hanging out with friends. That's just not worth the money.

A second youth, an 18-year-old lower-class African American male from New York, similarly stated:

> I got no interest in taking any job that sweeps away my time with my friends. I was offered one two months ago at a factory making bedspreads in Brooklyn, but they wanted me to work second shift from 4 to 12 at night and I didn't want to do that cause then I'd have no time to play with friends. So I just had to pass on that one cause working that shift ain't worth it.

Of the 19 percent (16) who said they would take jobs below their present status, all of whom were from lower-class families, 84 percent (14) said these jobs were not easy to find because immigrant labor dominated this slice of the market through well-established and powerful networks. This statement, from a 21-year-old African American male from New York, was emblematic:

> me and my friends been looking for legal jobs and we don't care much about what they are, but the ones that we hear about are always taken by immigrants because they're connected. I mean, them immigrants gots all kinds of networks helping them so I don't stand much of a chance getting a good job where they're working.

In sum, it was not simply a lack of jobs that contributed to unemployment in the legal sector of the economy but the idea that available jobs were undesirable or that acceptable ones were currently taken by immigrant labor. As a 22-year-old white male from Oakland put it:

> Well it's true I'm unemployed and I guess I could take some jobs that are around here, but I prefer to wait for what I'm considering a good job to come along. I mean, I'm not going to work at a job that's not going to give me what I want out of it. I'd rather stay unemployed and deal [sell drugs] for some spending money.

The next set of questions focused on what made the person decide to become involved in the illicit economy: how, more specifically, did that happen? Two broad theses are often presented as to why individuals become involved, centering on some factors that push individuals toward crime and on others that lure or pull them into it. As this relates to individuals from different social classes, the general working hypothesis is that lower-class individuals are more likely to be pushed into the illicit economy because they need money to live and have fewer opportunities to obtain it (Sampson and Wilson 1995; Sullivan 1989). On the other hand, middle-class individuals are more likely to have been pulled into illegality through some form of social temptation. Here, rather than financial stress being the issue, the idea is that some level of greed has enticed them to participate in order to make significant amounts of money. In addition, or instead, they may find the feeling of doing something illegal and not getting caught to be seductive and exhilarating, like consuming an illegal drug; in other words, they experience a thrill that ensues from taking risks (Katz 1988).

Data from the interviews produced some surprising results related to these hypotheses. First, most of the youth interviewed—across class—said they did not feel pressured by life's events to become involved in the illicit economy. When asked if they went into this economy because they needed money to get by in life, 56 percent (47) said that they did not feel desperate and in need of radically changing what they were doing prior to becoming involved. All of the respondents said they had some money that was provided to them by family members, and all lived at home or with family members where they did not have to pay rent. Thus, despite repeated queries, not one respondent, irrespective of class background, reported feeling in any way pushed into participating because of his or her unemployed status. Perhaps this is because the current state of unemployment for youth, compared with previous generations, is not thought to be as socioeconomically detrimental in sustaining either young people's immediate physical needs or their long-term social goals.

For example, all of the youth interviewed stated that no one with whom they were currently living pressured them, in the past or presently, to leave their current homes and find their own living arrangements. Rather, the major point communicated to them by their parents or older family members was that social norms had changed from when they—these families and friends—were young. To illustrate, take the example of a 19-year-old white middle-class male in Los Angeles who lives at home and is involved in producing methamphetamine for sale. As he explained:

> My dad, and occasionally my mom will say, after they ask if I'm looking for work, that I'm lucky I don't have to go out and get a job and apartment

because their parents [his grandparents] thought that's what they should do if they weren't in school. I told them "well things have changed," and they said, "they certainly have!"

Another instance emerges in the thoughts of a 21-year-old lower-class African American male, living in New York with his brother and sister-in-law (both 18 years older), who is part of a group which steals expensive cars and sells the parts:

> I hear all the time from my brother and sister-in-law how I got it made. They both go on and on about how when they were my age it was expected that when men got to 18, they had to leave the house and get their own place to live. They ain't telling me to leave or nothing, and I know that it's different now, but I wish I didn't have to listen to this shit over and over again!

The youth gave two reasons as to why the attitudes of their parents or guardians had changed. One was parents/guardians understood that fewer jobs were available for today's youth, regardless of whether they had achieved a high school or college degree; as a result, young people needed to be patient and either wait for a job or continue in school to get the training and/or credentials necessary to secure "adequate" employment in the current labor market. The second reason, provided only by lower-class subjects, was that their parents/guardians believed racial prejudice and immigrants willing to work for less made finding a good job with wages capable of supporting a person and family at a "reasonable level" difficult to find quickly. The comments from two respondents living in different parts of the country highlight the point. One, a 20-year-old white male from a middle-class New York family background, explained:

> Both my dad and mom get that it's not so easy to find jobs that's got good pay and benefits these days. They tell me things have changed so much since they were young and everybody could get a job and stay with it for their whole life . . . so [now] they just tell me not to quit trying and they'll support me as long as it takes to get a good job.

Another, a 21-year-old African American Oakland resident from a lower-class family background, similarly said:

> My moms and pops understand it's really hard to get a good job now cause of all the racism that employers got toward hiring black men. My dad especially gets upset and says they'd rather hire an illegal than us blacks cause they're so racist about thinkin' black males won't work hard and stuff. That's why they tell me to just keep going for jobs, and if I don't get 'em I'll still have a place to sleep and eat.

Another important factor was that all the respondents said they had received modest amounts of spending money from their family before becoming involved in the illicit economy. Of course, this varied as to when a young person was provided this support, with some receiving a weekly stipend and others given money randomly over a 30-day period. Nonetheless, the vast majority of those from both middle- and lower-class backgrounds reported they were not in any extremely desperate financial situation when they decided to enter the illegal economy. The following two comments grow out of the experiences of youth from both social class backgrounds, the first coming from a 20-year-old white female from a middle-class family in New York:

> There's never been a real need for me to worry about money 'cause I'm still living with my parents and they'll give me money when I ask. So all I need to do is just wait for what I want to work at professionally, and in the meantime I can make some extra money with my clothing deals [the fraud scam she is involved in].

A 22-year-old male from an African American lower-class family in Oakland expressed a related point, answering:

> No, I never felt like I had to go do stuff off the books. Like I got a roof over my head and food here at my mom's place and she's always giving me some spending money, but when some opportunities came up to sell some high-end drugs I decided to do it cause the money was real good compared to the other jobs I was applying for.

Although economic issues were not significant "push" factors explaining these young people's participation in the illegal economy, other social factors did appear to create a "push" into it. One factor involved family obligations: of the 10 (12 percent) interviewed who said they did feel pressured into this market, all indicated they had family members active in this economy; in each case, it was the family member who had asked them for assistance with the family member's illegal activity. Consequently, in these cases, the pressure of family obligations resulted in youth feeling the "push" to become actively involved in the illicit economy. Exemplifying youths' decision to honor family obligations and participate in the illicit economy are two comments, the first from a 21-year-old Latino male from a lower-class family background who lives in Los Angeles:

> When my dad left to hook up with this other woman, my mom was left with me and my three sisters to feed. She hadn't worked since marrying my dad, so it was hard for her to get a job that could pay the bills. I really had to find something that would help us, but there was not too much that was out there. So I decided to work for this guy who strips cars that are stolen for the parts. I have been working there for about 10 months and the pay has been real good. I'd like to get a good regular job, but there's not too much around and this really helps my mom.

Relatedly, according to a 20-year-old lower-class African American male living in New York:

> I started dealing drugs when my brother was having some trouble with paying his rent and needed to make more money selling drugs. He'd been doing that for about two years, but then he needed more sales to pay off his personal stuff and asked me if I could help him sell in another area. I didn't really feel like doing it, but then again he's my brother and needed help so I did it. Now I'm doing it because it gives me good money until I can get a job [in the legal market] making the same—'cause I ain't interested in making less, you understand?

A second factor behind 17 percent (14) of the respondents saying they felt pushed into becoming active in the illicit market involved anxiety they felt to contribute a share toward their social group's entertainment. For these young people, being part of a group meant each member was expected to provide some financial contribution toward recreational events like purchasing or renting motor vehicles and paying for gas, food, and so on. For example, as a 20-year-old middle-class white male living in Los Angeles, explained:

> You know, we [the group he associated with] go out and things. There's always stuff going on and people chip in to share the expenses so if the same people do it all the time, it gets obvious and embarrassing so being unemployed left me kind of with just a little bit of money that my folks would give and that was not enough to help as much as I should've. So when I asked around about how to get some money, there was this guy who said if you want to put in some work, I know where you can get some money. That's pretty much how I got started in the business I'm in [credit card fraud]. . . . The money is good so I can do my own thing or contribute to group stuff without anybody in the group looking down at me.

Another factor influencing individuals to become active in the illicit economy entailed managing self-respect and social norms related to the fashion standards of their group. These individuals felt stress at the perceived need, as one respondent mentioned, "to up my fashion game" (i.e., to have clothing that kept up with the level the peer group considered "stylish"). This, of course, required a consistent source of income, as described by a 20-year-old African American female from a lower-income family living in New York:

> My friends been getting some nice clothes and showing up to parties looking good, you know what I mean? Now I do the same thing cause I got money to do that, too, but before I was "muleing" [carry drugs] for my cousin. I'd show up wearing the same clothes and that was just getting so embarrassing for me, you know? . . . yea, so I don't plan to look for another job now cause money

and time thing is both good, but you never know I could still see myself doing other things too.

The last factor mentioned by the respondents in this study was the need to share material objects/possessions with their peers (or provide them for their peers) so as to regain or maintain social status within the social group through, for example, the use of a car, drugs, alcohol, and/or electronic equipment. For these youth, their social rank within their primary group and what this provided was the prime motivator and related directly to feelings of personal identity and empowerment within the group. The comments of a 20-year-old Latino male from Oakland were typical of those who felt this:

> Now that I got money from my business stuff [he makes a cocaine–methamphetamine mixture—i.e., "crank"—for sale] I can give people stuff to use or just give them stuff like a gift. I like being able to do that [give a gift] cause before I couldn't and I wanted to. I gave a couple of my friends my drone [electronic flying apparatus] to play with and they had a lot of fun with it. It's nice that my friends think I'm the gadget guy and I want to keep making money to stay that guy! You know?

In sum, the data from the interviews were consistent in revealing social factors, and not the usual economic ones, that had "pushed" individuals toward the illicit economy. In fact, the data presented here indicate that a number of the working-, lower-, and middle-class youths' motivations to participate in the illicit economy converged. Basically, the social desires and concerns expressed by these youths were instrumental in instigating their illicit economy involvement by exposing each of these individuals to the reality that their current financial situation was not capable of achieving their desired social rewards.

Pull Factors

Although youth identified the previously cited factors as "pushing" them toward participation in the illicit economy, at least four major factors were cited as having "pulled" them in the direction of illegal work (Natarajan 2011). First, young people said they knew that individuals involved in this economy had opportunities to gain a considerable amount of money and material possessions. For another, they understood that a great deal of social recognition (i.e., status and privilege) could result from participating in this economy within a particular network and/or extended peer group. Moreover, the social recognition they so wanted was linked to the sharing of any profits they accumulated from their dealings in the illegal economy.

The comment of a 20-year-old middle-class white male living in New York was representative:

> I thought about running the business [he steals credit card numbers] I'm in for a while before getting started. I knew for sure there was going to be some risks with the law, but then again I really liked that people would look up to me for things I could give them . . . yea, I was considered important to people I was hanging around with and I really liked that feeling and will continue to like that feeling as I go on [in the business].

Others who said they were pulled into this economy as a result of wanting social recognition included women from the lower class who had been involved in prostitution. Here social recognition sometimes took the form of wanting the affection of a significant other, as in the case of one woman whose boyfriend suggested she get involved to "temporarily" help them as a couple to manage their current "financially difficult" situation. All of the women from lower-class backgrounds in the sex trade recounted versions of a boyfriend's line that wanting them to be involved in the "business" signified that the boyfriend really "loved her and wanted to protect her" from physical harm; they were convinced that their entering prostitution was like "an act of love that the boyfriend affectionately acknowledged." However, while all of these women were romantically involved with men who had become a "pimp" for them, none were presently with the same man who had pulled them into the business (Dank et al. 2014). What is more, all the women in this situation maintained that what they really wanted to do was show their desire to take care of "their man"; consequently, and even though they remained in the sex trade and the same physical location, they felt betrayed when the responsibility for controlling the business was transferred by their former lover to a new "pimp" with whom they did not become romantically involved. The comments of Yvette, a 22-year-old white female from a lower-class family living in Los Angeles, exemplify this point:

> Donnie was my boyfriend at the time I started. At the time his car was broken and he needed to fix it to find work, so he asked me for a loan, but I didn't have any money. So then he says maybe I could do a trick or two [sex for money] to just make enough for him to get the car fixed and then when he got the job we could get married. I had a hard time deciding, but he kept acting sad and anxious so I said I'd do it a couple of times. . . . Then there was always some other money problem for me to keep doing it. Finally, when I said I had enough, he got pissed off and just left without any contact information. Then, if you can believe it, a pimp comes to me and says that Donnie said that I might be interested in working for him, and I said screw you and went my own way. . . .

> You ask me how I think of life now and what my future might be. I don't know about the future, but what I think now is like, I don't know, kind of like the song by Dylan "Like a Rolling Stone"? I don't know if I understand all the phrases right, but it seems to spell out my life to this point.

A second pull factor cited by respondents related directly to feelings of empowerment. For these individuals, the potential to accumulate a good deal of wealth in the illicit market presented them with the ability to control other individuals and situations, providing them more status than they presently possessed. Two examples of this pull factor follow: one involved a 21-year-old male from New York who said he had consumed drugs recreationally for about 5 years and was asked by a friend if he wanted to invest in buying a large amount of marijuana. He decided to do it because it would save him money; after the first time doing this and making a great deal of money selling to others, he decided to continue because now he was able to provide it to his friends and this made him feel in control of his relationships. As time went on, individuals who were friends of friends came to him for drugs—he also expanded to sell oxycodone and other pain pills—deferring to him about other social issues like who should be responsible for organizing social events and what was appropriate in certain social situations. This made him feel powerful, and his status within the group increased as he could often dictate the outcome of a situation that had nothing to do with the consumption of drugs. This same "pull" factor was at play with a 22-year-old middle-class African American male living in Los Angeles, who said:

> I'm doing well in the business [illegal prescription drug resales] and I got some privileges that come with money. People recognize that I got the means to make things happen and that's got its benefits. But the big thing is that people will come to me to fix problems of all kinds and that is what is powerful, you know? That kind of respect is powerful.

A kindred instance involved a 20-year-old middle-class female from Los Angeles who was a junior in college and had been involved in the escort business (upper-class prostitution) for a year. She said that while at a fraternity party a man she did not know asked a group of men and women if they knew anyone who was an escort. Everyone in the group said no, but she recounted that this put the idea in her head for the first time. After about 6 months, a time when she had been very actively dating, she and a friend decided to learn more about the escort business and went on the Internet for information; in this way, they made contact with a 30-year-old female who introduced them to the "nature of the business" (i.e., the routine and remuneration). This woman also reported that after three talks with her friend—the last of which included discussing that this niche of the sex trade business involved more "upper-class" men, greater financial rewards, and little risk of being hurt or given a disease—they would try it. After they began, she said, they liked it for both the money and an exciting sense of control they felt over their male clients that they did not experience in other sexual situations with their male peers.

A third "pull" factor several youth articulated was that the process of making extra money would "require little of their daily time." While some time investment was required at the beginning to learn the routines to make money, after this period—on average, about 15 days—minimal time was entailed for executing the business and making a profit. The average amount of time an individual devoted to work varied with drug production/sales, with prostitution involving the most time. Times cited for differing illicit work venues were (1) drug sales/production, averaging about 4 hours a day, 7 days a week for those from the lower class and 2.5 hours a day, 3 days a week for those from the middle class; (2) prostitution, averaging 4 hours a day 2 days a week for the middle class and 5 hours a day, 5 days a week, for the lower class. For the other activities the range was from 1 to 3 hours, 1.5 days a week.

The fourth and last factor that individuals cited as pulling them into this economy was that not much was required as initial capital investments, allowing for a calculated chance to be taken with minimal financial risk. For example, those who stole car parts mentioned that their primary investment was tools to gain access by disabling the alarm/anti-theft protection systems to drive the car away, house it, and strip the desirable parts. For stick-ups, purchasing guns and bullets was combined with continuing to rotate them so as not to be identified (especially if a round was required) and locating a car that could be used to escape. For drug production, a physical space had to be rented to establish a lab, and products had to be purchased to produce the drug; for drug sales, an initial investment was needed to buy the drugs for retail; for credit card fraud, computers and different services had to be purchased so as to camouflage the source (Contreras 2012). As an 18-year-old middle-class white female drug dealer living in Los Angeles explained, characteristically:

> well, when I decided to get started selling drugs to friends, I had to use some money to buy my first couple of shipments and after that I had enough to pay myself back and work off the profits. So to start I had to make a little investment, but luckily it was not a big amount. I mean I used the money that I had saved from doing secretary work during the summer to buy at first. That made my two friends' suggestion that we do it seem possible, and so we took the chance. Now, we're really doing good.

Estimated Length of Participation

The next question that I asked was how long they expected to continue in the business. Seventy-two percent (61) said they had no idea how long they would continue. Of these individuals, 31 (51 percent) said they would do so until something in the legal sector could give them the same amount of money they were presently making or close to it. Another 30 (49 percent) said that they would stay until it was too physically and/or legally risky to continue. Interestingly, 93 percent (37) of the respondents from the middle class said that when they became active in the illicit economy they intended to stay only for a short time. Yet, when asked how long they had been involved, no noticeable difference distinguished their responses from those of lower-class respondents, all of whom also indicated they intended to stay until something better came along or the risks became too high. More specifically, lower-class youth reported that they had participated on average for 26 months, while middle-class youth reported on average 24 months. Thus, regardless of the reason a person joined the illicit economy—in other words, whether because of "push" or "pull" factors—once active, the positive benefits received were sufficiently significant to hold them regardless of social class background.

When I asked the youth if they had ever quit, 14 (17 percent) said they had but then later rejoined. Here, too, four major factors were cited to explain quitting. The first was anxieties associated with being arrested. The second involved fears of being injured or killed by a competitor or client. The third reason given was that peers might perceive their involvement as something negative, and this could result in social avoidance of the youth. Those engaged in stick-ups, prostitution, and stealing clothing mentioned this factor most often. The fourth reason was that the risk of morally implicating their family and/or loved ones had become too great to continue. However, all 14 of these individuals also declared that they had returned to this economy down the road.

What factors, then, persuaded them to re-enter? All respondents mentioned these three reasons: (1) the money one could accumulate from this economy was quite good, and no alternative had been found in the legal market; (2) while inactive, it occurred to them that there were opportunities to advance within the illegal economy so as to make greater sums of money than they had previously recognized, exciting them to want to try again (Venkatesh and Levitt 2000); and (3) recognizing, in retrospect, that compared to jobs in the regular economy they could make "good money" and not have to spend much time doing it. All of the 14 youth interviewed about returning considered their illegal activities to be "easy jobs" that allowed them the freedom to pursue additional education at local community colleges or universities and to engage in various leisure activities while securing enough money to fulfill their related needs. Two examples follow. The first is from a 21-year-old middle-class white female living in New York:

> I'm very ok about continuing the escort business thing while I'm finishing up [college] because I only need to do it a couple times a week at most for a few hours and then I can do whatever I want or need to do. Money's great and it's like super easy.

A further example comes from a 20-year-old lower-class African American female living in Oakland:

> I go and deliver some drugs to the three college guys once or twice a week, and that takes me a couple of hours and I'm done. Then I go to my own classes at [college] and study. I got about a year and a half before I get my degree in physical therapy. Now, I call that an easy way to make money and get ahead!

Participation and the Future

I ended my interviews by asking the respondents how long they expected to continue. The answer to this question varied by social class. Nearly all of those in the lower class said that no time consideration figured into their projections of future involvement. All but two said they would stay active as long as profits and financial opportunities existed for them.[1] Interestingly, while the risks associated with being arrested and/or injured by competitors, clients, and creditors were understood and mentioned, these risks did not figure into any rational decision that might cause them to cease and desist participation in the illegal economy. A small number mentioned that if they were to be injured or if an opportunity to make similar amounts of money arose in the legal economy, they would consider the option of quitting. Nonetheless, all voiced doubt that there would be the same opportunities to make money in the legal economy. The statement of this 23-year-old lower-class Latino male living in Oakland was typical:

> I mean, I could get rid of any worries [I have] and just quit making and selling the drugs, but then I'd be unemployed cause there ain't shit out there for work that's going to pay anything decent. So then I'd be safe and everything, but not living much at all. I ain't sayin' that I'm interested in dying, but not being able to do much because you ain't got no money ain't really living either.

When it came to how long the middle-class youth intended to stay involved, one answer given was that they would only work temporarily in the current underground economy to secure coveted possessions and afford desired leisure activities before moving on to a job in the legal economy. Most of these individuals were in college or had been on the job market for a while without finding the type of occupation that met their expectations. Another middle-class response was that youth intended to continue involvement but at a very low level in the illicit economy as a means of supplementing their present incomes. This response came from those who thought that an entry-level job in the legal economy was unlikely to produce the amount of income they desired. Examples included people working in the private sector in computer programming, medical assistants, and apprentices to business investors. Each of these positions had the potential to yield considerable income but required being internally promoted to a position with more authority, which would take time. Take the comments of a 22-year-old middle-class white male from Los Angeles as illustrative here:

> I'd say I'm going to stay working in some limited way in the card business [credit card fraud] 'cause I got a regular job in this travel company and I know I'll need the extra money until I'm promoted to some higher level that's higher in pay, and that could take a while.

A last middle-class response involved explaining that, while looking for work in the legal economy (and stopping illegal work), youth would remain associated with co-workers from the illegal economy. In so doing, they could still fall back on illegal work if nothing worked out in the legal economy. As a 21-year-old middle-class white male from New York elaborated:

> I been running the credit card numbers for about two years and I'm going to stop and get on to see if I can land a job with one of the clothing production companies. But I'm going to stay in touch with the guys I've been working with because, if nothing good comes up or something doesn't work out, I may need to do it again.

Particularly striking here is the lack of any difference in amounts of time spent in the illegal economy for those who said they had no intention of stopping, those who reported that their engagement was temporary, or those for whom work was a means to supplement their present income at jobs in the legal sector. Moreover, sociologically, little variance surfaced between middle- and lower-class respondents in terms of times reported doing illicit activities when controlling for specific occupational demands. The fact that individuals who want to stop, slow down, or believe they are only involved on a part-time basis all commonly report spending roughly the same amount of time in the illicit economy suggests several possibilities by way of explanation. One is that youth like what they are doing and the resources illicit activities provide them; another is that the jobs in the illicit economy take similarly small amounts of time, rendering them appealing across otherwise different class backgrounds of young people interviewed.

Still a third possibility is that youth want to work less but are unable to make that happen, creating an inaccurate delusion about the hours they are actually putting in; and, finally, perhaps they are lying to themselves (or the interviewer) about staying involved to avoid moral conflict. Probing questions were not able to eliminate, or definitively ascertain, which of these possibilities was most accurate.

CONCLUSION

What are some of the sociological takeaways from the interview data presented? First, part of the cultural landscape that directly applies to employment has changed and will likely continue to change. No longer do young people in the United States appear to believe it is simply good to work no matter what that work entails; this view may have shifted in large numbers, which is an empirical question further research needs to address using large randomized survey data. Presently, there are individuals in both the lower and middle classes who think it is only acceptable to work at a job worthy of their labor, that is, that the job's status should approximate what they believe is appropriate for their current social identity and/or can provide the income required for their desired lifestyles. Therefore, it is now considered more acceptable to forgo working and assume the unemployment designation while waiting for the best job fit.

Second, this cultural shift has expanded to such an extent as to currently allow individuals from divergent income groups the ability to justify their participation in the illicit economy. In essence, more tolerance exists within the society for being active in the illegal economy; or, in other words, less social disapproval operates to stigmatize and negatively affect socioeconomic prospects for the remainder of those who participate. Therefore, with limited moral risks, there is less cause for self-regulation or the ability of individuals to exercise personal social control.

Third, aspects of the underground economy have expanded to offer additional products and services, which patrons from all classes find attractive to consume. This provides opportunities for those who participate and is a strong incentive for youth to invest time and risk both legal prosecution and physical harm so as to capitalize on potentially significant profits. What is particularly revealing is that there are middle-class youth who have more educational and occupational opportunities active in this market, suggesting attractive aspects of the illicit market unrelated to any immediate stress they feel about being unemployed and/or that they are no longer willing to defer gratification until they complete their education.

Fourth, clear economic incentives pull individuals into this economy, but additional social (obligations and status) and psychological (feeling empowered) factors influence involvement as well. Thus, although clear differences pertain in how youth from different social class backgrounds assessed the amount of time they would continue their involvement in this economy, both were active for relatively the same amount of time. This suggests considerable holding power associated with their current illegal activities. This finding is reinforced by the fact that a number of individuals had ceased being active but then returned to illegal activities. Oddly, the options currently existing within the illicit economy afford young people a type of socioeconomic and psychological safety net for some period of their economic lives (Venkatesh 2009). In other words, greater convergence between middle-class and working-/lower-class understandings of what is happening in the economy, and the choices available to manage, appears to be occurring.

Fifth, opportunities available in the illicit economy tend to both inflate the unemployment rate (by maintaining numbers higher than might be occurring) and provide youth the ability to realize some of their contemporary cultural expectations about time devoted to working, quantity and quality of their desired material possessions, and the establishment of a coveted social life. Further, the changing cultural connotations of work, as well as the multifaceted aspects of this economy, muddy our assessment of the impact of unemployment on youths' current and future economic situation. In turn, it presents some challenging questions associated with policy issues related to job creation and unemployment for this segment of the society.

Lastly, the data in this chapter showcase the need for researchers and policymakers to reconceptualize the interrelationship between the economy and contemporary culture; to create new understandings about the nature of time, leisure, and work; and to blend traditional and new approaches to work (employment) and nonwork (unemployment) so as to better appreciate their meaning for both the individual and the society.

NOTE

1. The two respondents who did not say this were both involved in the sex trade, and they said they wanted to move to something else in the legal economy. One had applied to work as a receptionist in a medical practice and was offered the job when the present employee retired in the next 3 months. The other had applied to work as a receptionist at a local car dealership, a telephone company, and a dentist's office.

REFERENCES

Belfield, Clive R., Henry M. Levin, and Rachel Rosen. *The Economic Value of Opportunity Youth*. Washington, DC: Corporation for National and Community Service, 2012.

Bourgois, Philippe. *In Search of Respect: Selling Crack in El Barrio*. New York: Cambridge University Press, 1995.

Bureau of Labor Statistics. *Employment and Unemployment Among Youth Summary*. Washington, DC: US Department of Labor, 2016.

Contreras, Randol. *The Stickup Kids: Race, Drugs, Violence, and the American Dream*. Berkeley: University of California Press, 2012.

Dank, Meredith, Bilal Khan, P. Mitchell Downey, Cybele Kotonias, Debbie Mayer, Colleen Owens, Laura Pacifici, and Lilly Yu. *Estimating the Size and Structure of the Underground Commercial Sex Economy in Eight Major US Cities*. Washington, DC: Urban Institute, 2014.

Dexter, Lewis Anthony. *Elite and Specialized Interviewing*. London: European Consortium for Political Research, 2012.

Duster, Troy. "Crime, Youth Unemployment, and the Black Urban Underclass." *Crime and Delinquency* 33, no. 2 (1987): 300–16.

Estevão, Marcello, and Evridiki Tsounta. "Has the Great Recession Raised U.S. Structural Unemployment?" Working Paper 11/105, International Monetary Fund, Washington, DC, 2011.

Gregg, Paul, and Alan Manning. "Skill-Biased Change, Unemployment and Wage Inequality." *European Economic Review* 41, no. 6 (1997): 1173–1200.

Harrison, Bennett, and Barry Bluestone. *The Deindustrialization of America: Plant Closings, Community Abandonment and the Dismantling of Basic Industry*. New York: Basic Books, 1982.

Kasarda, John D. "Structural Factors Affecting the Location and Timing of Urban Underclass Growth." *Urban Geography* 11, no. 3 (1990): 234–64.

Katz, Jack. *Seductions of Crime: Moral and Sensual Attractions in Doing Evil*. New York: Basic Books, 1988.

Natarajan, Mangai, ed. *Crime Opportunity Theories: Routine Activity, Rational Choice and their Variants*. New York: Routledge, 2011.

Sampson, Robert J., and William Julius Wilson. "Toward a Theory of Race, Crime, and Urban Inequality." In *Crime and Inequality*, edited by John Hagan and Ruth Peterson, 37–54. Stanford, CA: Stanford University Press, 1995.

Scarpetto, Stefano, Anne Sonnet, and Thomas Manfredi. "Rising Youth Unemployment During the Crisis: Long-Term Consequences on a Generation." OECD Social Employment and Migration Working Paper DELSA/ELSA/WD/SEM(2010)6, Organisation for Economic Co-operation and Development, Paris, France, 2010.

Sullivan, Mercer. *Getting Paid: Youth Crime and Work in the Inner City*. Ithaca, NY: Cornell University Press, 1989.

Venkatesh, Sudhir Alladi. *Off the Books: The Underground Economy of the Urban Poor*. Cambridge, MA: Harvard University Press, 2009.

Venkatesh, Sudhir Alladi, and Steven Levitt. "An Economic Analysis of a Drug Selling Gang's Finances." *Quarterly Journal of Economics* 115 (2000): 757–85.

Wilson, William Julius. *The Truly Disadvantaged: The Inner City, the Underclass, and Public Policy*. Chicago: University of Chicago Press, 1987.

8

Effects of Incarceration on Labor Market Outcomes Among Young Adults

David J. Harding, Anh P. Nguyen, Jeffrey D. Morenoff,*
and Shawn D. Bushway

Over the last three decades, the number of individuals incarcerated in prisons and jails in the United States has risen dramatically. As a result, over 700,000 prisoners are released each year (West, Sabol, and Greenman 2010). Released prisoners are disadvantaged educationally, economically, and socially; and the prison boom has been linked to increasing inequality in the United States, due primarily to purported effects of incarceration on employment and wages (Western 2006). Incarceration is disproportionately experienced by young, low-skill, African American males and has potentially important consequences. For example, declining labor force participation by young black men during the late 1990s, when a strong economy pulled other low-skill workers into the labor market, has been attributed to incarceration and its effects (Holzer, Offner, and Sorensen 2005). For those seeking to understand the labor-market experiences of young adults from poor urban communities, the criminal justice system is arguably now as important as schools, neighborhoods, and families.

We should be concerned about the effect of incarceration on labor-market outcomes for young adults because of the potential for both long-term consequences and spillover effects into other life domains. The life-course framework—which focuses on the role of salient life events in structuring developmental trajectories and life transitions (Elder 1988)—suggests that

* Harding, corresponding author, can be contacted at Department of Sociology, University of California at Berkeley, 410 Barrows Hall, Berkeley, CA 94720, or via email at dharding@berkeley. edu. This study was funded by a grant from the National Science Foundation (SES1061018), with additional support from center grants from the Eunice Kennedy Shriver National Institute of Child Health and Human Development to the Population Studies Centers at the University of Michigan (R24 HD041028) and at the University of California, Berkeley (R24 HD073964). We thank Charley Chilcote and Paulette Hatchett at the Michigan Department of Corrections for facilitating access to the data and for advice on the research design.

incarceration may be particularly consequential for young people making the transition to adulthood. During this period critical life events typically occur, including school completion, first full-time employment, leaving the childhood household, and marriage and childbearing (Shanahan 2000). The life-course framework emphasizes the sequential connections between critical life events (for example, the connection between first employment and leaving the childhood household) and the role of early events in establishing trajectories of advantage or disadvantage over the life course. "Each [life] stage represents a launching point for the next" (Hogan and Astone 1986, 110). Thus, we view employment in young adulthood as a key indicator of—and prerequisite for—long-term social and economic well-being more generally.

Another possible reason to be concerned with the effect of incarceration on labor-market outcomes is the potential role of employment in future involvement in criminal behavior and the criminal justice system. Conventional wisdom and social science theory suggest the importance of employment for recidivism or desistance from crime. For example, Sampson and Laub (1993) argue that employment creates stakes in conformity by increasing the costs of reincarceration, reduces the material motivations for crime, and structures one's time and social networks. Yet prior research clearly shows that although employment is a statistically significant predictor of recidivism (e.g., Engelhardt 2010; Hagan 1993; Sampson and Laub 1993; Tanner, Davies, and O'Grady 1999; Thornberry and Christenson 1984; Uggen 2000), employment is far from determinative, and the evidence is decidedly mixed (Petersilia 2003). For example, there is some evidence that employment merely delays recidivism rather than preventing it, and in some samples employment and recidivism are only weakly associated (Tripodi, Kim, and Bender 2010; Petersilia 2003). Moreover, the direction of the causal relationship (if any) between employment and recidivism is far from clear as recidivism has the potential to affect future employment through the incapacitative effects of subsequent prison terms.

In this study we examine the effect of being sentenced to prison—compared to a probation sentence—on various labor-market outcomes among white and nonwhite young adults aged 14–25. We leverage a natural experiment involving the random assignment of judges with different "tastes" for harsh sentencing to isolate effects of incarceration in prison that are uncontaminated by pre-sentence differences among those sentenced to prison versus probation (whether those differences are observed or unobserved in our data).[1] We draw on administrative data on all individuals sentenced for a felony in Michigan between 2003 and 2006 and followed over time through 2012 in correctional and unemployment insurance records.

Our analysis considers multiple measures of labor-market outcomes, including point-in-time employment, employment in the primary versus secondary labor market, stability of employment, and employment at wages above the poverty line for a single person.

INCARCERATION AND THE LABOR MARKET

Low Rates of Employment Among Former Prisoners

Studies of incarceration and employment find that offenders who have been incarcerated or served longer sentences tend to have weaker labor force attachment after prison (Bushway and Reuter 2002; Bushway and Paternoster 2009; Nagin, Cullen, and Jonson 2009; Wakefield and Uggen 2010). However, some studies have also shown that prisoners experience temporary employment increases after their release relative to their employment status just before going to prison, which may be partially attributable to the effects of post-prison parole supervision and reentry programs (Bloom et al. 2007; Pettit and Lyons 2007; Tyler and Kling 2007; Kling 2006; Loeffler 2010).

Figure 8.1 shows rates of formal employment before and after sentencing for both nonwhites and whites aged 14–25 at sentencing, separately among

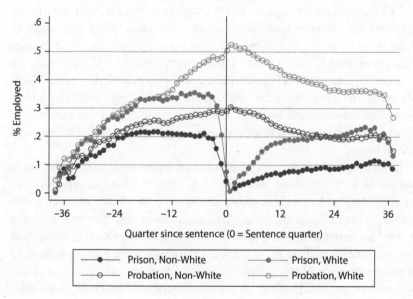

Figure 8.1 Employment Among Offenders Aged 14–25, by Sentence Type and Race

those sentenced to prison and those sentenced to probation. This figure is based on our administrative data from Michigan for felony sentences between 2003 and 2006. The first thing to note is the generally low rates of employment across all prisoners and probationers of both racial groups. Even among the group with the highest employment rates, white probationers, employment peaks at just over 50 percent. These low rates of employment are important because they suggest that individuals with felony convictions face steep barriers to employment even before they are sentenced. They are also important to keep in mind as we discuss the magnitude of effects of incarceration on employment. Figure 8.1 also shows stark temporal trends in employment probabilities. For all groups, employment increases as they age up until sentencing (76 percent of nonwhites and 83 percent of whites have no prior felony sentences before the focal sentence in the figure), although employment among nonwhite prisoners levels off long before sentencing. This increase is far steeper for whites than nonwhites, likely reflecting broader inequalities beyond those generated by felony sentencing. Moreover, those who will eventually be sentenced to probation rather than prison experience better pre-sentencing employment trajectories among both nonwhites and whites. This illustrates the challenge of estimating a causal effect of incarceration in prison on employment due to preexisting differences between those sentenced to prison and those given probation.

The point of sentencing marks a shift in employment trajectories for all groups. Those sentenced to prison experience a sharp drop in employment in the two or three quarters prior to sentencing. We believe this at least partially reflects pretrial detention in jail for those accused of the more serious crimes that are most likely to lead to a prison sentence. The employment rates of both nonwhite and white prisoners plunge to basically zero immediately after sentencing to prison and slowly increase as prisoners are released from prison. The steeper increase in employment rates after sentencing among whites reflects in part shorter prison terms among whites, a product of shorter minimum sentence lengths among whites than nonwhites (by the fourth quarter after sentencing 87 percent of nonwhites and 85 percent of whites were still in prison; by the twentieth quarter, 42 percent of nonwhites but only 28 percent of whites were still in prison). For neither white nor nonwhite prisoners does the rate of employment ever return to pre-sentence levels, despite the fact that aging would normally lead to improved labor-market outcomes over this period of the life course.

It might be tempting to compare pre-prison and post-prison employment among either nonwhite or white prisoners and conclude that prison negatively affects employment (by about 10 percentage points in both race groups), but examining the employment trends of probationers post-sentencing complicates such an interpretation. Both nonwhite and white probationers also experience a drop in employment that begins around the time of sentencing, and this downward trend continues for the rest of the observation period. The immediate effects may reflect employment disruption due to criminal justice system contact. The longer-term decline could be explained by the stigma of a felony conviction or by the heightening risk of removal from the labor market due to incarceration in the future as both probationers and former prisoners on parole are at heightened risk of incarceration from technical violations of supervision conditions. This downward trend in employment probabilities among probationers contrasts markedly with the upward trend among prisoners and suggests that had the prisoners been sentenced to probation instead, their pre-sentencing trend in employment would likely not have continued.

Stark racial differences are also evident post-sentencing. Perhaps most striking is that white former prisoners are more likely to be employed in the formal labor market than nonwhite probationers at about 5 years after sentencing. This may reflect differential stigma by race, general differences between blacks and whites in employment prospects, or high rates of future incarceration among nonwhite probationers. Together, the descriptive information provided in Figure 8.1 illustrates the complexities of estimating causal effects of incarceration in prison and motivates our use of a natural experiment to estimate such effects. However, before we describe our methodology, we discuss possible explanations for the poor labor-market outcomes of former prisoners, both those attributable to incarceration itself and those attributable to preexisting disadvantages.

Explanations for Poor Labor-Market Outcomes Among Former Prisoners

Why are employment rates so low among former prisoners? One important explanation is that individuals who serve time in prison tend to have poor labor-market prospects before they even enter prison (Bushway, Stoll, and Weiman 2007). Indeed, the most consistent predictors of post-prison employment among former prisoners across studies are criminal history, pre-prison employment, and pre-prison education levels (Bushway, Stoll, and Weiman 2007). This means that even had they not been incarcerated in prison, many former prisoners would have had little chance, at least in the short term, of acquiring employment outside the low-skill labor market, where real incomes across all workers have fallen over the last few decades. Weiman, Stoll, and Bushway (2007) argue that larger-scale changes in our political economy have created a low-wage labor market that has made employment challenging for former prisoners and other disadvantaged workers, particularly the shift to the knowledge economy and the decline in manufacturing, falling rates of unionization, a decline in the real value of the minimum wage, movement of jobs out of central cities, and declines in the enforcement of antidiscrimination and minimum wage laws.

Poor health may also be a significant barrier to labor-market success among former prisoners, who have high rates of mental illness, substance abuse, and associated problems such as homelessness (Visher and Travis 2003).

Another set of explanations focuses on the effects of incarceration on readiness for the labor market. As summarized in Bushway, Stoll, and Weiman (2007), human capital may erode while in prison; the conditions of prison may lead to problems with physical health, mental health, and substance abuse; and "soft skills" may be damaged by the harsh social environment of prison, what has been termed "prisonization." With regard to soft skills, Caputo-Levine (2013) argues that the strategies and interaction styles that men develop to deal with the interpersonal violence of prison life become internalized and persist after release, making it difficult to perform well in job interviews or in a socially demanding work environment. For instance, former prisoners may be more sensitive to confining physical spaces, perceive accidentally bodily contact as threatening, resist making small talk, and hesitate to display outward signs of friendliness such as smiling. These problems are likely to be most serious immediately after release and may dissipate as the former prisoner has time to adjust to the new social environment (Harding, Morenoff, and Wyse 2019).

A third set of explanations is the intensity of complying with parole requirements, especially in the early period after release. Being on parole can feel like a full-time job, especially when transportation to and from the required meetings, social service appointments, and check-ins is taken into account. These requirements tend to become less onerous after the first month or two on parole, but other requirements persist. Parole conditions can limit the types of jobs that a parolee can hold, for example. Certain industries may be off limits because they tend to pay workers under the table, while parole officers want to see a pay stub as proof of formal employment.

A fourth set of explanations for low employment after release from prison—and probably the most researched—is the stigma of a felony record and incarceration. We can distinguish between two types of stigma: formal and informal. Formal stigma prevents individuals with a criminal record, or a record of certain types of crimes, from working certain types of jobs or from obtaining the licenses or other certifications needed for whole classes of jobs.[2] Although variation across states and the sheer number of occupations involved make an exact count all but impossible, those with a criminal record are barred from working in a very large number of occupations, even long after they have completed their sentences (Petersilia 2003).[3] Formal barriers extend to other domains as well, such as housing and public benefits (Travis 2005). One that is particularly important for employment is a driver's license, particularly in a state like Michigan with a relatively weak public transportation infrastructure. Federal law requires states to revoke or suspend driver's licenses for drug offenders or risk losing federal highway funds (Petersilia 2003).

Informal stigma affects employment prospects when employers prefer not to hire those with felony or prison records. A series of recent audit experiments employed testers with fictitious résumés that vary in whether they signal a recent prison term. They are trained to pose as job applicants for real job openings. These studies show that having a criminal record reduces one's chance of a callback after applying for a job (Pager 2003, 2007; Pager, Western, and Bonikowski 2009; Uggen et al. 2014).[4] A critical aspect of this informal stigma is the use of criminal background checks by employers. With the computerization of criminal records and easier access to them online through both private companies and public records searches, use of criminal background checks among employers has been steadily increasing (Holzer, Raphael, and Stoll 2007), despite questions about the accuracy of these records, particularly those obtained through private companies (Bushway et al. 2007), and the inability of a criminal record to predict future criminal behavior in the long term (Blumstein and Nakamura 2009).

To fully understand the role of stigma in the labor-market experiences of former prisoners, we must also consider the ways in which a criminal record affects the types of jobs that former prisoners are able to obtain and which former prisoners are most likely to be affected. Audit studies and surveys of employers show that different types of firms are more or less likely to do background checks. Smaller firms are less likely to do background checks than larger firms and those with separate human resources departments. Firms covered by formal bans on hiring ex-offenders are more likely to do background checks, as are those that hire for jobs with child contact, cash handling, or customer contact (Holzer, Raphael, and Stoll 2007). Restaurants are among those least likely to conduct background checks (Pager 2007), likely because they are small firms with high job turnover.

Surveys of employers also suggest that characteristics of the former prisoner play a role in how information about a criminal record is used in hiring decisions. Employers are most open to hiring drug offenders, then property offenders, and finally violent offenders. They also consider mitigating circumstances like work history since conviction or release, enrollment in rehabilitation programs, and time since release (Pager 2007). Indeed, there is some evidence that firms that use background checks are more willing to hire ex-offenders than those that do not, although this applies only to those using private background check companies and not public records checks (Holzer, Raphael, and Stoll 2007). This also suggests that such firms are using background checks to exclude only offenders with particular criminal histories or to exclude them from only particular types of jobs.

Although the evidence on the importance of stigma is powerful, it is still unclear how stigma in the labor market translates into lower employment rates. First, Bushway, Denver, and Kurlychek (2014) point out that if only some employers in an industry do background checks or refuse to hire former prisoners, and that rate is relatively low, the effect could be small if most jobseekers are applying for many jobs and only need to be hired into one. They find, however, that among employers of low-wage healthcare workers in New York State, who are required to check backgrounds before hiring, denial of a job due to a criminal record has a very large effect on employment and wages because it excludes the job applicant from a whole class of jobs. Second, stigma may also affect employment by discouraging former prisoners from looking for jobs or looking as actively. For example, Apel and Sweeten (2010) find that the negative effect of incarceration on employment among first-time offenders is entirely due to not searching for work rather than searching but not finding work (see also Smith and Broege 2016).[5] Sugie (2016) finds that some former prisoners observed for the first 3 months after release stop looking for work after a period of unsuccessful job searching, particularly older former prisoners, namely those in their 30s and 40s. Third, stigma may not just affect whether and where one finds a job but also whether one can keep a job, for instance, if former prisoners are subject to greater scrutiny or are the first to be laid off when layoffs occur. Moreover, interviews with former prisoners suggest that they worry about background checks done after hiring, perhaps after a probationary period or before one's first scheduled pay raise (Harding 2003).[6]

When they do find formal employment, former prisoners tend to work in what is called the "secondary labor market," jobs that are characterized by lower wages, greater turnover, poor working conditions, and fewer possibilities for upward mobility (Bushway, Stoll, and Weiman 2007; Western 2007). For example, Western (2002) provides evidence that incarceration does not just reduce employment and wages in the short term but also lowers wage growth over the long term, suggesting that former prisoners may be relegated to the secondary labor market as a result of their incarceration. Moreover, prior research shows that an important feature of involvement in the labor market among former prisoners is the high degree of volatility in employment (Cook 1975; Sugie 2016), which could also be explained by employment in industries with high turnover more generally (such as the service sector and temporary labor). However, to our knowledge, no prior research has directly examined the types of jobs in which a representative sample of former prisoners is employed; and we have found only one study that has attempted to estimate the impact of incarceration in prison on employment stability (Loeffler 2010).

Finally, incarceration in prison may increase the risk of future reincarceration through the greater surveillance and scrutiny that comes with post-release parole supervision. Those under parole supervision are at risk of reincarceration not just for new felony crimes but also for technical violations of parole such as curfew violations, absconding, and positive drug or alcohol tests. Because future reincarceration removes former prisoners from the labor market (through what criminologists call "incapacitation"), it will reduce their probability of employment at least somewhat if some of them would have been employed. Probationers are also potentially subject to incarceration for technical violations, but probation supervision is less intense than parole supervision, at least in Michigan. (Over 90 percent of released prisoners are released onto parole in Michigan.)

Racial differences in post-prison employment among former prisoners cannot simply be explained by pre-prison characteristics (supplementary analyses not shown). One explanation is discrimination in the labor market against blacks in general. Another is the heightened stigma attached to felony conviction and incarceration experienced by black former prisoners compared to white former prisoners (Pager 2003, 2007). For example, Pager (2007) finds that restaurants, which tend not to do background checks, are most likely to hire white ex-offenders but least likely to hire black ex-offenders. This suggests that when employers do not do background checks, race may stand in as a proxy for a criminal record, disadvantaging black applicants in general. There is also some evidence that formal disqualification from jobs based on a criminal record is more common among jobs typically occupied by blacks, such as employment in the public sector. Racial differences in employment could also reflect greater reliance on informal employment among blacks, although if that were the case, we would view that as a further indicator of racial differences in outcomes, given the desirability of, and legal protections provided by, formal employment. Finally, blacks may face greater scrutiny on parole than whites, increasing their chances of removal from the labor market due to reincarceration. This could occur through individual-level discrimination by the criminal justice system or because of different parole supervision practices in counties where blacks are concentrated.

METHODOLOGY

Our goal is to estimate the causal effect of being sentenced to prison rather than to probation on various labor-market outcomes. Due to the threat of unobserved differences between young people sentenced to prison and probation, we rely on a natural experiment based on the random assignment of judges to criminal cases. In other words, our identification strategy is based on the random assignment of judges within counties. Judge identifiers serve as instruments for sentence type. Because they are randomly assigned to offenders, they provide a source of exogenous variation in sentence type, or variation that is uncorrelated with offender and offense characteristics that might be predictive of labor-market outcomes. The intuition behind an instrumental variable design is to estimate the causal effect of interest (prison vs. probation sentence) using only the variation in the "treatment" produced by the instrumental variables. This approach also assumes (as explained below) that the variation in treatment assignment is independent of both observed and unobserved predictors of the outcome. Counties may differ on a number of institutional factors (e.g., prosecutor practices, including use of plea bargaining), and outcomes and offenders may vary systematically across counties, so we remove all between-county variation by including county fixed effects in our models. This will ensure that only variation in sentencing practices between judges in the same county will be used in the identification of causal effects.[7]

A valid instrument must meet two conditions (for a review, see Angrist and Pischke 2009, chap. 4). First, it must affect the causal variable of interest or the "treatment" (here, sentence to prison rather than probation). This is often referred to as the "relevance" condition. Second, it can only be correlated with the outcome through the treatment. In other words, the instrument's effect on the treatment must be the only pathway through which the instrument affects the outcome, and there are no other variables that create an association between the instrument and the outcome. This second condition is known as the "exclusion restriction." While the first condition can be examined empirically, the validity of the exclusion restriction must be argued based on theory or knowledge of the institutional rules that generate the instrument.

The relevance condition is based on the idea that judges have considerable discretion in sentencing and that different judges systematically sentence more or less harshly than others. Although Michigan does have sentencing guidelines, these guidelines are advisory only and leave considerable room for judicial discretion. The result is considerable variation across judges within counties in Michigan. For example, the probability a judge will sentence an offender to prison rather than probation, net of criminal history and offense type, varies from 30 percentage points below other judges in the same county to 60 percentage points above other judges in the same county.

Even when there is variation in the treatment across instruments, estimates from an instrumental variables design can be biased when the

instruments are weak, in other words, when they are only slightly correlated with treatment (Bound, Jaeger, and Baker 1995). The danger is that
chance relationships in a sample can be mistaken for true correlations in
the population and instrumental variables estimates may be no better than
ordinary least squares regression (Angrist and Pischke 2009). This can be
a problem especially when there are many instruments relative to endogenous variables (overidentification), as is the case here with the many judge
identifiers (dummy variables) that serve as our instruments. Bound, Jaeger,
and Baker (1995) recommend examining two indicators of the strength of
the first stage, an F test for the joint significance of the instruments in the
first-stage equation and the proportion of variation in the treatment independently explained by the instruments. Appendix Table A8.1 shows that
either the F statistic or the proportion of variance explained (or both) is large
for all treatments in our models.

The exclusion restriction has two requirements: (1) that the instruments
are as good as randomly assigned and (2) that the instruments are correlated
with the outcome only through the treatment. We are confident that judges
are randomly assigned in Michigan. Criminal cases are assigned to judges by
the court clerk when cases are initially filed (at indictment). Therefore, initial
charges are filed before the prosecutor knows which judge will be assigned.
Michigan's Administrative Rules of Court specify in section 8.111(B) that
judges be assigned to all cases "by lot," but the chief judge of each court is
responsible for issuing orders on the exact procedures. All felony cases in
Michigan are handled by circuit courts, and all circuit courts have a computerized case management system that assigns cases at filing to judges using
a random number generator. This procedure assigns cases at random based
on the proportion of cases a judge is supposed to receive over the course of
a year, rather than when the case is filed. Our conversations with both pros-
ecutors and defense attorneys indicate that random assignment of judges
when charges are filed is taken extremely seriously as a core tenant of fair
and just operations of the court. While experienced attorneys are typically
aware of the sentencing styles of particular judges and one might imagine
that some degree of "judge shopping" occurs for high-profile or extremely
serious cases, circumventing the computerized random number generator
sounds implausible on its face; and moreover, it is hard to believe that such
efforts, if even possible, would be taken in the more routine cases that make
up the vast majority of felony cases. While we cannot empirically verify that
judge assignment is random with respect to unobserved variables, we can
check that the covariates we observe are uncorrelated with judge assignment. Appendix Table A8.2 shows that this is indeed the case. While F tests
of the joint significance of the instruments in predicting the covariates net of
county fixed effects are often statistically significant due to our large sample

size (picking up chance variation in offender characteristics across judges), the F statistics are small. In order to correct for chance differences in judge caseloads, we condition on these covariates in all models.

The exclusion restriction also requires us to assume that the instruments are correlated with the outcome only through the treatment. For this analysis, this means that the judge to whom one is assigned only affects recidivism or employment through the sentence the judge imposes. This assumption would be violated, for example, if judges who sentenced more harshly also treated defendants more harshly in court, leading them to question the legitimacy of the criminal justice system, which might make them more likely to return to crime. However, this would only be a violation of the assumption if the legitimacy of the system is undermined by the judge's actions beyond sentencing. Given the very small amount of time that defendants actually interact with the judge, such effects seem unlikely to be consequential.

A violation of the exclusion restriction could also occur due to the selection of cases into our data set, which only includes cases that result in conviction and sentencing. We do not observe defendants indicted but not convicted, but judge assignment occurs at indictment. While many offenders whose cases do not result in conviction are unlikely to be comparable to those who are convicted (based on actual guilt, for example), defendant plea bargaining could be influenced by the harshness of the judge to whom the case is assigned. For example, a defendant who draws a harsh judge may be more willing to plea-bargain knowing that a conviction at trial will result in a more severe sentence, while an otherwise similar defendant who draws a lenient judge may be more willing to risk a trial knowing there is some chance of acquittal and, in the event of a guilty verdict, a less severe sentence would result anyway. One might also suspect that a judge's sentencing practices would be positively correlated with probability of conviction at trial. Under these scenarios, defendants who appeared before lenient judges would be less likely to appear in the data since more will go to trial and more of those will be acquitted. The result could be that, among the cases in our data set, more lenient judges have sentenced cases with offenders more likely to recidivate, a correlation between judge harshness and the outcome that is not due to sentence type. This would introduce a downward bias into the effect of incarceration on recidivism. One way to examine whether these scenarios occur is to see if more lenient judges have more trials and fewer plea bargains among the cases that appear in our data. This does not seem to be the case.

The above discussion assumes that treatment effects are constant, yet it is more reasonable to assume that the effects of prison versus probation vary by offender, what is termed "heterogeneous treatment effects" in the literature.

When treatment effects are heterogeneous, instrumental variables methods estimate the "local average treatment effect," which means that the estimated effects apply not to the entire population of those actually treated but rather to those whose treatment status is changed by the instrument. Here, this means we are estimating the effects of prison on those whose sentence is influenced by the judge to whom they were assigned. Some offenders, based on their crimes and their histories, would be sentenced to prison by all judges and some to probation by all judges. Our estimates capture the effect of prison among those on the margin, who were sent to prison because they were randomly assigned to a more punitive judge. By definition, it is not possible to identify these individuals in the data, but we discuss this to be clear about what parameter we are estimating.[8]

A key issue is determining the appropriate start of the "risk" period for measuring outcomes. Probationers will be "at risk" for recidivism and employment outcomes immediately following sentencing, but those sentenced to prison will not be at risk until their first release (or parole) due to incapacitation. We believe that the policy effect of most interest is the total effect of incarceration, which includes the effect of incapacitation and can be captured by starting the risk period at the sentence date for all cases. Any reform in sentencing for the marginal prisoner would correspond to effects estimated by starting the risk period at sentencing. This also provides the cleanest counterfactual comparison between those who receive different types of sentences as delaying the start of the risk period until release from prison potentially reintroduces bias due to parole decisions and confounds age and time period with sentence type.

To implement our instrumental variables estimator of the effect of incarceration in prison versus probation on white and nonwhite young people aged 14–25 at sentencing, we use two-stage least squares estimation. Our instruments are a set of dummy variables for the assigned judge plus interactions between judge dummies and pre-sentence characteristics (see note 8). Our treatments are dummies for prison versus probation as well as the other two possible sentences one can receive for a felony (jail and jail with probation). Although we include the other treatments in the model to avoid introducing sample selection bias, we focus on the prison versus probation comparison because it is the cleanest comparison of incarceration versus no incarceration. We estimate these models on all cases in the data and interact our treatments with a set of dummy variables for combinations of race (white or nonwhite) and age group (14–25, 26–35, and 36 and above at sentencing). Since the focus of this chapter is young people, we report only effect estimates for whites and nonwhites aged 14–25. Unfortunately, there are too few Latinos or members of other racial/ethnic groups in Michigan to examine effects separately for those groups. The vast majority of those who are nonwhite are in fact African American. Robust standard errors are reported for all treatment effect estimates.

Data

We collected, cleaned, and coded data on all individuals sentenced for felonies in Michigan between 2003 and 2006 based on administrative databases at the Michigan Department of Corrections (MDOC). A primary source of data is the pre-sentence investigation report prepared for judges before sentencing, which provides our pre-sentencing covariates as well as judge identifiers. (In Michigan these reports are prepared by employees of the MDOC for all felony cases.) We also collected pre- and post-sentence employment information from the Michigan Unemployment Insurance (UI) Agency to assess quarterly employment, quarterly earnings, industry, and employer in the formal labor market for our analytic sample between the third quarter of 1997 and the second quarter of 2012.[9]

Our analytical sample excludes individuals for whom judges have no discretion in sentencing. This excludes individuals sentenced for first-degree murder or for flat sentences, in which the minimum sentence is the same as the maximum sentence and is set by statute (mostly felony firearm crimes). We also exclude individuals whose cases are handled by specialty courts as judges are not randomly assigned in such courts and individuals who were on probation and were resentenced for a technical probation violation. This leads to a final analytic sample of 111,110, of whom 18,298 are nonwhite and aged 14–25 and 22,820 are white and aged 14–25.

Outcome Variables

We constructed multiple labor-market outcomes from the UI records. The most basic is whether the individual had any formal employment in the fourth or twentieth full-calendar quarter after sentencing (we refer to these hereafter as "focal quarters"). This was the measure presented in Figure 8.1. Because this simple employment measure does not take into account the amount of earnings, we also constructed a measure of whether the individual had earnings above the poverty line for a single person in the quarter. To measure employment stability, we constructed a measure of whether the individual was employed in the focal quarter and the two prior consecutive quarters.

To examine directly the hypothesis that incarceration in prison increases the probability of relegation to the secondary labor market, we classified employers as secondary labor-market employers based on two-digit North American Industry Classification System (NAICS) industry codes.[10] Employers classified as forestry, fishing, hunting, and agriculture support

(NAICS code 11), retail trade (codes 44 and 45), administrative and support and waste management and remediation services (code 56), and accommodation and food services (code 72) were classified as employers in the secondary labor market. Together these employers accounted for 49.8 percent of employed person-quarters in the overall sample (all ages, races, and sentence types) between 2003 and the second quarter of 2012.[11] Based on this classification, we constructed a measure of whether or not the individual was employed in an industry not associated with the secondary labor market in each of the focal quarters. Descriptive statistics for all outcomes are presented in Appendix Table A8.3.

Pre-Sentence Variables

In addition to year of sentence, race, and age, our pre-sentence variables include measures of criminal history, gender, pre-sentence employment in the formal labor market, education, marital status, and histories of mental illness and drug and alcohol abuse. Descriptive statistics are provided in Appendix Table A8.4. These variables serve as controls in the two-stage least squares estimation models we present below.

RESULTS

Table 8.1 shows our estimates of the causal effects of incarceration in prison compared to a probation sentence on our four employment outcomes, separately for nonwhites and whites at the fourth and twentieth quarters since sentencing. Each estimate can be interpreted as the change in the probability of the outcome due to incarceration in prison versus probation. It is important to remember that these effects represent the effect on the "marginal" prisoner, that is, the prisoner who was sentenced to prison rather than probation due to the judge he or she was randomly assigned; and they do not represent an average treatment effect that applies to all prisoners compared to all probationers (see the discussion of the local average treatment effect above).

Table 8.1 shows results at the fourth quarter following sentencing (1 year since sentencing). At this point, 87 percent of nonwhite prisoners and 85 percent of white prisoners have not yet been released from prison, so the estimates almost entirely reflect incapacitation effects of the original prison sentence. In other words, how much employment are prisoners missing due to their incapacitation in prison? When we examine the probability of any employment in the calendar quarter, we see that there are large effects for both nonwhites and whites, although the effects are larger for whites. The larger effects are not surprising given the higher rates of employment

Table 8.1 Two-Stage Least Squares Estimates of Effects of Incarceration on Labor Market Outcomes, Among Young Offenders (14–25)

	Nonwhite		White	
4th quarter after sentence date	b	SE	b	SE
Any employment	–0.188***	(0.024)	–0.314***	(0.043)
Consecutive employment in last 3 quarters	–0.074***	(0.020)	–0.279***	(0.036)
Total earnings above poverty for a single person	–0.009	(0.017)	–0.264***	(0.033)
Employment in industry not in the secondary labor market	–0.022	(0.018)	–0.171***	(0.033)
20th quarter after sentence date				
Any employment	–0.078***	(0.023)	–0.129**	(0.042)
Consecutive employment in last 3 quarters	–0.035	(0.020)	–0.172***	(0.037)
Total earnings above poverty for a single person	0.010	(0.018)	–0.133***	(0.034)
Employment in industry not in the secondary labor market	–0.006	(0.017)	–0.072*	(0.033)
% Prisoners still incarcerated in 4th quarter after sentence	87%		85%	
% Prisoners still incarcerated in 20th quarter after sentence	42%		28%	

Robust standard errors (SE) in parentheses.
*$p < 0.05$, **$p < 0.01$, ***$p < 0.001$.

among white probationers than black probationers we saw in Figure 8.1. For nonwhites, prison reduces employment by about 19 percentage points, while for whites the effect is about 31 percentage points. Considering the relatively low rates of formal employment in this population generally, we view these as substantial effects.

For nonwhites, these effects are smaller when we look at more nuanced and more stringent indicators of labor-market success. The effect of prison on stable employment (employment for three consecutive quarters) for nonwhites is 7 percentage points. This is still a substantively meaningful effect, given the low rates of employment in this population and the aggregate effects given the number of young blacks who experience incarceration in the United States. Among nonwhites, the effects of prison on formal labor-market earnings above the poverty line for a single person and on employment outside the secondary labor market are substantively small and not statistically significant. Among whites we continue to see large effects of incarceration in prison on these more nuanced outcomes. Prison reduces the probability of stable employment by 28 percentage points, the probability of earnings above the poverty line by 26 percentage points, and the probability of employment outside the secondary labor market by 17 percentage points. Because the vast majority of both nonwhite and white prisoners are still in prison at this point, these racial differences in prison incapacitation effects reflect racial differences in the labor-market success of probationers. White probationers experience vastly better labor-market success than nonwhite probationers (see Appendix Table A8.3 for more detail). This could reflect generally better employment prospects among young whites than among young blacks or differential effects of felony stigma between blacks and whites. Given the divergent employment outcomes between white and nonwhite probationers even before sentencing shown in Figure 8.1, we suspect that the former explanation is the more salient one.

Table 8.1 also shows our estimates of the effect of prison versus probation at the twentieth quarter since sentencing (5 years since sentencing). At this point in time, 42 percent of nonwhites and 28 percent of whites are still in prison on the original prison term, so these estimates reflect primarily post-release labor-market outcomes. Given that incapacitation is much reduced, it is not surprising that the effects are smaller; but effects on any employment are still substantively large and statistically significant for both nonwhites and whites. Among nonwhites, prison reduces the probability of any employment by about 8 percentage points, while it reduces employment among whites by 13 percentage points. Among nonwhites, we no longer see statically significant effects on the more nuanced measures; but among whites, we continue to see large and statistically significant effects on employment stability (17 percentage points), earnings above the poverty line (13 percentage points), and employment outside the secondary labor market (7 percentage points). Again, we believe that these racial differences in effects of prison reflect the generally more advantaged position of young whites relative to young blacks in the labor market. Simply put, young whites with a felony conviction have more to lose from incarceration in prison than young nonwhites when it comes to employment outcomes. The comparison group for young nonwhites sentenced to prison, young nonwhites with a felony conviction who are sentenced to probation, is faring very poorly on employment stability, earnings, and employment in the primary labor market even when they do manage to find employment (see Appendix Table A8.3 for more detail).

CONCLUSION

In this chapter we have examined the effect of incarceration in prison compared to being sentenced to probation on the employment outcomes of young adults by leveraging a natural experiment based on the random assignment of judges to criminal cases in Michigan. This research design addresses one of the main threats to causal inference about the effects of incarceration, the potential for unobserved individual characteristics to confound differences in outcomes between prisoners and probationers. Our main finding is that compared to probation, being sentenced to prison has substantively large negative effects on employment for both nonwhite and white young adults (aged 14–25). These effects are largest 1 year after sentencing (in the fourth calendar quarter following sentencing), when incapacitation removes most prisoners from the labor market entirely, but persist to the 5-year point (the twentieth quarter), when the majority has been released from their initial prison term. These effects are larger for whites than nonwhites, likely reflecting the better labor-market position of young whites compared to young nonwhites.

To test the hypothesis that prison relegates ex-offenders to the secondary labor market where turnover is high, wages are low and show little growth over time, and there are few prospects for advancement, we also examined the effect of prison on more nuanced employment outcomes. These effects are almost exclusively experienced by young whites, primarily because young blacks are unlikely to experience stable employment, earnings above the poverty line, or employment in an industry outside the secondary labor market even when they are sentenced to probation rather than prison. The one exception is that incarceration in prison reduces not only any employment but also stable employment 1 year after sentencing for nonwhites, when incapacitation in prison is driving prison effects.

We can speculate about possible explanations for the larger effects of prison among whites than nonwhites. The first is that young whites generally have more success in the labor market than young nonwhites, so whites have more to lose from incarceration in prison than nonwhites. Our data show that white probationers have relatively more success on the labor market than nonwhite probationers. Alternatively, the mark of a prison record could signal something different to employers for young whites compared to nonwhites. This would be consistent with Pager's audit study research that found larger effects for whites than nonwhites, but that work estimates the combined effect of a felony conviction and a prison sentence, whereas everyone in our sample has a felony conviction. Finally, whites and nonwhites could experience different risks of future incarceration, either while on probation or while on parole after release from prison. For example, if nonwhite probationers experienced a higher risk of future incarceration than white probationers, the smaller effects of original prison sentences among nonwhites we see in our analysis could result from the low rates of employment that come from future incapacitation in prison among nonwhite probationers.

This discussion suggests multiple implications for future research. First, our differential findings by race and employment outcome suggest that issues of employment stability and the secondary labor market deserve greater attention in the study of labor-market experiences of young adults, particularly young adults of color. Simple indicators of employment at one point in time, or even wages at one point in time, may understate the challenges that young adults face in the labor market with job stability and eventual upward mobility if they struggle to find employment outside the secondary labor market or can find only temporary employment. These experiences could play a large role in discouragement and dropping out of the labor market entirely. Second, the poor labor-market outcomes of those sentenced to probation, especially among nonwhites, suggest that the effect of the stigma of a felony conviction itself deserves greater scrutiny, even when that felony does not result in a prison sentence. Our research design cannot shed light on the effect of a felony conviction itself, and prior audit study research has conflated effects of felony conviction and incarceration in prison, which theoretically might carry different types or degrees of stigma.

What are the policy implications of our findings? First, they suggest to us that the problems with nonwhite youth unemployment are as much created by more structural and systemic disadvantages in the labor market as they are a product of mass incarceration itself. One caveat to this statement, however, is that because everyone in our sample has been convicted of a felony, we cannot examine racial differences in the effect of a felony, and such an effect could be stronger for nonwhites than whites. Another caveat is that if racially disproportionate mass incarceration has stigmatized all young nonwhites in the labor market, as young men of color have become fundamentally associated with criminality and prison, then whether an individual is sentenced to prison or not may have little effect.

Second, our results also suggest that at the margin one could put fewer young people in prison (among both whites and nonwhites) and not do any harm because there are no positive effects of incarceration on employment for either group. This change would make both nonwhites and whites better off as our results suggest it would produce an increase in white and nonwhite youth employment. Given the high cost of incarceration compared to alternative sentences such as probation, our findings suggest that we could spend less on prisons and improve the employment outcomes of many disadvantaged young people. A caveat to this conclusion is that it does not take into account any possible deterrent, rehabilitative, or incapacitation effects of prison on reducing future crime among young adults, a question which awaits further analysis with our data. However, estimates of the effect of prison on future offending from other studies of the entire adult population suggest that any deterrent or rehabilitative effects are likely to be small or zero (Berube and Green 2007; Green and Winik 2010; Abrams 2011; Loeffler 2013).

NOTES

1. Only three studies of which we are aware have leveraged natural experiments to estimate the effects of incarceration on labor-market outcomes. With data from Florida state inmates and federal inmates in California, Kling (2006) instruments for prison sentence length using judges and finds no effects of longer compared to shorter prison sentences on employment or earnings in the medium term, although he does find positive effects in the period immediately after release. Using data from Cook County, Illinois, Loeffler (2013) instruments for incarceration in prison using judges and finds no effects on employment or job tenure. Using data from Harris County, Texas, Mueller-Smith (2015) instruments for incarceration in prison or jail for a felony and finds substantial effects on employment. None of these studies looks specifically at young people, examines differential effects by race, or examines industry of employment.

2. Another potential barrier to hiring ex-offenders is so-called negligent hiring lawsuits. If an employer is sued over the behavior or actions of an employee and it is demonstrated that the employer should reasonably have known the employee was likely to engage in such behavior, the employer can be liable for negligent hiring. An employee's past criminal record can be used against the employer in such cases, though only if the crime is directly related to the job responsibilities (Petersilia 2003). One question is whether employers are actually aware of these legal issues. Pager's (2007) employer surveys suggest that most are not.

3. According to the American Bar Association, there are over 30,000 state laws, provisions, and exclusions from employment related to criminal records across the United States (National Research Council 2014). Another estimate suggests that over 800 occupations are closed to those with a criminal record somewhere in the United States (Bushway and Sweeten 2007). In Michigan specifically, there are 593 such laws and regulations related to employment, occupational and professional licenses, and business licenses (American Bar Association 2015).

4. For an earlier generation of audit studies on the effect of a criminal record, see Schwartz and Skolnick (1964), Buikhuisen and Dijksterhuis (1971), and Boshier and Johnson (1974). These studies were conducted before the large increase in the incarceration that started in the mid-1970s and before technology that allowed for fast and cheap record checks.

5. One qualification is that the Apel and Sweeten study seems to be capturing mostly incarceration in jail, which may be a very different population from those incarcerated in prisons, especially when looking only at first-time offenders.

6. It is also unclear whether stigma is attached to the criminal record, incarceration, or the combination. Audit studies and employer surveys tend to focus on

felony criminal records (though see Uggen et al. 2014 on misdemeanors). One might hypothesize that incarceration amplifies the impact of a criminal record because it signals a more serious crime, because employers worry about prisonization and other effects of prison, or because incarceration makes it harder to conceal a criminal record (due to résumé gaps).

7. An additional reason to include county fixed effects is that tighter labor markets and more manufacturing employment are associated with better employment and recidivism outcomes for former prisoners, particularly for first-time offenders and those who were employed before prison (Bushway, Stoll, and Weiman 2007; Wang, Mears, and Bales 2010; Bellair and Kowalski 2011; Nguyen, Morenoff, and Harding 2014). Thus, it is important to remove variation in employment outcomes across counties.

8. The local average treatment effect interpretation of instrumental variables requires an additional assumption, which is termed "monotonicity." This means that the instrument only affects the treatment in one direction—the harshness of judges always affects the treatment in the same direction. In other words, a judge who imposes more punitive sentences than her or his colleagues to some offenders does not also impose more lenient sentences than her or his colleagues to others. (This is also sometimes referred to as "no defiers" in the instrumental variables literature [Angrist, Imbens, and Rubin 1997].) This might occur if a judge treats some types of offenders, say drug offenders, more harshly but other types of offenders, such as property offenders, less harshly than her or his colleagues. Following Mueller-Smith (2015), we relax this assumption by interacting judge dummies with pre-sentencing offender characteristics and treating those interactions as instruments. We also note that when there are more instruments than endogenous regressors and when we assume treatment effect heterogeneity, the instrumental variables estimates provide a weighted average of the effects that would be produced by using each instrument individually. Angrist and Pischke (2009) show that the weights are the relative strength of the effects of the judges on the treatment (in other words, the strength of the "first stage" for each instrument).

9. To match individuals with their quarterly employment records, all social security numbers (SSNs) available in the MDOC databases were sent to the Michigan UI Agency and Workforce Development Agency for matching. In some cases, more than one SSN and name were available for each subject, due to the use of aliases. We prioritized SSNs that were also listed in Michigan State Police records, to which we also had access. Returned UI records were matched with names from the MDOC databases, including aliases, to eliminate incorrect SSNs. If more than one SSN that the MDOC had recorded for the same person matched records in the UI data, project staff selected the best match by comparing employer names listed in the UI records with those listed in the MDOC records.

10. Unfortunately, the UI data do not contain occupation, so there is potential to misclassify individuals who work in industries associated with the secondary labor market but who themselves are not in the secondary labor market, such as managers of restaurants or retail stores.

11. Only 0.7 percent of employed person-quarters in 2003–12 had employers without valid NAICS codes.

REFERENCES

Abrams, David S. "Building Criminal Capital vs Specific Deterrence: The Effect of Incarceration Length on Recidivism." Unpublished manuscript, University of Pennsylvania Law School, 2011. https://www.law.upenn.edu/cf/faculty/dabrams/workingpapers/AbramsRecidivism.pdf

Angrist, Joshua D., Guido W. Imbens, and Donald B. Rubin. "Identification of Causal Effects Using Instrumental Variables." *Journal of the American Statistical Association* 91, no. 434 (1997): 444–55.

Angrist, Joshua D., and Jorn-Steffen Pischke. *Mostly Harmless Econometrics: An Empiricist's Companion.* Princeton, NJ: Princeton University Press, 2009.

Apel, Robert, and Gary Sweeten. "The Impact of Incarceration on Employment During the Transition to Adulthood." *Social Problems* 57, no. 3 (2010): 448–79.

Bellair, Paul E., and Brian R. Kowalski. "Low-Skill Employment Opportunity and African American–White Difference in Recidivism." *Journal of Research in Crime and Delinquency* 48, no. 2 (2011): 176–208.

Berube, Danton, and Donald P. Green. "The Effects of Sentencing on Recidivism: Results from a Natural Experiment." Presented at the Second Annual Conference on Empirical Legal Studies, New York, NY, November 9–10, 2007.

Bloom, Dan, Cindy Redcross, Janine Zweig, and Gilda Azurdia. *Transitional Jobs for Ex-Prisoners: Early Impacts from a Random Assignment Evaluation of the Center for Employment Opportunities (CEO) Prisoner Reentry Program.* New York: Manpower Demonstration Research Corporation, 2007.

Blumstein, Alfred, and Kiminori Nakamura. "Redemption in the Presence of Widespread Criminal Background Checks." *Criminology* 47, no. 2 (2009): 327–59.

Boshier, Roger, and Derek Johnson. "Does Conviction Affect Employment Opportunities?" *British Journal of Criminology* 14 (1974): 264–68.

Bound, John, David A. Jaeger, and Regina M. Baker. "Problems with Instrumental Variables Estimation When the Correlation Between the Instruments and the Endogenous Explanatory Variable Is Weak." *Journal of the American Statistical Association* 90, no. 430 (1995): 443–50.

Buikhuisen, Wouter, and Fokke P. H. Dijksterhuis. "Delinquency and Stigmatisation." *British Journal of Criminology* 11 (1971): 185–87.

Bushway, Shawn, Megan Denver, and Megan Kurlychek. "Estimating the Mark of a Criminal Record." Unpublished manuscript, 2014.

Bushway, Shawn, and Raymond Paternoster. "The Impact of Prison on Crime." In *Do Prisons Make Us Safer? The Benefits and Costs of the Prison Boom,* edited by Steven Raphael and Michael A. Stoll, 119–50. New York: Russell Sage Foundation, 2009.

Bushway, Shawn, and Peter Reuter. "Labor Markets and Crime Risk Factors." In *Evidence-Based Crime Prevention,* edited by Lawrence Sherman, David Farrington, Brandon Welsh, and Doris MacKenzie, 198–240. New York: Routledge, 2002.

Bushway, Shawn D., Michael A. Stoll, and David Weiman, eds. *Barriers to Reentry? The Labor Market for Released Prisoners in Post-Industrial America.* New York: Russell Sage Foundation, 2007.

Bushway, Shawn D., and Gary Sweeten. "Abolish Lifetime Bans for Ex-Felons." *Criminology & Public Policy* 6, no. 4 (2007): 697–706.

Caputo-Levine, D. D. "The Yard Face: The Contributions of Inmate Interpersonal Violence to the Carceral Habitus." *Ethnography* 14, no. 2 (2013): 165–85.

Cook, Philip J. "The Correctional Carrot: Better Jobs for Parolees." *Policy Analysis* 1, no. 1 (1975): 11–54.

Council of State Governments Justice Center. 2015. National Inventory of the Collateral Consequences of Conviction. https://niccc.csgjusticecenter.org/. Accessed September 28, 2015.

Elder, Glen H., Jr. "The Life Course as Developmental Theory." *Child Development* 69 (1988): 1–12.

Engelhardt, Bryan. "The Effect of Employment Frictions on Crime." *Journal of Labor Economics* 28, no. 3 (2010): 677–718.

Green, Donald P., and Daniel Winik. "Using Random Judge Assignments to Estimate the Effects of Incarceration and Probation on Recidivism Among Drug Offenders." *Criminology* 48, no. 2 (2010): 357–87.

Hagan, John. "The Social Embeddedness of Crime and Unemployment." *Criminology* 31, no. 4 (1993): 465–91.

Harding, David J. "Jean Valjean's Dilemma: The Management of Ex-Convict Identity in the Search for Employment." *Deviant Behavior* 24, no. 6 (2003): 571–95.

Harding, David, Jeffrey D. Morenoff, and Jessica J. B. Wyse. *On the Outside: Prisoner Reentry and Reintegration.* Chicago: University of Chicago Press, 2019.

Hogan, Dennis P., and Nan Marie Astone. "The Transition to Adulthood." *Annual Review of Sociology* 12 (1986): 109–30.

Holzer, Harry J., Paul Offner, and Elaine Sorensen. "What Explains the Continuing Decline in Labor Force Activity Among Young Black Men?" *Labor History* 46 (2005): 37–55.

Holzer, Harry, J., Steven Raphael, and Michael A. Stoll. "The Effect of an Applicant's Criminal History on Employer Hiring Decisions and Screening Practices: Evidence from Los Angeles." In *Barriers to Reentry? The Labor Market for Released Prisoners in Post-industrial America,* edited by Shawn Bushway, Michael A. Stoll, and David F. Weiman, 117–50. New York: Russell Sage Foundation, 2007.

Kling, Jeffrey R. "Incarceration Length, Employment, and Earnings." *American Economic Review* 96 (2006): 863–76.

Loeffler, Charles. "Does Imprisonment Alter the Life Course? Evidence on Crime and Employment from a Natural Experiment." *Criminology* 51, no. 1 (2013): 137–66.

———. "The Effects of Imprisonment on Labor Market Participation." Presented at the Annual Meeting of the American Society of Criminology, San Francisco, CA, November 17–20, 2010.

Mueller-Smith, Michael. "The Criminal and Labor Market Effects of Incarceration." Unpublished manuscript, Department of Economics, University of Michigan, 2015. http://sites.lsa.umich.edu/mgms/wp-content/uploads/sites/283/2015/09/incar.pdf

Nagin, Daniel S., Francis T. Cullen, and Cheryl Lero Jonson. "Imprisonment and Reoffending." *Crime and Justice* 38, no. 1 (2009): 115–200.

National Research Council. *The Growth of Incarceration in the United States: Exploring Causes and Consequences,* edited by Jeremy Travis, Bruce Western, and Steve Redburn. Washington, DC: National Academies Press, 2014.

Nguyen, Anh P., Jeffrey D. Morenoff, and David J. Harding. "The Effects of Local Labor Markets on Prisoner Reintegration: Formal Employment Among Former Prisoners in Michigan, 2003–2012." Presented at the Annual Meeting of the American Sociological Association, San Francisco, CA, August 16–19, 2014.

Pager, Devah. *Marked: Race, Crime, and Finding Work in an Era of Mass Incarceration.* Chicago: University of Chicago Press, 2007.

———. "The Mark of a Criminal Record." *American Journal of Sociology* 108, no. 5 (2003): 937–75.

Pager, Devah, Bruce Western, and Bart Bonikowski. "Discrimination in a Low-Wage Labor Market: A Field Experiment." *American Sociological Review* 74, no. 5 (2009): 777–99.

Petersilia, Joan. *When Prisoners Come Home: Parole and Prisoner Reentry.* New York: Oxford University Press, 2003.

Pettit, Becky, and Christopher J. Lyons. "Status and the Stigma of Incarceration: The Labor-Market Effects of Incarceration, by Race, Class, and Criminal Involvement." In *Barriers to Reentry? The Labor Market for Released Prisoners in Post-Industrial America,* edited by Shawn Bushway, Michael A. Stoll, and David F. Weiman, 203–26. New York: Russell Sage Foundation, 2007.

Sampson, Robert, and John Laub. *Crime in the Making: Pathways and Turning Points through Life.* Cambridge, MA: Harvard University Press, 1993.

Schwartz, Richard D., and Jerome H. Skolnick. "Two Studies of Legal Stigma." In *The Other Side: Perspectives on Deviance,* edited by Howard S. Becker, 87–101. London: Free Press, 1964.

Shanahan, Michael J. "Pathways to Adulthood in Changing Societies: Variability and Mechanisms in Life Course Perspective." *Annual Review of Sociology* 26 (2000): 667–92.

Smith, Sandra S., and Nora Broege. "The Role of Mental and Physical Health Concerns on Ex-Offenders' Job Search." Working Paper, Department of Sociology, University of California at Berkeley, 2016.

Sugie, Naomi F. "Pounding the Pavement: Job Search and Work After Prison." Working Paper, University of California, Irvine, 2016.

Tanner, Julian, Scott Davies, and Bill O'Grady. "Whatever Happened to Yesterday's Rebels? Longitudinal Effects of Youth Delinquency on Education and Employment." *Social Problems* 46 (1999): 250–74.

Thornberry, Terence P., and Robert L. Christenson. "Unemployment and Criminal Involvement: An Investigation of Reciprocal Causal Structures." *American Sociological Review* 49, no. 3 (1984): 398–411.

Travis, Jeremy. *But They All Come Back: Facing the Challenges of Prisoner Reentry.* Washington, DC: Urban Institute Press, 2005.

Tripodi, Stephen, Johnny S. Kim, and Kimberly Bender. "Is Employment Associated with Reduced Recidivism?" *International Journal of Offender Therapy and Comparative Criminology* 54, no. 5 (2010): 706–20.

Tyler, John H., and Jeffrey R. Kling. "Prison-Based Education and Reentry into the Mainstream Labor Market." In *Barriers to Reentry? The Labor Market for Released Prisoners in Post-Industrial America,* edited by Shawn Bushway, Michael A. Stoll, and David F. Weiman, 227–56. New York: Russell Sage Foundation, 2007.

Uggen, Christopher. "Work as a Turning Point in the Life Course of Criminals: A Duration Model of Age, Employment, and Recidivism." *American Sociological Review* 67 (2000): 529–46.

Uggen, Christopher, Mike Vuolo, Sarah Lageson, Ebony Ruhland, and Hilary Whitham. "The Edge of Stigma: An Experimental Audit of the Effects of Low-Level Criminal Records on Employment." *Criminology* 52 (2014): 627–54.

Visher, Christy A., and Jeremy Travis. "Transitions from Prison to Community: Understanding Individual Pathways." *Annual Review of Sociology* 29 (2003): 89–113.

Wakefield, Sara, and Christopher Uggen. "Incarceration and Stratification." *Annual Review of Sociology* 36 (2010): 387–406.

Wang, X., D. P. Mears, and W. D. Bales. "Race-Specific Employment Contexts and Recidivism." *Criminology* 48 (2010): 1171–1211.

Weiman, David F., Michael A. Stoll, and Shawn Bushway. "The Regime of Mass Incarceration: A Labor-Market Perspective." In *Barriers to Reentry? The Labor Market for Released Prisoners in Post-Industrial America*, edited by Shawn Bushway, Michael A. Stoll, and David F. Weiman, 29–79. New York: Russell Sage Foundation, 2007.

West, Heather C., William J. Sabol, and Jennifer J. Greenman. *Prisoners in 2009*. NCJ 231675. Washington, DC: Bureau of Justice Statistics, US Department of Justice, 2010.

Western, Bruce. "Mass Imprisonment and Economic Inequality." *Social Research* 74, no. 2 (2007): 509–32.

———. *Punishment and Inequality in America*. New York: Russell Sage, 2006.

———. "The Impact of Incarceration on Wage Mobility and Inequality." *American Sociological Review* 67, no. 4 (2002): 526–46.

Appendix Table A8.1 First-Stage F Tests (Joint Significance of Instruments)

	Judge Indicators		Judge Indicators and Judge–Covariate Interactions	
	Partial F Test	Shea's Partial R^2	Partial F Test	Shea's Partial R^2
Prison vs. probation, nonwhite, 14–25	44.69	0.003	4.30	0.106
Prison vs. probation, nonwhite, 26–35	10.78	0.002	4.46	0.110
Prison vs. probation, nonwhite, 36+	12.08	0.002	4.44	0.112
Prison vs. probation, white, 14–25	6.07	0.002	2.61	0.083
Prison vs. probation, white, 26–35	6.11	0.002	3.34	0.100
Prison vs. probation, white, 36+	9.79	0.003	3.61	0.102
Jail vs. probation, nonwhite, 14–25	107.85	0.003	7.52	0.184
Jail vs. probation, nonwhite, 26–35	13.12	0.001	5.64	0.160
Jail vs. probation, nonwhite, 36+	12.05	0.002	4.99	0.152
Jail vs. probation, white, 14–25	38.15	0.003	9.00	0.194
Jail vs. probation, white, 26–35	15.27	0.002	5.73	0.171
Jail vs. probation, white, 36+	19.43	0.002	5.40	0.166
Jail + probation vs. probation, nonwhite, 14–25	51.68	0.002	4.33	0.086
Jail + probation vs. probation, nonwhite, 26–35	14.03	0.001	5.22	0.098
Jail + probation vs. probation, nonwhite, 36+	15.34	0.001	5.07	0.097
Jail + probation vs. probation, white, 14–25	6.82	0.001	2.31	0.067
Jail + probation vs. probation, white, 26–35	7.05	0.002	3.01	0.080
Jail + probation vs. probation, white, 36+	8.32	0.002	2.88	0.080

Note: $p < 0.001$ for all F statistics

Appendix Table A8.2 Check of Randomization (Joint Significance Tests of Instruments)

Pre-Sentence Characteristics	F Statistic	p Value
Prior juvenile commitment	2.58	0.0000
Prior juvenile probation	2.62	0.0000
Prior adult jail	3.43	0.0000
Prior adult prison	8.97	0.0000
Prior adult probation	2.98	0.0000
Prior criminal sexual offense	2.70	0.0000
Prior misdemeanor	3.35	0.0000
0 prior felony	5.13	0.0000
1 prior felony	1.00	0.4120
2 prior felonies	1.52	0.0008
3 prior felonies	1.47	0.0004
4+ prior felonies	5.40	0.0000
0 prior arrest	4.08	0.0000
1–2 prior arrests	3.49	0.0000
3–4 prior arrests	1.77	0.0000
5–7 prior arrests	0.98	0.4566
8 or more prior arrests	6.41	0.0000
Drug abuse history	2.89	0.0000
Alcohol abuse history	2.23	0.0000
Mental health illness history	2.36	0.0000
Juvenile offender	1.94	0.0000
Age at first arrest	3.09	0.0000
Age at sentence	3.03	0.0000
Female	4.36	0.0000
Nonwhite	9.34	0.0000
Age 14–25	3.87	0.0000
Age 26–35	1.68	0.0000
Age 36+	1.86	0.0000
Age 14–25 × nonwhite	9.08	0.0000
Age 26–35 × nonwhite	2.47	0.0000
Age 36+ × nonwhite	1.81	0.0000
Age 14–25 × white	3.29	0.0000
Age 26–35 × white	1.74	0.0000
Age 36+ × white	2.58	0.0000
Less than high school	1.87	0.0000
GED	1.69	0.0000
High school	1.60	0.0000
More than high school	1.96	0.0000
Not single	2.07	0.0000
Pre-prison employment—23 quarters prior	4.09	0.0000
Pre-prison wages—23 quarters prior	2.47	0.0000

Appendix Table A8.3 Summary Statistics of Employment Measures, Among Young Offenders (14–25)

	Nonwhite		White	
	Prison	Probation	Prison	Probation
4th quarter after sentence date				
Any employment	0.03	0.29	0.07	0.52
Consecutive employment in last 3 quarters through 4th quarter	0.01	0.17	0.02	0.36
Total earnings above poverty for a single person	0.01	0.10	0.03	0.25
Employment in industry not in the secondary labor market	0.01	0.10	0.03	0.23
20th quarter after sentence date				
Any employment	0.09	0.20	0.21	0.39
Consecutive employment in last 3 quarters through 20th quarter	0.05	0.14	0.12	0.29
Total earnings above poverty for a single person	0.03	0.10	0.10	0.25
Employment in industry not in the secondary labor market	0.03	0.09	0.10	0.20

Appendix Table A8.4 Descriptive Statistics of Pre-Sentence Variables, Among Young Offenders (14–25)

	Nonwhite		White	
	Mean	SD	Mean	SD
Female	0.13	0.34	0.15	0.36
Less than high school	0.58	0.49	0.49	0.50
GED	0.09	0.29	0.11	0.31
High school	0.27	0.44	0.33	0.47
More than high school	0.06	0.23	0.07	0.25
Pre-prison employment (% employed 23 quarters before sentence)	0.23	0.25	0.35	0.29
Single	0.03	0.18	0.07	0.25
Drug abuse history	0.50	0.50	0.56	0.50
Alcohol abuse history	0.18	0.38	0.37	0.48
Mental health illness history	0.09	0.29	0.24	0.43
0 prior felony	0.76	0.43	0.83	0.37
1 prior felony	0.13	0.34	0.09	0.29
2 prior felonies	0.06	0.24	0.04	0.19
3 prior felonies	0.03	0.16	0.02	0.13
4 or more prior felonies	0.02	0.15	0.02	0.13
0 prior arrest	0.05	0.22	0.05	0.22
1–2 prior arrests	0.33	0.47	0.35	0.48
3–4 prior arrests	0.24	0.42	0.23	0.42
5–7 prior arrests	0.20	0.40	0.19	0.40
8+ prior arrests	0.18	0.39	0.18	0.38
Sentenced in 2003	0.27	0.44	0.27	0.44
Sentenced in 2004	0.26	0.44	0.26	0.44
Sentenced in 2005	0.24	0.42	0.24	0.43
Sentenced in 2006	0.24	0.43	0.24	0.42
	18,298		22,820	

Part IV

WHAT IS TO BE DONE?

9

Transforming High School and Addressing the Challenge of America's Competitiveness

Stanley S. Litow and *Grace Suh*

INTRODUCTION

The United States once boasted the world's fastest-growing middle class, a signal of its national prosperity. Our workforce has always been known for its dedication and hard work. But as other economies have superseded us in middle-class growth, the strength of our overall economy is in serious jeopardy. Why? Because motivation and hard work, while important, are no longer enough. To succeed, our next generation needs improved academic preparation and broader skills. Reinvigorating the American workforce by providing a clear path to the middle class is critical in addressing income inequality, revitalizing our economy, and strengthening America's competitiveness.

American workers need higher skill levels more than at any time in our history. In the heyday of manufacturing and skilled labor, vocational education or career and technical education (CTE) provided the critical workplace skills that promoted youth employment and economic mobility. But today's, and tomorrow's, knowledge-based jobs require more than a high school diploma. To succeed, workers need an integrated approach to post-secondary education and career preparation tailored to global market demands, stressing skills including problem-solving, communications, and teamwork, coupled with high-quality academics. Therefore, the task for today's CTE is to create a clear path to student success, ensuring college and career readiness. With high-quality preparation for college and career, graduates can pursue meaningful, long-term career opportunities and a hopeful future.

* This is a revised and updated version of an earlier report prepared by the authors in conjunction with Opportunity Nation.

To move forward, we need a national debate among business leaders, educators, policymakers, and the general public about CTE reforms that addresses the nagging "skills gap" and high rates of youth unemployment. This debate should provide an important historical context and a cogent argument for an updated and transformed CTE system to strengthen America's global competitiveness. The P-TECH 9–14 School Model, which has already achieved significant results in raising education attainment levels while bolstering the American economy, is one needed solution. P-TECH offers a roadmap to enabling a broader set of reforms that, if implemented, would significantly strengthen US competitiveness and support economic growth.

Change can happen. We have faced, and have overcome, similar challenges before—revising our educational standards as we evolved from an agrarian nation into an industrial superpower. At the end of World War II, America made high school mandatory and universal, opening the door to higher education. Some reforms were fueled by major public policy actions, such as the GI Bill of Rights or the Elementary and Secondary Education Act. Others were brought about by business and civic leadership. In the late 1940s, for example, the academic discipline of computer science was created by IBM in partnership with Columbia University. Today, we have an opportunity to compete more successfully in the global arena, but the key will be the degree to which we embrace innovation in education and workforce development together across various economic sectors. Now is the time for business, government, education, and community leaders to rewrite the narrative for American CTE and blaze the pathway forward for our next generation.

MAKING IT IN AMERICA

Ask the majority of Americans—especially our young people—and they will tell you that it is getting harder to make it in America. A 2011 nationwide poll of 18- to 34-year-olds by Demos and Young Invincibles found that half of young adults believe that they will be worse off than their parents and 77 percent believe that the middle class is disappearing (Draut et al. 2011, 3). A survey of older Americans for the fiftieth anniversary of the American Association of Retired Persons showed that 55 percent believe they are leaving the world in worse condition than they inherited it, with only 20 percent believing they are leaving a better world (Bridgeland, Putnam, and Wofford 2008, 4).

According to the Congressional Budget Office (2016), while the top 1 percent of earners grew their share of the nation's income (average inflation-adjusted market and before-tax income) by 188 percent from 1979 to 2007, those in the other four income quartiles grew their household income by only 18 percent over the same 28-year period. Income over this period became less equally distributed because of significant growth at the top. Meanwhile, economic mobility for low-income Americans almost completely stalled, with only 4 percent of those born into families earning in the lowest quintile making it to the top (Pew Charitable Trusts 2012). By comparison, rates of economic mobility were higher in both Canada and many European countries (Organisation for Economic Co-operation and Development 2010).

According to the Center for Labor Market Studies, employment rates for teens (ages 16–19) and young adults (ages 20–24) have dropped to new post–World War II lows. During the 2-year period from late 2007 to late 2009, the number of employed teens in the United States declined by nearly 25 percent, while the number of employed young adults fell by nearly 11 percent (Sum and Khatiwada 2010, 2). These employment rates are more than 18 percent below their year 2000 values and nearly 23 percent below their values in 1989—the peak of the 1980s labor-market boom (Sum, Khatiwada, McLaughlin 2009, 3). The prospects are particularly bleak for black and other low-income young males. In late 2009, unemployment among black male teens topped 86 percent. According to a 2016 report by the Brookings Institution, black and Latino youth are three to six times more likely than white youth to be unemployed and not in school (Ross and Svajlenka 2016).

While race differences are significant, the difference in education attainment levels are even more so. In 2014, the employment rate of young adults with a bachelor's degree was 87 percent, while the rate for young adults with a high school diploma was 66 percent. For those with less than a high school diploma, the rate was 52 percent (Ross and Svajlenka 2016).

With fewer than half of college graduates younger than 25 holding jobs requiring a college degree, less educated young people increasingly are displaced from the job market by their better-educated peers (Sum, Khatiwada, and McLaughlin 2009, 3). Ironically, teen unemployment reinforces itself in an endless cycle. Employers complain about the lack of workplace skills among young workers, but those workers are unable to develop and master their workplace skills without appropriate job opportunities.

POSTSECONDARY EDUCATION: THE NEW ECONOMIC IMPERATIVE

America's labor market is rapidly changing, demanding that more workers have at least some post-secondary education or training. In 1973, when manufacturing was in its heyday, nearly 72 percent of the labor market was made up of people with a high school diploma or less (Symonds, Schwartz, and Ferguson 2011, 2). Ten years later, manufacturing jobs began to decline, along with opportunities for less educated workers. The 2007–09 recession saw 5.6 million workers with a high school education or less lose their jobs, with only 80,000 of those jobs returning in 2010 (Carnevale 2016).

Today, with the shift from a manufacturing to a service and information economy, there are more than 29 million middle-education jobs that pay middle-class earnings in the United States. These jobs require more education and training than a high school diploma but often less than a bachelor's degree and, on average, pay $35,000 or more per year. Some pay significantly more. Nearly 10 million middle-education jobs pay more than $50,000 annually, and 3.6 million pay more than $75,000 annually (Carnevale, Hanson, and Jayasundera 2012).

The five major pathways to these jobs—many of which are part of CTE—are employer-based training, industry-based certifications, apprenticeships, post-secondary certificates, and associate's degrees. These pathways are opportunities, not dead ends. For example, 23 percent of students who earn a post-secondary certificate go on to earn an associate's degree or better (Carnevale, Hanson, and Jayasundera 2012).

WANTED: A NEW AMERICAN WORKER

Today's workers need deep content knowledge along with comprehensive workplace skills. They must be well rounded and possess expertise in their specific fields, along with a set of foundational competencies enabling them to apply their knowledge effectively. These workplace skills include critical thinking, problem-solving, teamwork, communication, leadership, and creativity. A high regard for ethical behavior and the ability to work cross-culturally also are required.

A near-record 5.6 million middle-education jobs were available in December 2016 (Gillespie 2016). Employers complain that young workers are unprepared for the evolving demands of the workforce. Specifically, many have demonstrated insufficient basic skills, such as oral and written communication, literacy, professionalism, critical thinking, and problem-solving (Symonds, Schwartz, and Ferguson 2011, 4). A national survey of 450 chief executive officers and 751 post-secondary leaders found that business leaders experience high levels of frustration in hiring. While unemployment was close to 10 percent at the time of the survey, 53 percent of business leaders said that their companies were facing a "very" or "fairly major" challenge in recruiting non-managerial employees with the skills, training, and education required. The challenge was even greater for the heads of smaller companies, which created more than 50 percent of new jobs in 2007; 67 percent of these leaders said finding the right talent was difficult (Bridgeland, Milano, and Rosenblum 2011).

The burden of preparing workers cannot be the sole responsibility of schools. A fully prepared workforce requires a multifaceted and integrated approach. Employers, educators, government, and community leaders cannot proceed in silos but must work together—each contributing specific expertise and resources to solve complex employment needs and prepare the new generation of workers for twenty-first-century jobs.

WHERE US STUDENTS STAND

America's youth are woefully unprepared to meet the increasingly high demands of the skilled labor market. In 2015, just 33 percent of US eighth-graders were rated proficient or higher in a national math assessment, and more than one in four scored below the basic level. The same test found that only one-third of high school seniors were college-ready in math and reading. In the same year, in an international exam given to 15-year-olds, US high school students ranked nineteenth behind other industrialized nations in science and thirtieth in math (Desilver 2017). While progress has been made and good examples exist in some schools and states, the United States continues to face a dropout epidemic. Twenty-five percent of all students and 60 percent of nonwhite students leave high school before graduation (Balfanz et al. 2012, 5).

Given these statistics, it is no surprise that 34 percent of all students at 4-year public colleges and universities enroll in at least one remedial course, while 43 percent of our nation's community college students require remediation. These numbers are much higher for low-income students and students of color.

Raising education prospects for all Americans would significantly impact the national economy. On average, high school graduates earn $130,000 more over their lifetimes—and college graduates up to $1 million more—than their peers who drop out of school (Balfanz et al. 2012, 16). Transforming just one student from dropout to graduate would yield more than $200,000 in higher tax revenue and savings for the government over the course of that person's life. If each state had a graduation rate of 90 percent, 580,000 additional students would have graduated in the class of 2011 alone, increasing the GDP by $6.6 billion and generating $1.8 billion in additional revenue from increased economic activity (Balfanz et al. 2012, 6).

THE PROMISE OF CTE

Clearly, high school is only a stepping stone to economic security. We must prepare youth and young adults with a higher level of skills to fill the knowledge-based jobs that require more than a high school degree.

CTE can be an agent of change, offering students three key benefits: academic knowledge, especially as applied to actual occupations; workplace skills such as communication, ethics, and teamwork; and technical skills, which are unique to specific occupational areas (Stone and Lewis 2012). By providing students with a variety of academic and workplace skills, CTE can become more relevant by directly linking academic training to job-market requirements. And CTE need not only prepare students for associate's degrees. Quality CTE programs prepare students to complete bachelor's degrees or higher.

To raise the education prospects of more young people and lift the American economy, CTE quality must also be significantly raised. Teachers and administrators have noted that in the past many underserved students were pushed into CTE programs because they lagged academically or were considered "hard to teach." While many CTE programs have moved far beyond this, the perception of CTE as a second-class track rather than as an alternative pathway remains a real concern.

CTE: A SNAPSHOT

CTE is a complex and diverse system, designed to prepare youth and adults for a wide range of careers and further educational opportunities. Programs serve a wide range of individuals at virtually all levels of the system—from middle school and high school to area career and technical centers, community and technical colleges, and other post-secondary institutions.

Within CTE, occupations and career specialties are grouped into 16 "career clusters" with each defined by a common set of knowledge and skills. These clusters are broken down further into programs of study, which combine academic and technical content in a sequence of secondary and post-secondary courses. The link between secondary and post-secondary is purposeful and necessary as a continuum of study that prepares students for college and career. Students graduate from these programs with varying educational attainment, ranging from industry-recognized credentials and post-secondary certificates to 2- and 4-year college degrees.[1]

CTE is a huge enterprise. As of 2011, 12 million students were enrolled in secondary or post-secondary CTE programs. Students' depth of experience with CTE varies significantly. Almost all high school students take at least one CTE course, and one in four students takes three or more in a single program area. One-third of college students are involved in CTE programs, and as many as 40 million adults engage in short-term post-secondary occupational training.[2]

Courses fall into three categories: general labor-market preparation (keyboarding, introductory technology education, career education, general work experience), family and consumer sciences (courses intended to prepare students for roles outside the paid labor market), and specific labor-market preparation (courses that teach skills and knowledge required in specific occupations such as healthcare or business). Most CTE courses provide specific labor-market preparation.[3]

At the secondary school level, students have access to CTE in a variety of settings. According to the latest data (2002), 900 of America's 18,000 public high schools were devoted to full-time CTE programs featuring a specific career focus in addition to academic coursework. An additional 8,000 schools were comprehensive high schools that had an academic focus but also provided both on-site and off-site CTE programs (US Department of Education 2008, 8). There also were 1,200 area or regional CTE schools (each serving several high schools) that provided CTE to students who also were receiving most, or all, of their academic instruction at their home high school (US Department of Education 2008, 13).

Approximately 5,700 institutions provided post-secondary CTE in 2005 (US Department of Education 2008, 76). Thirty-six percent of career education programs are provided by public and private institutions offering 2- and 4-year degrees (US Department of Education 2008, 78). Of the 1.9 million post-secondary career credentials awarded in 2005, 44 percent were bachelor's degrees, 21 percent were associate's degrees, and 36 percent were certificates. The highest percentage of degrees were awarded in the healthcare field (26 percent), with business and marketing following close behind (24 percent) (US Department of Education 2008, 161).

Funding

CTE is funded at the federal, state, and local levels. Federally, funding is through the Carl D. Perkins Career and Technical Education Act (Perkins). Perkins represents one of the largest federal investments in high schools and is the largest federal source of support for community colleges. In 2011, Perkins received 7.8 percent ($1.1 billion) of the nation's $14.5 billion education spending (US Department of Education 2011). Perkins funds represent about 6 percent of funds for secondary CTE programs but only about 1 percent of funds for post-secondary CTE education. The remaining funding is primarily from state and local appropriations. At the post-secondary level, the breakout is roughly 32 percent state and local appropriations, 31 percent from federal student aid, 16 percent from tuition and fees, 18 percent from federal tax expenditures for post-secondary education, 2 percent from veterans' educational benefits, and less than 1 percent from the Perkins Act.[4]

At a minimum, states are required to match Perkins state administration funds. The amount they provide beyond Perkins varies from state to state. According to the National Association of State Directors of Career and Technical Education Consortium (NASDCTEc), 48 percent of states reported decreased funding on the secondary level and 50 percent of states reported a decrease in funding on the post-secondary level in 2010. Rural states, in particular, reported minimal state education budgets (National Association of State Directors of Career and Technical Education Consortium 2010a).

Governance

CTE programs administered at the state level vary widely. Each state selects one agency to be its Perkins-eligible agency. The Department of Education is the eligible agency in 40 states and US territories, but 13 states and one territory designate a department of workforce development or a community college system to serve this role.

State leadership for CTE does not necessarily reside within the eligible agency. While the majority of states administer CTE through their education departments, seven relied on other governmental or post-secondary agencies in 2010 (National Association of State Directors of Career and Technical Education Consortium 2010b). And while it is critical, given that it is the source of most jobs, the role the private sector offered in the governance of these efforts is minimal.

State governance at the post-secondary level is more varied, with administrative and programmatic leadership encompassing a range of institutions that includes state community college boards and individual campuses (National Association of State Directors of Career and Technical Education Consortium 2010b). Post-secondary and workforce development agencies can also support programs for adult learners and other nontraditional students (National Association of State Directors of Career and Technical Education Consortium 2010b).

QUALITY CTE FOR ALL STUDENTS

It is impossible to discuss CTE without examining outcomes. In the past, CTE has been called a "dumping ground" for underserved and special-needs students (National Association of State Directors of Career and Technical

Education Consortium 2010c). The latest data on students in CTE show that as a group they are largely disadvantaged, suffering from high levels of poverty. According to a 2005 report from the US Department of Education, 52 percent of full-time CTE high schools reported moderately high levels of poverty, with 31 to 50 percent of students eligible for the National School Lunch Program (NSLP). This contrasts with comprehensive high schools, which reported that 19 to 21 percent of students qualified for NSLP (US Department of Education 2008, 10).

Data also suggest that CTE students may be taking less rigorous courses—particularly in mathematics, which is increasingly linked to success in college and career. According to data from the US Department of Education that compared high school graduates from the class of 2005, graduates who took geometry or higher-level mathematics in grade 9 took less occupational coursework (90 versus 93 percent), were less likely to complete an occupational concentration (16 versus 22 percent), and earned fewer occupational credits on average during high school (2.6 versus 3.1 credits) than their peers who took algebra or lower-level mathematics (US Department of Education 2008, 40). In addition, graduates who accumulated four or more occupational credits in high school earned 1.2 fewer core academic credits on average than their classmates who took no occupational coursework (14.8 versus 16.0 credits) (US Department of Education 2008, 44).

Based on these findings, CTE garnered its reputation as a second-class track. Just like the general education system, the quality of CTE schools varies significantly. Numerous CTE programs show promise in reducing high school dropout rates, increasing high school graduation rates, and improving labor-market outcomes. According to the NASDCTEc, high-risk students are 8 to 10 times less likely to drop out in 11th or 12th grade if enrolled in a CTE program versus a general education program. More important, students with a CTE concentration had a higher graduation rate, with an average rate of 90 percent in school year 2007–08 (Blosveren n.d.). This could be attributed to CTE students' being more motivated and interested in hands-on, relevant coursework. The NASDCTEc also reports that, to a much greater extent than their non-CTE peers, CTE students develop a range of academic and workplace skills that are essential to college and career success, including problem-solving, project completion, research, math, communication, time management, and critical thinking skills.

CTE students can also have stronger labor-market outcomes. The NASDCTEc reports that students who earned a CTE-related associate's degree or certificate earn an average of $9,000 more per year than those with associate's degrees in the humanities or social sciences. Those with credentials in high-demand fields such as healthcare can average earnings of almost $20,000 more per year.[5]

CTE: A HISTORY

To understand CTE today, we must first understand its history.

Vocational Education and Its Roots in Early America

The first forms of vocational education trace to colonial times when young people learned specialized trades through apprenticeships, which served as the primary form of training for employment while also providing basic education and instruction in ethics. For the poor, apprenticeships were the only avenue for receiving access to education (Gordon 2007, 4).

The Industrial Revolution brought an end to the apprenticeship system as factories required workers who could operate machines. Instead of specialized education learned through masters, workers could learn on the job. To provide workers with education beyond job skills, charities and societies of mechanics institutes established schools (Gordon 2007, 9).

Land Grant Universities: Vocational and Academic Education Merge

In the 1860s, clearer links between vocational and academic education developed. The nation's small but growing post-secondary institutions were not producing graduates who could serve the economy, particularly in agriculture and industry. At the same time, politicians and educators wanted to make it possible for all Americans to receive an education. In response, Congress passed the first Morrill Act in 1862, giving every state a grant of 30,000 acres of public land for every member in its congressional delegation based on the 1860 census. States were to sell this land and use the proceeds to establish colleges in agriculture, home economics, mechanical arts, and other professions for the current and future needs of the economy (Gordon 2007, 43).

The Smith-Hughes Act of 1917: Vocational Education Finds a Place in the Public Schools

The Smith-Hughes Act of 1917 became the first legislation supporting vocational education in the public schools in agriculture, trades, industry, and home economics (Gordon 2007, 66). It was based on a report by the Commission on National Aid to Vocational Education that found that more than 26 million Americans worked in agriculture and manufacturing but less than 1 percent had adequate training. The act created the Federal Board of Vocational Education to establish and oversee vocational education, providing funding for vocational programs for Americans from the age of 14 to below baccalaureate level.[6]

The act helped vocational education programs flourish but at a cost. The number of students grew from 200,000 and less than \$3 million spent annually prior to 1917 to 3.4 million with \$176 million spent annually by the end of the 1950s.[7] However, the act unwittingly separated vocational from academic education. Funding was only for the salaries of vocational teachers, not academic teachers; and students receiving instruction from these vocational teachers could receive only up to 50 percent academic instruction.[8] In addition, each state was required to establish a state board for vocational education, which in some states led to a board separate from the state board of education (Gordon 2007, 88).

The Servicemen's Readjustment Act of 1944

At the end of World War II, the country grappled with helping millions of returning veterans assimilate into civilian life. The Servicemen's Readjustment Act of 1944 (or the GI Bill of Rights) provided this support through education and training; loan guarantee for homes, farms, or businesses; and unemployment pay. Signed by President Franklin D. Roosevelt, it made college, including technical training, a viable option for many who would have sought employment by providing tuition assistance along with living allowances to servicemen and -women pursuing study. At its peak in 1947, veterans accounted for 49 percent of college admissions. By the time the original GI Bill ended in 1956, 7.8 million of 16 million World War II veterans had participated in education or training programs (US Department of Veterans Affairs 2012).

The National Defense Education Act of 1958

The National Defense Education Act of 1958 was the first federal acknowledgment that education was critical to US national security and specifically underscored the importance of science, mathematics, and technical skills. The act followed the Soviet launch of Sputnik I into space in 1958. With America in recession and fearing that Soviet technology was superior, the federal government took aggressive steps to provide vocational training for youth and adults (Gordon 2007, 90).

The Vocational Education Act of 1963

The Vocational Education Act was passed in 1963 to authorize federal, state, and local spending to establish new, as well as maintain existing, vocational programs. The act set forth multiple features, with the goal of providing high-quality vocational training that met the diverse needs, interests, and

abilities of people of all ages, rather than just addressing the needs of industry. Additionally, it stipulated that funding be provided to people with
disabilities and populations with academic or socioeconomic needs that
prevented them from participating in regular vocational education programs
(Gordon 2007, 92).

A Nation at Risk and the Perkins Act

In 1983, *A Nation at Risk: The Imperative for Educational Reform*, a report
of President Ronald Reagan's National Commission on Excellence in
Education, was published, recommending higher standards and more rigorous academics at the elementary and secondary school levels. As a result, states increased the academic requirements for graduation, which led
to declining enrollments in vocational programs over the next two decades
(Cohen and Besharov 2002).

In 1984, as a result of the educational reforms occurring in the United
States, including creating an equal opportunity for all to pursue education, the first Perkins Act was passed, giving states federal support of CTE
programs and prioritizing access to populations that were previously underserved, including people with disabilities, immigrants, women, people
of color, and adult learners, by requiring that they be equally served and
represented in enrollment, recruitment, and placement in a full range of
programs.[9] The act was later amended to require states to develop performance outcomes and standards as a means of improving accountability (US
Department of Education 2005).

In 1994, a disturbing report from the US Department of Education's
National Assessment of Vocational Education warned that vocational education was becoming "a dumping ground" for disadvantaged students and
students with disabilities. The report cited teachers without adequate formal
education and courses lacking academic rigor, pointing to insufficient
homework and weak requirements for program completion. The report
called for changes that moved from occupational preparation to preparation for broader industry careers and post-secondary education (Cohen and
Besharov 2002).

The Perkins Act was amended in 1998 and 2006 in order to continue
to strengthen the CTE system. The Perkins Career and Technology Act of
1998 sought to further improve CTE through academics, advancing CTE
students to higher-level CTE careers (US Department of Education 2012c).
The Carl D. Perkins Career and Technical Education Improvement Act of
2006 (Perkins IV) saw the integration of academics and technical standards,
creating separate performance indicators for secondary and post-secondary
programs and specific and separate requirements for areas of CTE studies for

secondary and post-secondary programs that did not exist (US Department of Education 2012b).

Acknowledging that Perkins was in need of significant improvement, the US Department of Education released in April 2012 a blueprint for CTE, stating that reforms are required to meet the twenty-first-century educational and economic needs of young people and adults and emphasizing that "postsecondary education and training are prerequisites for jobs of the new economy" (US Department of Education 2012). The blueprint called for a rigorous, relevant, and results-driven CTE. While so much in education reform has been divisive, with respect to the core elements of Perkins reform, the Department of Education's blueprint had bipartisan support and cross-sector support from business, labor, student, and parent organizations (US Department of Education 2012).

AN INNOVATION MODEL: P-TECH

Complementing continuing efforts at the federal level, many forward-looking states have moved beyond traditional CTE policies and programs, choosing to invest in a range of innovative models. Some examples are proven. Others are in nascent stages but show great promise. This section provides one example, the P-TECH[10] 9–14 School Model, which uses CTE funding as a component.

P-TECH was created by IBM in response to a request from the City of New York and its school system. It began as a unique collaboration among the New York City Department of Education, The City University of New York, the New York City College of Technology, and IBM. While beginning in one school in Brooklyn, New York, the intent was never to create a single successful school. It was to create an innovative, fully replicable model.

P-TECH schools are innovative grade 9–14 public schools offering a pathway from high school to college to career for young people from all academic backgrounds. In 6 years or less, students graduate with a high school diploma and a no-cost, 2-year associate's degree in a growth industry field. Each P-TECH school works with a corporate partner or partners and a local community college to ensure an up-to-date curriculum that is academically rigorous and economically relevant. Hallmarks of the program include one-on-one mentoring, structured workplace visits and skills instruction, paid summer internships, and first-in-line consideration for job openings with a school's partnering company.

P-TECH graduates are fully prepared to begin middle-class careers in the twenty-first-century workplace or to continue their educations at the 4-year college and university level and beyond, or both. In 2017 the replicable and sustainable P-TECH model encompassed a network of nearly 100 schools, serving tens of thousands of students across 7 states in the United States, and outside the country as well, with another 100 schools anticipated over the next year. Together, these schools are providing the model for an international effort to reform and revitalize CTE.

P-TECH is distinct from "early college" schools in significant ways:

- P-TECH schools are public schools. They are "open admissions," meaning there is no testing for admission. P-TECH does not "cream" or "cherry-pick" its students.
- As part of a scope and sequence connected to an associates degree in an in-demand STEM (science, technology, engineering, math) field, P-TECH students, who demonstrate readiness, take full-credit college courses beginning in the summer between grades 9 and 10.
- Each P-TECH school is a collaboration among a school district, a community college, and a corporate partner to ensure a rigorous curriculum that maps directly to current and future job-market needs.
- Each P-TECH student has a mentor, experiences workplace learning embedded in a strong academic curriculum, and benefits from structured workplace visits and paid internships. Successful graduates are placed "first in line for jobs" with the school's industry partner.
- Because P-TECH schools serve primarily historically underserved young people, the college degree is provided at no cost to students.

Skills Mapping

A critical component of P-TECH is "skills mapping." Mapping curricula to labor-market and college criteria allows P-TECH to prepare students for evolving industry needs. Skills mapping is informed by actual job requirements to ensure that programs are preparing students with the credentials, knowledge, and clear understanding of workplace expectations needed for real jobs. This does not replace a set of core academic requirements. P-TECH stresses academics, but by mapping to skills it makes the academic program rigorous and relevant. This involves identifying foundational workplace competencies and technical skills in key job areas. After these skills are identified, they inform curriculum decisions that are relevant to current and future job-market demands.

Workplace Learning

Workplace learning is a key aspect of the integrated sequence of high school and college coursework leading to a 2-year postsecondary degree. Workplace learning provides a seamless pathway to career. The workplace learning sequence of coursework, mentoring, work site visits, internships, and apprenticeships is intertwined with requirements for a post-secondary degree. As students move through the sequence, they shift the balance of their time and focus from school to work, just as they shift their balance from high school core requirements to college degree completion.

Mentoring provides students with meaningful academic, workplace learning, and emotional support. Each student is paired with a mentor from industry who serves as a professional role model, working with students on a range of workplace learning activities integrated into student learning.

Industry partners help teachers develop workplace learning coursework focused primarily on workplace competencies, such as leadership, teamwork, problem-solving, communication, and critical thinking. To enable students to fully understand the world of work, students participate in structured workplace site visits and meet with employees who are in jobs that students may graduate into, as well as engaging with executives who will encourage and inspire students.

Beginning the summer after year 3, students engage in skills-based, paid internships providing them with the opportunity to apply their technical and professional skills as they on real-world problems in actual workplace settings. This is key to ensuring that students have the experience necessary to attain an entry-level job and be first in line for jobs with their industry partner.

Integrated Scope and Sequence of High School and College Coursework

In addition to career preparation and skills mapping, P-TECH focuses on college readiness—mapping its curriculum with college admissions criteria, creating a college culture within the school. P-TECH student learning is focused on a 6-year scope and sequence of blended high school and college coursework to ensure that students will earn an industry-recognized, 2-year post-secondary degree. P-TECH students take college courses as early as the summer between grades 9 and 10 once they are college-ready. None of the courses are remedial, and all are credit-bearing.

P-TECH's curriculum is also aligned with educational standards as the foundation for learning in college—particularly higher education institutions with strong math, science, and engineering programs. As part of creating the early college culture, students have opportunities to visit the college campus and engage with college faculty and students, even before they begin college coursework. This provides students with firsthand knowledge of the expectations of post-secondary college and career environments.

P-TECH RESULTS

While only P-TECH Brooklyn, the first school, has completed the full six years of the model, schools across geographies are seeing significant results. School leaders—like P-TECH's founding principal Rashid Davis and some of his counterparts like Armando Rodriguez in Chicago, IL, Kevin Rothman in Newburgh, NY, and Karen Amaker in Norwalk, CT—have demonstrated that faculty can embrace and be motivated to deliver this innovative model with success.

The first P-TECH school completed the 6-year model in summer 2017. The school has more than 600 overwhelmingly minority (96 percent black or Hispanic) and low-income students. More than 80 percent qualify for free or reduced lunch, and 16 percent have individualized education programs.

By June 2017, more than 50 percent of the initial cohort of students had completed their high school and college degrees on time or earlier. By 2018, 17 graduates have jobs at IBM, and most are completing their bachelor's degrees while working. The majority of the other graduates are already enrolled in 4-year degree programs. College readiness, college completion, and grades on college courses are significantly higher than national averages. The dropout rate is near zero.

Other P-TECH model schools experience similar results. In Chicago, the Sarah E. Goode STEM Academy, a partnership between the Chicago Public Schools, City College of Chicago, Richard J. Daley College, and IBM, completed year 5 of the model, with attendance higher than the district average and more than a dozen students completing 1 or 2 years ahead of schedule. Its population is 98% children of color and is the second highest rated high school in the city. Other schools have similar results. For example, Norwalk Early College Academy in Norwalk, CT, finished its third year with promising data that include the following:

- 40 percent of students placed into college-level English and mathematics by the end of year 1
- 37 percent of rising 10th-graders and rising 11th-graders enrolled in a 10-week college session in summer 2016, with over 90 percent of students passing
- 38 percent of all students enrolled in college courses in fall 2016

Similarly, Excelsior Academy in Newburgh, NY, finished year 3 as well, with 95 percent attendance, along with the following data:

- 52 percent of current year 3 students will have access to higher-level math (calculus) before they finish the program, compared to only 26 percent who were on track entering ninth grade
- Of the 99 year 2 and year 3 students,
  - 73 percent are currently enrolled in college coursework
  - 70 percent have met the college-ready benchmarks for math before their third year in high school
  - 37 students have earned at least four college credits
  - 15 students have earned at least 19 college credits
  - 40 percent of students have met the college-ready benchmarks for English during their first year of access

P-TECH REPLICATION

In education we have always had high-functioning schools. The challenge has been to replicate and expand success and make it sustainable. P-TECH was designed to eliminate barriers to replication. It was created as an open enrollment school to guard against critics who might say that its success was dependent on "creaming" the student population. It encouraged support of all key stakeholders, teachers and principals, along with administrators, parents, and advocates. By building these core elements into the model, its replication began almost from the outset.

There are now close to 100 schools across seven states (New York, Illinois, Connecticut, Colorado, Maryland, Rhode Island, Texas), as well as Australia and Morocco. New schools are set to launch in the state of Louisiana and Taiwan, and many are more are anticipated in additional states and countries. IBM is lead industry partner for eight schools, with more than 450 businesses, many working in consortiums, partnering in the remaining schools. IBM is providing thought leadership, technical assistance, and guidance to ensure high-quality implementation.

Broad replication is continuing, fueled by the results and the needs addressed by the P-TECH design. However, broader and more rapid expansion allowing thousands, as opposed to hundreds, of schools to develop depends on a full understanding of the actions needed for further expansion.

P-TECH requires strong leadership, from the public and private sectors, beginning with government leaders. P-TECH's visibility grew significantly after President Obama, who featured P-TECH in his State of the Union address, visited a P-TECH school in October 2013. The Trump administration has similarly supported P-TECH.

Governors have also led, following the lead of New York governor Andrew Cuomo, who established the first and largest network of P-TECH schools, by building P-TECH replication into their statewide economic development plans. To date, Governor Cuomo has supported four rounds of state grants, funding close to 40 schools statewide.

From the private sector, businesses large and small have demonstrated leadership by changing the way that they work with schools. By engaging with P-TECH, companies commit to a long-term investment, offering mentors, paid internships, skills mapping, and more, following IBM's model. Businesses understand that by partnering with educators and playing a direct role in developing their talent pipelines, they can build the skills they need for future leaders and workers.[11]

PATHS FORWARD

We must ensure that America's education and workforce training systems meet the demands of our students, employees, and employers. Too much is at stake: individual opportunity and economic mobility, a productive workforce and robust economy, and a country that can compete in the global economy. Accomplishing these goals will require leadership from all levels of government and from business and educators.

Many reforms can be instituted to accelerate career and technical education as an attractive, prestigious path for many students. Below is a set of core actions to accelerate the focus on career and technical education, advance a plan to create more effective systems and policies, and foster a spirit to work across sector and party to fulfill the promise of pathways to career.

First and foremost is the opportunity to reauthorize the Perkins Act using federal funds as an incentive for incorporating the reforms that are desperately needed. In that reauthorization we have a clear opportunity to link to labor-market data, meaningfully engage employers, close the link between high school and post-secondary education, and establish clear metrics for performance.

Improve Data Availability to Measure Success and Demonstrate Return on Investment

The College Programs to Career Pathways

The federal government can promote stronger alignment between secondary and post-secondary study and labor markets. Student loans and grants under Title IV of the Higher Education Act can serve as leverage for the federal government to promote systematic reform. It should use this leverage to link post-secondary education data with employment outcomes, promoting greater accountability throughout our higher education system. The rationale is not greater government control but transparency and the provision of essential information promoting employment opportunities, efficiency, and productivity.

Leverage Existing Transcript and Earnings Data to Create a Transparent Matching System Between CTE Programs and Career Pathways

At the state and federal levels, policymakers should promote an education–employment matching system. Such a system would tie job exchanges (on-line job-search engines) with learning exchanges that match job and career pathways with available courses offered at post-secondary institutions, minimizing the need for additional oversight or state regulation.

Some states have developed the capability to connect wage records reported to state agencies that administer unemployment insurance and transcript records at secondary and post-secondary institutions. Connecting these data can show the effectiveness of specific programs at promoting positive employment outcomes, such as employment in field, wages, hours worked, and duration of employment. Additionally, using these data would inform students of the cost of dropping out of school or pursuing other courses of action.

Although many states have made the connection between wage and transcript data, most states have only just begun to use the data effectively to inform the youth or encourage program accountability. The federal government already distributes money to states to improve education data systems, but states limit access to the data for the purpose of connecting secondary and post-secondary programs to employment and earnings. This lack of transparency prevents individuals and institutions from utilizing the data to improve program delivery and placement services.

Significantly Expand the Role of Employers

The changing economy demands a highly trained workforce. Employers must be fully engaged in the development of programs and curriculum, training teachers and workers, and providing work-based learning and on-the-job training for students. Given the wide range of employers, by size, location, and industry, opportunities for meaningfully engaging employers will need to be equally diverse. Policies should be developed that provide incentives to employers and educators to work together.

Employers have recognized the need for a highly trained and well-educated workforce to help their businesses and our economy compete in the global marketplace. To ensure that employers are actively engaged in the development of curriculum, training of teachers and staff, and engagement of students in work-based and on-the-job training, federal policymakers should establish a tax credit for business and industry employers who directly engage with high schools and post-secondary institutions to create or strengthen enterprising pathways. This credit should also encourage employers to provide work-based learning opportunities for students and externships for teachers as part of a career pathway or program of study.

Improve Federal and State Policies to Strengthen CTE

Federal and state policymakers can accelerate the quality and availability of rigorous, high-quality career and technical education through legislative and policy reforms. At the federal level, Congress can update the Carl D. Perkins Career and Technical Education Act and the Higher Education Act and use this opportunity to not only reauthorize these laws but integrate CTE into the larger education system to meet the demands of an ever-changing economy. Concurrently, state policymakers must develop policies and legislation to improve CTE programs in their states. Although federal funding is a relatively small percentage of the total funding for CTE, it can leverage significant changes. Given this unique opportunity for reform and the clear economic imperative for action, the following are strategies to accelerate the progress of CTE.

Collaboration and Coordination Between Secondary,
Post-Secondary, and Industry

As discussed throughout this chapter, the changing economy demands that more employees have some post-secondary degree or industry-recognized credential. The current silos of secondary and post-secondary education systems, and the funding streams that perpetuate their separation, will not prepare enough students to meet the demand for middle- and high-skilled employees. There must be increased coordination among secondary and post-secondary institutions and the workforce to ensure smooth transitions for students and to improve successful post-secondary completion and employment. Models of this type of coordination, like P-TECH, can be found in many rigorous, high-quality programs.

Federal policymakers should require the creation of career pathways, including programs of study directly linking secondary and post-secondary programs to ensure that students graduate from high school and complete a post-secondary degree. Federal funding for CTE should support the development and implementation of these career pathway programs.

Expand CTE Programs of Study That Link High School CTE with Post-Secondary Programs

Career and technical programs form connections between secondary and post-secondary institutions. They are intentional and designed to result in industry-based certification or a college degree. They offer dual-enrollment activities, which have been shown to promote post-secondary enrollment and completion and avoid remediation. Apprenticeships and other programs geared toward working learners allow students to mitigate financial barriers by earning an income while earning credit or mastering skills toward a career pathway.

Alignment of Programs with Regional and State Workforce Needs

CTE offers a pathway for all students to obtain a high-quality education to connect them to a career with sustaining wages. However, if these pathways are not aligned to workforce needs and students graduate with a credential that does not have value in the labor market, the promise of high-quality CTE will not be realized.

Federal and state policies should require career pathways programs, including programs of study, to work with workforce development agencies, business leaders, and industry representatives to identify high-demand, high-skill, and high-growth occupations. This alignment should not be limited to the development of programs but should also ensure that programs and curriculum are updated to address changes in technology and other workforce changes.

Integrate Academic and Technical Education, Curriculum, and Instruction

High-quality CTE programs provide students with opportunities to gain academic and technical skills by integrating core academic courses and concepts with the principles of CTE through relevant, project-based learning. By integrating these two concepts that often operate in silos, the lessons can be more relevant and reinforced by each other.

Federal and state policies should encourage integration of CTE and academic courses to ensure that students are provided with a comprehensive education program to help them be college- and career-ready. This should include reforming curriculum to integrate rigorous academics with real-world, project-based content; supporting professional development for CTE and academic teachers to understand how integration can and should occur; and developing evaluations to more effectively measure student mastery of academic and technical skills.

Ensure Students Attain College and Career Readiness Skills

As programs integrate academic and technical education, it is important to evaluate a student's level of proficiency in both college and career readiness. Federal and state policies should encourage programs to develop methods of evaluating students on a wider range of college and career readiness standards to ensure that assessments more fully capture the skills gained in CTE classes. These policies should also create more flexibility for programs to measure student success through competency, rather than focusing on time in school.

Professional Development of Teachers, School Leadership, and Counselors

High-quality CTE requires that teachers, school leaders, and counselors are prepared to support students moving through the system. When teachers collaborate to integrate content across academic and technical disciplines, it results in strong positive outcomes. School counselors are a critical link in the process of helping students identify and enroll in programs that cultivate their interests and aspirations. A recent study of school counselors found that counselors are eager to receive additional professional development, particularly around college and career readiness.

Federal and state policies should support professional development opportunities for teachers, school leaders, and counselors and provide flexibility for schools to target the funds as they see fit.

Rural Programs

Like all students, those in rural areas should have access to high-quality CTE programs regardless of the proximity of post-secondary institutions or workforce partners. In Massachusetts, a consortium of rural high schools has formed one larger career and technical high school, which has allowed students to have access to greater resources, greater variety, and a larger number of industry partners. While this example involves a geographical consortium, other rural partnerships can utilize technology to connect students and industry to ensure relevance and rigor.

Reform Federal College Work–Study

Research has shown that work-based learning opportunities can help students gain the essential skills needed to succeed in the workforce. Federal Work–Study (FWS) provides nearly 800,000 undergraduates at 3,400 postsecondary institutions the opportunity to gain work experience while earning critical financial aid. The federal government invests nearly $1 billion in this program every year, approximately the same level of funding as the entire Perkins program. Through FWS, students can work on campus or at a public, non-profit, or for-profit organization, with federal funding covering 75 percent of student wages. Despite large participation, the majority of students work in on-campus positions, in largely minimum wage positions, and only 7 percent of all students engage in opportunities that allow them to collect wages while performing community service or working in the offices of private non-profits. A greater push to tie work opportunities to developing skills and opportunity is essential. Moving forward, the FWS program should be reformed to (1) ensure that work opportunities are linked to career aspirations and skill development, (2) increase the number of study–serve opportunities, and (3) make comprehensive changes to the allocation of aid to ensure that the students who need help the most are given preference.

Reauthorization of the Higher Education Act must tie FWS dollars directly to opportunities that make post-secondary education and work opportunities more efficient, rigorous, and relevant. Students participating in FWS should have the opportunity to earn independent study credits for the work experience and knowledge they gain in private sector jobs. This will allow some students to progress through credit attainment at a quicker rate and minimize the amount of time they must spend earning a post-secondary degree or credential. Universities, students, and employers must collaborate to develop individualized plans to ensure that students' work is related to their academic course of study, that students are challenged in their work, and that there is measured progress in hard and soft skills that leads to long-term employment. To maximize the potential of FWS, it cannot be viewed only through the lens of college affordability but also as a way to prepare students to be successful in career and community after college. Consequently, there should be an effort to increase off-campus work–study placement with employers who will offer higher wages and real work experience tied to career success.

Currently, the Higher Education Act, which authorizes the FWS program, specifies that all federal investment be allocated to universities based on "prior allocation." While individual award is determined using the Free Application for Federal Student Aid, many more recipients are eligible for

FWS grants than Pell grants, meaning the aid is not used to efficiently target the students who need it most. In reforming FWS, funding should be allocated to universities based on proportion of student need and allocated to students with the greatest need.

CONCLUSION

The education-to-workforce equation has completely flipped within a generation—most jobs in the 1970s required a high school diploma or less, and today, and into the future, the overwhelming majority of jobs require some college and many a 2- or 4-year college degree. As we have made clear, this is not the first time education has needed significant change to address changes in the economy. However, the pace of change now requires us to act and act quickly.

A reinvention of education to address both the skills crisis and the youth unemployment challenge, with CTE at its core and P-TECH as the linchpin, clearly can provide a pathway to economic mobility and success. In particular, P-TECH serves as a roadmap for how systems can be reformed to produce results that address economic and social needs: partnerships that align secondary and post-secondary institutions and industry, attainment of industry-recognized post-secondary degrees tied to labor-market outcomes, rigorous academic expectations blended with workplace learning, and a commitment to serve *all* students, giving them the support and motivation to be competitive in twenty-first-century STEM careers. Embrace of this model can be achieved quickly and systematically.

Innovations like P-TECH will carry multiple benefits. Students who might question the relevance of high school and college to their career dreams can link learning with career; students worried about the affordability of college can choose paths that accelerate the time to degree and lower the cost of college; students graduating with occupational certificates, associate's degrees, or more will have stronger currency in the labor market; employers who have worked with secondary and post-secondary institutions on curriculum and the skills they need in the workforce will experience lower training and remediation costs; and, most important, America can be more competitive and on a better path to close its skills gap to draw on more talent here at home. Increase in college and career readiness and increase in the number of students going into the workforce with a college degree and career preparation as opposed to only a high school diploma will strongly impact the economy.

Importantly, P-TECH results offer a significant return on investment. The elimination of large investment in remediation, a faster pathway to completion, and, most important, the significant tax revenues added as a consequence of improved college completion and the seamless transition from school to college and career make P-TECH not only the right solution but one that reaps significant financial benefit.

The growing network of P-TECH schools is eliciting exciting, real results. But this effort must move from a multiple of schools across several states into a national movement, connecting school to career and addressing in a substantive way the issue of income inequality and economic competitiveness. While much of the education reform agenda has been politicized, resulting in a lack of consensus, this is largely not the case with CTE reform or P-TECH. It has broad bipartisan support fueling its expansion. Now is the time to translate this support into swift action at the federal, state, and local levels. Our nation can seize this moment to redesign pathways that include career and technical education in ways that engage students, strengthen their learning and skills, and meet the growing demand of our economy.

NOTES

1. Association for Career and Technical Education. "About CTE." https://www.acteonline.org/aboutcte/#secondary.

2. Ibid.

3. Office of Vocational and Technical Education, e-mail, August 14, 2012.

4. Ibid.

5. National Association of State Directors of Career Technical Education Consortium. "Learning That Works!" https://careertech.org/sites/default/files/CTE-TalkingPoints-Basics.pdf.

6. Wikipedia. "Smith-Hughes Act." https://en.wikipedia.org/wiki/Smith%E2%80%93Hughes_Act.

7. Ibid.

8. Ibid.

9. GovTrack. "S. 2341 (98th): Vocational Education Act of 1984." http://www.govtrack.us/congress/bills/98/s2341. Accessed August 2012.

10. P-TECH stands for Pathways in Technology Early College High School.

11. In order to support replication, IBM created the P-TECH 9–14 School Model Playbook website (www.ptech.org), a central hub for public–private partnerships interested in learning about and implementing this groundbreaking school reform. The site focuses partnerships on the key elements that characterize the P-TECH model and provides action-oriented guidance and tools to enable them to implement the model with quality and fidelity. The site also features a series of

case studies from P-TECH model schools to ground the key elements in actual, effective practice.

REFERENCES

Balfanz, Robert, John Bridgeland, Mary Bruce, and Joanna Hornig Fox. *Building a Grad Nation: Progress and Challenge in Ending the High School Dropout Epidemic.* Washington, DC: Alliance for Excellent Education, America's Promise Alliance, Civic Enterprises; Baltimore, MD: Everyone Graduates Center at Johns Hopkins University, March 19, 2012.

Blosveren, Kate. "Career Technical Education: Learning That Works for America." National Association of State Directors of Career Technical Education Consortium, n.d. https://cte.careertech.org/sites/default/files/CTE-Learning-Works-NASDCTEc%26PIENetwork.pdf. Accessed August 2012.

Bridgeland, John, Jessica Milano, and Elyse Rosenblum. *Across the Great Divide: Perspectives of CEOs and College Presidents on America's Higher Education and Skills Gap.* Washington, DC: Civic Enterprises, Corporate Voices for Working Families, Institute for a Competitive Workforce, US Chamber of Commerce, Peter D. Hart Research & Associates, 2011.

Bridgeland, John, Robert Putnam, and Harris Wofford. *More to Give: Tapping the Talents of the Baby Boomer, Silent and Greatest Generations.* Washington, DC: Civic Enterprises, Peter D. Hart Research & Associates, 2008.

Carnevale, Anthony. "Trump Has Promised Manufacturing Jobs, but High School Grads Might Want to Seek Credentialed 'Middle-Skills' Posts Instead." The Hechinger Report, November 15, 2016. http://hechingerreport.org/trump-promised-manufacturing-jobs-high-school-grads-might-want-seek-credentialed-middle-skills-posts-instead/. Accessed August 2012.

Carnevale, Anthony, Andrew Hanson, and Tamara Jayasundera. *Career and Technical Education: Five Ways That Pay Along the Way to the B.A.* Washington, DC: Georgetown University Center on Education and the Workforce, 2012.

Cohen, Marie, and Douglas J. Besharov. *The Role of Career and Technical Education: Implications for the Federal Government.* Paper prepared for the Office of Vocational and Adult Education, Washington, DC. March 21, 2002. http://www.gpo.gov/fdsys/pkg/ERIC-ED466939/pdf/ERIC-ED466939.pdf. Accessed August 2012.

Congressional Budget Office. "The Distribution of Household Income and Federal Taxes, 2013." June 8, 2016. https://www.cbo.gov/publication/51361. Accessed August 2012.

Desilver, Drew. "U.S. Students' Academic Achievement Still Lags That of Their Peers in Many Other Countries." Pew Research Center. February 15, 2017. http://www.pewresearch.org/fact-tank/2017/02/15/u-s-students-internationally-math-science/. Accessed August 2012.

Draut, Tamara, Robert Hiltonsmith, Catherine Ruetschlin, Aaron Smith, Rory O'Sullivan, and Jennifer Mishory. *The State of Young America: Economic Barriers to the American Dream.* Demos, November 2, 2011. http://www.demos.org/publication/state-young-america-databook. Accessed August 2012.

Gillespie, Patrick. "America Has Near Record 5.6 Million Job Openings." CNN Money, February 9, 2016. http://money.cnn.com/2016/02/09/news/economy/america-5-6-million-record-job-openings/. Accessed August 2012.

Gordon, Howard. *The History and Growth of Career and Technical Education in America.* Long Grove, IL: Waveland Press, 2007.

National Association of State Directors of Career Technical Education Consortium. "A Synopsis of CTE Trends, Focus: Funding." November 2010a. https://cte.careertech.org/sites/default/files/SynopsisofCTETrends-Funding-2010.pdf. Accessed August 2012.

National Association of State Directors of Career Technical Education Consortium. "A Synopsis of CTE Trends, Focus: Governance." November 2010b. https://cte.careertech.org/sites/default/files/SynopsisofCTETrends-Governance-2010.pdf. Accessed August 2012.

National Association of State Directors of Career Technical Education Consortium. "Already At the Top: CTE Programs Show Positive Impact on Student Achievement, Focus: Suburban School (Three Part Series)." May 2010c. http://nrccte.org/sites/default/files/idea-center-files/suburban_final.pdf. Accessed August 2012.

Organisation for Economic Co-operation and Development. *Economic Policy Reforms 2010: Going for Growth.* Paris: OECD Publishing, 2010. http://www.keepeek.com/Digital-Asset-Management/oecd/economics/economic-policy-reforms-2010_growth-2010-en. Accessed August 2012.

Pew Charitable Trusts. *Pursuing the American Dream: Economic Mobility Across Generations.* July 9, 2012. http://www.pewstates.org/research/reports/pursuing-the-american-dream-85899403228. Accessed August 2012.

Ross, Martha, and Nicole Prchal Svajlenka. *Employment and Disconnection Among Teens and Young Adults: The Role of Place, Race and Education.* Washington, DC: Brookings Institution. May 24, 2016. https://www.brookings.edu/research/employment-and-disconnection-among-teens-and-young-adults-the-role-of-place-race-and-education/. Accessed August 2012.

Stone, James R., III, and Morgan V. Lewis. *College and Career Ready in the 21st Century: Making High School Matter.* New York: Teachers College Press, 2012. http://www.eric.ed.gov/ERICWebPortal/search/detailmini.jsp?_nfpb=true&_&ERICExtSearch_SearchValue_0=ED530690&ERICExtSearch_SearchType_0=no&accno=ED530690. Accessed August 2012.

Sum, Andrew, and Ishwar Khatiwada. *Dire Straits in the Nation's Teen Labor Market: The Outlook for the Summer 2010 Teen Job Market and the Case for a Comprehensive Youth Jobs Creation Strategy.* With Sheila Palma. Boston: Center for Labor Market Studies, Northeastern University, 2010.

Sum, Andrew, Ishwar Khatiwada, and Joseph McLaughlin. *Describing the Dimensions of the Current Labor Market Crisis in the U.S.* Boston: Center for Labor Market Studies, Northeastern University, 2009.

Symonds, William C., Robert B. Schwartz, and Ronald Ferguson. *Pathways to Prosperity: Meeting the Challenge of Preparing Young Americans for the 21st Century.* Cambridge, MA: Pathways to Prosperity Project, Harvard Graduate School of Education, 2011.

US Department of Education. *Career and Technical Education in the United States: 1990 to 2005.* NCES 2008-035. Washington, DC: National Center for Education Statistics, Institute of Education Sciences, July 2008. http://nces. ed.gov/pubs2008/2008035.pdf. Accessed August 2012.

US Department of Education. "Education Department Budget History Table." August 5, 2011. http://www2.ed.gov/about/overview/budget/history/edhistory.pdf. Accessed August 2012.

US Department of Education. *Investing in America's Future: A Blueprint for Transforming Career and Technical Education.* Washington, DC: Office of Vocational and Adult Education, April 2012a. http://www2.ed.gov/about/offices/list/ovae/pi/cte/ transforming-career-technical-education.pdf. Accessed August 2012.

US Department of Education. *Perkins III Accountability Primer.* Washington, DC: Division of Vocational Technical Education, Office of Vocational and Adult Education, Revised April 2005. http://cte.ed.gov/docs/DQI/Primer%206-30-05.pdf. Accessed August 2012.

US Department of Education. *Perkins IV—Frequently Asked Questions.* 2012b. http:// www2.ed.gov/about/offices/list/ovae/pi/cte/factsh/faq-080528.pdf. Accessed August 2012.

US Department of Education. "The Carl D. Perkins Vocational and Technical Education Act, Public Law 105-332." 2012c. http://www2.ed.gov/offices/OVAE/ CTE/perkins.html. Accessed August 2012.

US Department of Veterans Affairs. "Education and Training. History and Timeline." 2012. http://www.benefits.va.gov/gibill/history.asp. Accessed August 2012.

10

Time's Up! Shorter Hours, Public Policy, and Time Flexibility as an Antidote to Youth Unemployment

Katherine Eva Maich, Jamie K. McCallum, and Ari Grant-Sasson

INTRODUCTION

In 2015, Jeb Bush lost the Republican nomination for president with a simple gaff. In a meandering lesson about how to right the floundering US economy, he laid the responsibility at the feet of those already suffering: "People need to work longer hours" (Trudo 2015). Bush's remark sounded like a rehashed culture-of-poverty framework, positing that laziness and indolence explain why certain people are rich and others not. The Democrats and numerous journalists responded that Bush was "out of touch"; soon thereafter, he was out of the race. Yet Democrats had also proposed legislation that would allow workers to avoid the expected demotion to part-time status when certain requirements of Obamacare provided employers with an incentive to cut back their full-time staff. In other words, there was bipartisan support for the longer hours position (see Ponnuru 2015).

Some voters, too, agreed. Part of the reason involves many people wanting/needing to work longer hours. Hours of labor across the US economy rose by 9 percent between 1979–2013 (Golden 2016) and, according to a recent study by Project: Time Off (2016), Americans worked during more than 650 million of their earned vacation days last year. Over 6 million workers are today categorized as involuntarily part-time, meaning they would prefer to work full-time but cannot find employers to hire them. Researchers at the Federal Reserve feel that this seismic shift, one that has not returned to pre–Great Recession levels, is likely to persist (Valetta and van der List 2015).

In many ways, the controversy surrounding Bush's off-handed yet impactful remark is central to understanding the dilemma at the heart of this chapter: What is the relationship between the hours of work and unemployment? How does this relationship impact workers more generally, and how does it shape young workers' challenges and possibilities in the labor market? On the one hand, responses to Bush's comment suggest significant resentment and indignation that average workers are not struggling—a sentiment that could fuel interest in a movement to actually reduce the overall hours of labor, or at least stop them from rising. On the other hand, the dismal state of affairs for many workers means that any extra time in paid work translates into useful income, a powerful argument against reduction. With this tension in mind, we explore links between the youth unemployment crisis in the United States and the possibility of a movement to reduce the hours of labor. To the best of our knowledge, no such attempt exists.

Part of the way we approach these links is to take the struggle over time as central to our chapter; as Weeks (2011, 153) and others have pointed out, how time is organized has been central to the development of capital. We look at this struggle over and against time in two interrelated ways. First, we examine a policy called "work sharing" in which employers reduce hours of staff in order to avoid layoffs and save jobs, a policy that disproportionately benefits younger workers. Second, we explore the inchoate rumblings of resistance in the gig economy[1] and low-wage retail workplaces, where younger workers are channeling their anger toward digital labor platforms and unfair scheduling. Not content with simply winning shorter hours, they are exploring political and industrial solutions that will allow for greater control over their own time in general. We conclude by speculating on the implications of these policy prescriptions and resistance efforts that imagine innovative ways to bring about a more equitable and just world of work.

Overall, we find no evidence of the re-emergence of a coherent shorter hours movement. However, by looking at the content of recent policy measures and of varied protests, we note a renewed focus on time—albeit in small bursts, here and there—as a terrain of struggle for young workers that may increase as the character of work continues to shift through the twenty-first century.

Our chapter is *investigative* of several policy prescriptions that are worth exploring. It is also *speculative* about the possibilities for a shorter hours movement, broadly conceived, to address new problems of precarity and job losses that affect young people. And, finally, it is *suspicious* about the continued reproduction of the gig economy and low-wage sector as a work regime with potentially disastrous consequences for workers.

Research for this chapter was conducted through an analysis of current social science literature on precarious work, youth unemployment, and gig economy platform employment data. Additionally, we drew from recent journalistic pieces, news reports, policy briefs, and legislative transcripts. We begin by contextualizing our chapter in past struggles to control labor time.

HISTORICIZING STRUGGLES AGAINST LABOR TIME

When it comes to time spent working in the United States at present, two problems immediately come to light. First, an asymmetrical distribution of working time persists, with some people overworked and others under-employed. This makes perfect sense as overtime lowers demand for other workers (Boushey and Ansel 2016). Second, hours are increasingly unstable; precarious on-call work scheduling and gig economy–style employment relationships are the canaries in the coal mine of a labor market that producers fewer stable jobs. We believe it is possible that some kind of shorter hours movement, especially one that places an emphasis on young workers, has the potential to address these problems.

Looking back, American workers took an interest in decreasing the length of the working day as early as the late nineteenth century, both to reduce toil and to "spread the work" so as to reduce unemployment. In 1879, members of the Working Women's Union in Chicago brought together two important concerns of their membership: the 8-hour working day and the right to vote, as more than 300 seamstresses walked from shop to shop, protesting across the city to demand a shorter working day (Roediger and Foner 1989, 166).

The years following the turn of the century until World War I marked the greatest decrease in working hours in American history. While concerns over leisure remained relevant to workers, the movement for reduced work hours began to focus greater attention on worker safety (Hunnicut 1988). Concerns about overwork leading not only to injuries but also to diminished productivity enabled labor to gain the support of more liberal firm owners open to reform (Hunnicut 1988). Particular US states also utilized various schemas to determine which categories of workers should, or should not, be "allowed" to shorten their hours. In 1906, for instance, states as diverse geographically and ideologically as New York, Massachusetts, Indiana, and Nebraska prohibited women from working at night (Van Raaphorst 1988, 68–9).

However, in this state-issued, top-down forced shortening of working hours, domestic workers—consisting of nearly all women and often immigrants and women of color—were excluded (Van Raaphorst 1988, 68–9). During this period, however, women overall were participating in wage work at higher rates than previously, propelled by the depression-born trend to cut the workday from 10 hours to 8 (Kessler-Harris 1981, 53).

Yet it was not until unions were able to successfully pressure Roosevelt to pass the 1938 Fair Labor Standards Act that most workers were guaranteed a 40-hour workweek and safeguards from "starvation wages and intolerable hours" (Mayer, Collins, and Bradley 2013). The popular bumper sticker in union parking lots across the country is just one small testament to this history: "The Labor Movement: The Folks Who Brought You the Weekend." However, since that period, declines in hours of labor more or less stopped, even as increased productivity and more labor-saving technology rendered further declines possible. This may have happened because the comparably high wages in the post-war economy rendered increased hours more desirable for workers, and workers' increased consumption staved off overproduction and economic stagnation (Hunnicut 1988).

Does this same dynamic explain the stubbornness of long hours today? Arguably the incentive to work more to consume more does not analogously exist presently. According to Aguiar et al. (2017), workers are already delaying entering the workforce by remaining in education later. The labor force participation rate of American workers continues to remain stubbornly low by historical standards, and some young men are already showing a preference for video games and "leisure technology" over employment (Aguiar et al. 2017). The possibility of employment's reduced marginal utility, in turn, suggests an opportunity to criticize the de facto valorization of employment in the first place. As the following analysis of work-sharing programs suggests, now may be a perfect time to resurrect a movement for shorter hours and to "spread the work."

WORK-SHARING PROGRAMS

Work-sharing programs constitute the most robust policy instrument with which to spread work around, to maintain or elevate workers' incomes, and to reduce unemployment. The idea is simple enough. During economic downturns, employers and employees agree to reduce the labor hours of a firm's workers as opposed to laying off a select few. Such programs essentially spread the income losses that occur during recessions or downturns across a wider group of people, preventing more damaging consequences, like job losses, from occurring. However, as usual, it is the details that matter. We examine different work-sharing models and discuss the viability of various programs to reduce unemployment and increase leisure time.

German economist Axel Börsch-Supan has conducted research on work-sharing programs that rose to prominence in much of central and northern Europe during the 1980s and 1990s. In a study of German programs, Börsch-Supan (1999) finds that if workers' wages are not increased to compensate for lost work hours, less work for some does in fact make more for others. In other scenarios, however, the same study suggests that wage hikes concurrent with work-sharing programs caused some employers to seek out permanent replacements for workers in the form of automated technologies, leading to the very job losses work sharing sought to avoid. Consequently, work sharing presents a dilemma: during downturns, workers will have to either risk temporary unemployment with the hope of gaining a full-time job later or accept an indefinite pay cut until the economy recovers, something many cannot afford to do (Börsch-Supan 1999).

However, later research conducted in the immediate aftermath of the 2008 economic crisis suggests quite a different picture. An International Labour Office report on the German work-sharing program *Kurzarbeit* found that "work sharing has enabled German establishments to avoid layoffs and to practice flexibility by hours instead of flexibility by numbers as a human resource strategy" (Crimmann, Wießner, and Bellmann 2010, 35). This might have something to do with what Vroman and Brusentsev (2009) have identified as the role of short time compensation (STC) schemes that complemented work-sharing programs. STCs act as government-issued payments, a bridge between the full earnings of a worker and his or her income after the loss of wages that comes with reduced hours. In their study, the STC payment was 10 percent of a worker's wage so that an employee working 80 percent of his or her standard hours would be remunerated at 90 percent of his or her standard income (Vroman and Brusentsev 2009).

By reducing the amount of income workers lose when reducing their hours, this bridge increases the viability of work-sharing programs. If applied broadly, reduced labor hours should lower the production of firms while the STC payment raises consumer demand. Theoretically, this means consumer demand, fueled by the STC stimulus, would rise to meet and eventually outstrip supply, stimulating growth and hiring.

Work-sharing programs in the United States that include many of these features have existed since California inaugurated its own scheme in 1978 under then (as well as now) Governor Jerry Brown. The 1973 recession was the catalyst for Brown's program, designed to prevent additional layoffs generated by crises in the auto and energy sectors (Nemirow 1984). The program allowed employers to participate so long as they maintained employee health and fringe benefits for participating workers (State of California Employment Development Department 2017). The employee who had her or his hours reduced was then compensated by the state of California, which paid a portion of the standard level of unemployment insurance equal to the fraction of income lost by the hours reduction. Other states soon followed suit, and in 1983 the federal government passed its own program with amendments installed to guarantee union consent and the maintenance of proper health and pension benefits for affected workers (Stark n.d.). By 1992, 17 states across the country had passed their own work-sharing programs (Wentworth, McKenna, and Minick 2014).

As the Great Recession struck, work-sharing claims increased 10-fold in states with preexisting programs, and between 2010 and 2014 11 states created new programs (Wentworth, McKenna, and Minick 2014). A federal work-sharing scheme passed in 2012 by the Obama administration sought to increase the take-up of these programs by offering full federal compensation for the unemployment insurance payments paid out as part of the reduced hours compensation. The new national law also set national guidelines for how the programs should be implemented so as to receive federal funding; importantly, this was the first national bill that did not explicitly prohibit employees working fewer than 40 hours a week from participating (Wentworth, McKenna, and Minick 2014).

An STC scheme like the one described above would benefit young workers in particular. As Vroman and Brusentsev (2009) put it, it would help to "preserve the diversity of a company's workforce" by retaining the employees who are usually the first to be laid off—youth, women, and people of color. Others concur, claiming this is true of work-sharing programs more broadly. According to George Wentworth, interviewed for this research, "They [youth] are often the ones laid off first due to their lack of experience or their lack of seniority status in a union contract . . . work sharing could offer a way to keep them employed longer." Likewise, as Baker (2010b) notes, work sharing is especially useful in order to "target communities especially hard hit by chronic unemployment." A Brookings Institute report (Parilla and Berube 2014) argues that the German city of Munich, which experimented extensively with work sharing in the wake of the Great Recession and has a shockingly low youth unemployment rate, has "lessons . . . for America's youth employment crisis." A *Nation* article (Chen 2014) suggests that job-sharing programs, typically thought of as a way to avoid layoffs in manufacturing plants, are also very applicable in industries such as retail, with high percentages of young workers.

The National Employment Law Project's analysis of American work-sharing programs has revealed that take-up has been notably lower in the United States than in Europe during corresponding periods of economic distress. For workers, a major disincentive for participating in work sharing is that unemployment insurance paid out by the state counts against one's total entitlement claims cap (Wentworth, McKenna, and Minick 2014). Consequently, even though the payments are a fraction of what full unemployment claims would amount to, many workers are reticent to accept partial payments of unemployment insurance given the possibility that they could in the future become unemployed and with a smaller pool of insurance payments to count on (Wentworth, McKenna, and Minick 2014). Rectifying this problem will be a significant first step if expanding work sharing is to become an important part of a labor movement.

It is possible that the deficiencies of the careful legislation studied by Börsch-Supan can be remedied through a more radical bill that promises to both reduce unemployment and increase wages through a government payment issued to all citizens. A reduction in hours that occurred alongside a universal basic income (UBI) payment would have the effect of tightening the labor market and bidding up wages substantially (see Chapter 11). Such a labor market would fundamentally alter the terrain within which workers and employers currently negotiate and work. Potentially, workers would enjoy increased ability to report abuses at work and a greater voice on the shop floor if they do not fear the threat of unemployment. A UBI paid in conjunction with a radical work-sharing program thus has the capacity to greatly transform contemporary conditions of work.

Other potentially interesting policy proposals also aim to redress problems related to the time people spend at work. One such idea, promoted by progressive economist Dean Baker (2010a), is to offer tax breaks to employers who offer paid time off to workers and other family-friendly policies. Another would be to legally limit the ability of employers to use mandatory overtime (Golden and Jorgensen 2002). Early retirement schemes might also be a way to shorten the time a worker is at work over the life course of his or her job, if not the hours in a day. Does cutting the working life span of older workers necessarily make room for younger cohorts? The idea of a "lump of labor"—a fixed number of jobs in any given economic system—is often considered a fallacy by US economists, even though it may hold up in a very short time or during a relatively contained event, such as during the Great Recession (Munnell and Wu 2013). Yet, most studies find that young workers cannot simply replace older ones. Nor are they crowded out. In their research drawing on Current Population Survey (CPS) data between 1977 and 2011 in the United States and on available data in China, Munnell and Wu (2013) found "no evidence that increasing the employment of older persons reduces either the job opportunities or wage rates of young persons in the U.S. or China" (4).

The history of "sharing the work" and policy proposals to execute it offer some cautious hope that a reduction in hours would benefit young workers. Yet, most of these changes require government and employer cooperation to execute properly. In the next section, we examine how grass-roots worker resistance in the gig economy and low-wage retail sector embodies another dimension of a renewed focus on labor hours.

RESISTANCE IN THE GIG ECONOMY AND PRECARIOUS WORK

According to one view, the "sharing" or "gig" economy—think Uber, TaskRabbit, and Airbnb as examples—offers a convenient solution to young people without a job: rent yourself out. Since 2008 pundits, journalists, and scholars have proclaimed these Silicon Valley upstarts as the bright lights in an otherwise dreary economic sky. But that common-sense logic does not appear to hold up under scrutiny. By and large, the point of sharing economy companies is to create work tasks, not jobs. Also, a perceived race to the bottom in wages and conditions is causing more and more people to leave the labor market—or to challenge it (Griswold 2016). For these reasons, rather than argue that the make-work mentality of the gig economy will also make jobs, we argue that it is resistance to the basic fundamental principles underlining the gig economy that could be a driver of better employment— especially for youth.

Perhaps unsurprisingly, the gig economy currently depends on young, healthy workers, on those who are willing to push, hustle, and continue working without healthcare or benefits; in many cases, young workers are often knitting together several jobs so as to eke out a living. Based on an extensive, six-country study of online gig platforms and their workers, Mark Graham of the Oxford Internet Center notes,

> It is hard for us to say who is benefitting most and who is benefit[t]ing least. But I think some of the people who benefit most are those with good levels of education, those with good language skills, and of course those who are in good health, which is key to all of this. Those who benefit least are those with poor education, poor language skills, and sadly, if they're in poor health. (Lowrey 2017)

Graham's study is fairly unique as reliable data on the gig economy are generally difficult to attain. To this point, Bernhardt and Thompson (2017) note that part of the difficulty in understanding, theorizing, and potentially finding solutions to what gig work leaves wanting arises from the confusing character of definitions which evade easy categorizing and are continually (like the work itself) evolving. But how does gig work relate specifically to young workers and their various modes of organizing?

We focus our attention on youth since they comprise a significant proportion of gig workers: young workers between the ages of 18 and 29 years are five times more likely to have earned money from technology-enabled gig work than those 50 years and older (Smith 2016). The numbers increase drastically when looking specifically at online platforms: here, one finds that 18- to 29-year-olds have a rate of participation that is 12 times higher than those in the 50 years and older worker category (Smith 2016). This younger group is often comprised of workers of color as black workers participate in platform work three times as much as white workers; in 2016, Latino workers doubled the participation rate of white workers (Smith 2016). Thus, young workers, especially low-income workers of color, are those who increasingly are supplying the labor that is fueling the growing world of on-line platforms.

"The gig is up," some have declared (Van Grove 2016a), while other commentators wonder if the gig economy is a "fleeting fad or enduring legacy" (Storey, Steadman, and Davis 2016). However, recent work by Juliet Schor (2014) shows that levels of worker satisfaction were lower for those employed full-time in the gig economy than for those who were employed and had benefits (and, in the latter case, who only occasionally turned to "gig-ging" as a side job) (Heller 2017). In her 2015 qualitative study interviewing hosts, workers, chefs, and drivers involved with Airbnb, Taskrabbit, Kitchensurfing, and Uber, respectively, Alexandra Ravenelle (2017) also finds that workers are seduced by the "romance of entrepreneurialism to the masses" promised by the gig economy, often leaving them feeling vulnerable rather than independent (281). As a result, Schor (2017) reminds us that we cannot separate, either analytically or empirically, the gig economy from the "labour market context in which it operates" (277).

With this in mind, we turn in the last part of this chapter to a deeper look at the gig economy in relationship to current literature on precarious work and contemporary labor movement struggles. In so doing, we shift focus to examine a new terrain of resistance and pushback that uses the tools of the gig economy itself. Due to the relative newness of these platforms and their tendency to frequently change, a lack of data exists; consequently, commentators gloss over workers' experiences and celebrate the apparently ubiquitous character of the best-known online platform giants. This currently creates a steep power imbalance that shrouds most conversations around growing precarity and workers' involvement in the gig economy.[2]

As Standing (2011) and others have elaborated, the "sirens of labor flexibility" are still singing their sweet tune, though this time through an app that we believe needs an update (31). Recent examples of pushback against the gig economy and its consistent array of low-wage job options highlight the gig economy's failure to deliver quality jobs or offer a solid alternative to youth unemployment. Workers are taking control in order to "better manage their lives" (Elejalde-Ruiz 2017), and some Millennial workers have shown support for movement-oriented solutions to do just this. We see this phenomenon playing out through three trends: workers vying for more control over their schedules and their hours through fair workweek initiatives, worker-owned labor platforms, and nontraditional unions and collective bargaining strategies. We examine each in turn.

Controlling Schedules, Controlling Time

Chicago is one of many cities where a fair workweek ordinance is currently on the table as a result of worker support and the backing of the United Food and Commercial Workers Local 881. Alderman Scott Waguespack introduced legislation to amend the city's current municipal code by adding a chapter that details specific attempts to alleviate some of the most pressing difficulties around time for hourly workers. The ordinance specifically focuses on routinizing and clarifying workers' schedules that previously entailed uncertain schedules and erratic working hours. If passed, the ordinance would obligate employers to give workers 2 weeks' notice about their schedules; if employers later decide to change said schedules, they must then pay their workers extra wages and potentially other penalties. For instance, if an employer decides to change a covered employee's schedule less than 14 days but more than 24 hours before the worker's shift begins, the employer owes that worker 1 hour of "predictability pay" (City of Chicago 2017, 4).

Also notable about the Chicago ordinance is its introduction of a set of constraints and limitations on employers' abilities to contract out should there be extra work to distribute. This clause states that "Before hiring new Employees or Contract Employees, including hiring through the use of temporary services or staffing agencies, an Employer shall first offer additional hours of work to existing Employee(s)" (City of Chicago 2017, 5) Of course, when and how employers have to follow this rule entails subjective elements; yet, under the premise of predictability, the ordinance grants workers both more control over their time and the chance to pick up extra hours.

In the case of retail, salesclerks are not technically gig workers: at the heart of the distinction between them is scheduling. Retail workers have employers who leverage their power to prevent workers from controlling when they are able to work. Many gig workers, wrongly categorized as independent contractors, are compelled to work all the time because they are poor or in debt rather than because they have been scheduled to do so. However, we would argue that the two are more analytically similar than usually acknowledged for several reasons.

Major retailers who hire salesclerks are already considering using gig economy workers instead, and platforms are dedicated to facilitating this goal. One such platform, WeGoLook, advises the retail industry to not only replace its retail staff with gig workers but also hire gig workers as "secret shoppers" to report on the performance of the in-house sales force (WeGoLook 2017). Both giggers and retail workers have a shared interest in gaining greater control over their time. In this sense we see these two groups of workers as having sufficient overlapping interests in gaining control over their conditions of labor and their working time and have thus chosen to examine them in tandem.

As a case in point of that affinity, the Fair Workweek Initiative (FWI) began in 2012 as a response to increasing variability in on-demand scheduling practices in low-wage retail work (see Chapter 3). Take, for example, Aisha Meadows McLaurin, who works between 19 and 22 hours a week making $9.50 an hour at a fast-food restaurant in Chicago (Spielman 2017). She is a college student, a mother, and a worker simultaneously. Regarding time, she explains, "If I have to work on a day that I have school, something's got to give . . . I can't go to school that day. I choose work over school because I need money for things for my family. This bill is what we need to survive" (Spielman 2017). The first fair workweek protections, passed in 2014, are in place in San Francisco and Santa Clara County in California; 2 years later, a further wave of policies passed in Seattle, Washington; Emeryville and San Jose, California; Washington, DC; and New Hampshire. Then in 2017, Oregon and New York also won workweek protections (Fair Workweek Initiative 2017). Consequently, while the precise impact of the FWI movements taking place across these major cities remains to be seen, they set an important precedent for establishing state-supported worker control over the constantly shifting whims of employers.

Building a Better Platform

Another way that workers have pushed back is by wresting the central technological mechanism—the online platform—out of (solely) the gig economy's hands to create their own platform cooperatives. These platforms are dispersed through a number of different industries and generally move away from the traditional profit-based, top-down models of "Death Star platforms" like Airbnb and Uber (Gorenflo 2015).

Alternative cooperative platforms take a different approach. For instance, on their "About Us" page, the British Columbia-based Stocksy (2017) boasts elegant, black-and-white photographs of their youthful staff who cooperatively own and run this thriving photography and videography platform. After declaring themselves a cooperative, they hasten to add, "Think more artist respect and support, less patchouli. We believe in creative integrity, fair profit sharing, and co-ownership, with every voice being heard." Peerby, developed in The Netherlands and now existing in a number of other countries as well, allows people to borrow a range of items from one another for purposes of sharing. Then, too, several car-sharing cooperative platforms have popped up including Tapazz in Belgium and Modo in Vancouver, Canada. A platform has even been created to engender more cooperative platforms: this is Backfeed, which exists to produce further decentralization of cooperation in a host of different industries.

Up & Go is another cooperative platform: it connects clients to cleaning companies throughout New York City that are collectively owned by their workers. There are several co-ops working with Up & Go, and it has received widespread media coverage for its role in replacing the problematic franchise cleaning chain model (for example, Merry Maids) with a pro-worker platform model. Presently, workers earn an average of $22.25 when contracted through Up & Go compared to the industry average in New York City of $17.27 per hour (Rosenblum 2017). Thus, new platforms themselves have grown exponentially, creating their own demand for further platforms (Heller 2017).

Reinventing Bargaining and Strikes

Resistance is also taking shape through collective bargaining efforts that involve amending labor law to allow for gig workers—infamously understood as "independent contractors"—in contested battles over categorical definitions of employees to attain a status more akin to "real" workers as already defined in labor and employment law. It should be emphasized that the number of workers in this economy is large and growing: in 2015, at least 1 percent of the US working population was classified as gig economy workers, with large numbers concentrated in major metropolitan areas. For instance, in California, approximately 10 percent of the entire working population (comprising 1–2 million people) work in the gig economy. In San Diego alone, more than 12,000 people work as Uber drivers (Van Grove 2016a). Not surprisingly given these numbers, in 2016 Assemblywoman Lorena Gonzalez introduced the 1099 Self-Organizing Act to allow 10 or more independent contractors to collectively bargain with their employers. This involved the "hosting platforms" that are mainstays of the gig economy, encompassing Uber and Lyft drivers, Amazon Flex workers, and DoorDash and Postmates delivery drivers (Van Grove 2016a). If enacted, this legislation would change labor law such that these workers would newly be classified as part of a "minority"—rather than a majority—collective bargaining unit, a categorization that does not currently exist in the private sector in the United States.

Outside the United States, gig workers have recently taken more militant action. Since 2016, couriers at Deliveroo in the United Kingdom, a platform-based delivery service, and at Foodora, a similar service in Italy, have both waged successful strikes to win higher wages and more standardized working conditions (see Walker and Kaine 2016; Tassinari and Maccaronne 2017). In the United Kingdom, the couriers made common cause with an upstart union, the Independent Workers of Great Britain, that had ties to more traditional labor organizations and even crowd-funded its own strike support (Walker and Kaine 2016). Many of these examples suggest that workers are protesting and organizing through "union-like groups" and adapting "unionesque" tactics (Van Grove 2016b).

Is this necessarily a good thing, or might this indicate that workers are falling into institutional traps that resemble the often stereotypically bureaucratic, patriarchal, and exclusionary unions of the past? As labor leader Ed Ott (2014) remarks in his conclusion to *New Labor in New York*, "The old labor movement missed a lot, especially as the world changed around it" (291). Ott's point reminds us that todays' precarious workers are responding in ways quite similar to tried-and-true union methods. Harkening back to labor regulation in early twentieth-century America, we note with interest the continuities evident as workers either employ long-standing tactics of the labor movement itself (like collective bargaining as recognized workers rather than independent contractors) or align with organized labor and community organizations to demand more control and security over their working hours. Ott continues to say that *flexibility* is key—not the flexibility of labor, as most online platforms would have it, but the labor movement's flexibility in thinking through forms, tactics, strategies, and the very conception of what it means to be a union (2014, 291).

New York City's Freelancers Union, founded in 1995, echoes that notion in its slogan "Reexamine, Rethink, Reinvest. Join the Revolution" (King 2014, 150). Noting that more than a third of American employees (roughly 55 million) are "independent workers," the union is premised on combating the precarious nature of independent work and the expansion of the "precariat." Yet companies themselves are even borrowing labor and community organizing methods to campaign more effectively. Lyft, typically framed as the pro-worker protagonist platform compared to its monolithic competitor Uber, hired a community manager who draws on "traditional community-organizing models" in citywide campaigns against regulation (Heller 2017). Lyft has also significantly changed its mission as it has grown (Ravenelle 2017). Originally, the company touted itself as "your friend with a car," even going so far as to offer riders a fist bump; currently, they charge prices akin to those of Uber and dispatch field organizers across the country to identify up-and-coming political leaders who may be influential as allies in the coming years (Ravenelle 2017, 293; Heller 2017). For-profit, non-cooperative platforms, then, are also trying to recuperate the political aesthetics of grassroots organizing while they employ approaches similar to organizers.

Stepping back, we take these three particular moves as an indication that, indeed, simply saying that the "gig is up"—as does Van Grove (2016a)—may not sufficiently tell the entire story. All word plays aside, the simplistic term "gig economy" belies how seriously imbricated it has become in transforming the wider economy. In fact, research recognizes gig work as part of a larger trend toward informalization of the more "traditional" employment relations regime (De Stefano 2015). The mere range of serious contestation from several actors in various spheres including workers—mostly young, who were themselves contracted through a host of large companies, labor allies, and pro-worker legislative measures—attests to this. Young people are collectively standing up to combat the most inflexible and troubling parts of the gig economy.

Efforts to collectively bargain and consider gig workers "real" workers may not be straightforward in the future, nor will it be easy to regulate at a citywide scale workers' control over and knowledge of their own hours. But what we have just detailed shows two ways in which the (in)flexibility of the gig economy is being exposed and seriously criticized. Or perhaps capitalism, in its seemingly endless ability to innovate, will simply adapt to these new schemas and continue to employ a growing number of workers who are drawn to the seductive notions of controlling one's time and availability, as Scholz (2013) and others detail in their work on the "darker" aspects of digital labor and its effects on changing the working landscape for young workers.

At a minimum, though, we see significant and exciting possibilities in these three kinds of resistance—especially in the development of cooperatively owned platforms. The gig economy has seemingly changed the "rules of the game" for the growing sea of smart phone owners poised to hire someone to help with a random task or to sell their own labor in some creative manner. But we see even more potential for workers themselves to harness the best parts of digital capitalism—flexibility and part-time options that fit into their complex lives—as potentially changing the rules and the very outcome of the game going forward.

CONCLUSION

This chapter is the first attempt of which we are aware to theorize that a shorter hours movement might be a partial solution to youth unemployment. We have conceived of a "shorter hours movement" as part of a larger range of potential policy- and movement-based strategies aimed at offering workers, particularly but not exclusively young workers, greater control over how much and when they work. We also see such a movement offering the ability to design a work life that preserves "time off." Other contributors in this volume have proposed both full employment and a guaranteed basic income as other possible avenues. We feel the approach proposed here is a useful complement to these other positions. Via work sharing, policies and processes are already in place to transition into a shorter hours economy right now. Moreover, work sharing is likely to have the benefit of assisting young workers first since—again—they are usually the ones let go first when companies decide they need to shed employees. This said, though, it seems unlikely that the current level and intensity of work-sharing programs are actually robust enough to significantly impact the youth unemployment crisis. Currently, only half of US states have programs in place to offer employers a subsidy to retain workers at shorter hours, a crucial part of the equation.

However, the popular reaction against the Jeb Bush quote opening this chapter suggests a growing awareness of a "disconnect" between the kinds of work lives many Americans have and the kinds that elites often present workers as having. It remains to be seen if resentment at this disconnect can be transformed into a coherent labor movement focused on shorter hours. But the FWI, driven as it is by social desires to control labor time, offers a glimpse into what such a movement could look like. Campaigns for fairer scheduling are only a few years old, yet there are already a handful of states with actualized policies to help workers secure better working hours. This movement continues to grow.

There is no singular unified "future of work" (Scholz 2014). But the gig economy is probably the paradigmatic example of what happens when employers find themselves awash in an economy of un- or underemployed youth and take advantage of this "opportunity." Resistance and pushback in the forms this chapter describes, often enacted by organizations of young workers, have sought to thwart the growing trends of the gig economy in order to prevent the tendencies of precarity from spreading too pervasively and altering the terrain of more "traditional" labor and employment relations.

We see no clear signs that a shorter hours movement, one that would be recognizable to the early pioneers of hours reduction in the nineteenth century—and led by youth—is on the horizon. But while there may be a dearth of youth committed to renewing an old tradition, certainly a core exists in the form of young cohorts interested in reinventing new ones. David Rolff and Carmen Rojas are leading a movement jumpstarted from their Workers' Lab to bring young people into union circles that utilize app-based organizing platforms and other schemes targeting younger groups. This is in addition to other platforms like Coworker and UnionBase, pioneered by Millennials, which are encouraging unions to organize online.

While a robust shorter hours movement might not be close at hand, we nonetheless view such a prospect as being a useful antidote to long-term structural youth unemployment should this come to fruition or grow. Such a movement offers a path forward that is geared toward recognizing and redressing the contradictory character of a contemporary economy that increasingly offers longer hours for some and unemployment for others. By contrast, a shorter hours movement could share the work, allowing greater numbers of employees to have a job without being worked to death. The formal political arena may be neither amenable to nor advocating such a shift presently, but changes that brought about the weekend were hardly top-down gifts of an earlier age. Rather, improvements in the quality and length of working conditions of labor have been and will remain products of struggle, making us hopeful that the present conjuncture will force similar movements to the fore again.

NOTES

1. The "gig economy" is just one of a number of terms used to describe the growing percentage of work performed via online platforms or digital apps. Some prefer the "sharing economy" or "platform capitalism" or "app-based labor."

2. Newlands, Lutz, and Fieseler's (2017) recent article is a noted exception.

REFERENCES

Aguiar, Mark, Mark Bils, Kerwin Kofi Charles, and Erik Hurst. "Leisure Luxuries and the Labor Supply of Young Men." NBER Working Paper 23552, National Bureau of Economic Research, Cambridge, MA, June 2017. https://scholar.princeton.edu/sites/default/files/maguiar/files/leisure-luxuries-labor-june-2017.pdf. Accessed October 15, 2017.

Baker, Dean. "Between Overworked and Out of Work." *Yes! Magazine*, January 15, 2010a. http://www.yesmagazine.org/new-economy/between-overworked-and-out-of-work. Accessed October 15, 2017.

———. "Testimony of Dean Baker Before the Congressional Black Caucus." March 17, 2010b. http://cepr.net/documents/testimonies/baker-workshare-2010-03-17.pdf. Accessed October 15, 2017.

Bernhardt, Annette, and Sarah Thompson. "What do We Know About Gig Work in California? An Analysis of Independent Contracting." UC Berkeley Labor Center, June 14, 2017. http://laborcenter.berkeley.edu/what-do-we-know-about-gig-work-in-california/. Accessed October 15, 2017.

Börsch-Supan, Axel. "Reduction of Working Time: Does It Decrease Unemployment?" Presented at the 5th Meeting of the Deutsch-Französisches Wirtschaftspolitisches Forum/Forum Economique Franco-Allemand, Paris, France, July 1999. http://www.mea.mpisoc.mpg.de/uploads/user_mea_discussionpapers/dp03.pdf. Accessed October 27, 2017.

Boushey, Heather, and Bridget Ansel. *Overworked America: The Economic Causes and Consequences of Long Work Hours*. Washington, DC: Washington Center for Equitable Growth, May 2016. http://cdn.equitablegrowth.org/

wp-content/uploads/2016/05/16164629/051616-overworked-america.pdf. Accessed November 7, 2017.

Chen, Michelle. "Work-Sharing: A Socialist Alternative to Layoffs?" *The Nation*, October 20, 2014. https://www.thenation.com/article/work-sharing-socialist-alternative-layoffs/. Accessed October 15, 2017.

City of Chicago. "Legislative Notes, Office of the City Clerk, 2017-4947. Amendment of Municipal Code by Adding New Chapter Entitled 'The Chicago Fair Workweek Ordinance.'" June 28, 2017. https://chicago.legistar.com/LegislationDetail. aspx?ID=3091517&GUID=CD4A1D2E-CE8E-4EC4-B38D-4D3C38C14920z. Accessed October 15, 2017.

Crimmann, Andreas, Frank Wießner, and Lutz Bellmann. *The German Work-Sharing Scheme: An Instrument for the Crisis*. Conditions of Work and Employment Series 25. Geneva: International Labour Office, 2010. http://www.ilo.org/wcmsp5/ groups/public/---ed_protect/---protrav/---travail/documents/publication/wcms_ 145335.pdf. Accessed October 15, 2017.

De Stefano, Valerio. "The Rise of the 'Just-in-Time Workforce': On-Demand Work, Crowd Work and Labour Protection in the 'Gig-Economy.'" *Comparative Labor Law & Policy Journal*, October 28, 2015, Research Paper 2682602. https:// papers.ssrn.com/sol3/papers.cfm?abstract_id=2682602. Accessed November 7, 2017.

Elejalde-Ruiz, Alexia. "Proposed Fair Workweek Ordinance Would Mandate Predictable Schedules, Stable Paychecks." *Chicago Tribune*, June 27, 2017. http:// www.chicagotribune.com/business/ct-chicago-fair-workweek-ordinance-0628-biz-20170627-story.html. Accessed October 15, 2017.

Fair Workweek Initiative. "About Us." Center for Popular Democracy, 2017. http:// www.fairworkweek.org/. Accessed October 15, 2017.

Golden, Lonnie. *Still Falling Short on Hours and Pay: Part-Time Work Becoming New Normal*. Washington, DC: Economic Policy Institute, 2016. http://www.epi.org/ publication/still-falling-short-on-hours-and-pay-part-time-work-becoming-new-normal/. Accessed October 15, 2017.

Golden, Lonnie, and Helene Jorgensen. *Time After Time*. Washington, DC: Economic Policy Institute, 2002. http://www.epi.org/publication/briefingpapers_bp120/. Accessed October 15, 2017.

Gorenflo, Neil. "How Platform Coops Can Beat Death Stars Like Uber to Create a Real Sharing Economy." Shareable, November 3, 2015. https://www.shareable. net/blog/how-platform-coops-can-beat-death-stars-like-uber-to-create-a-real-sharing-economy. Accessed November 7, 2017.

Griswold, Alison. "People Are Getting Sick of Working in the 'Sharing' Economy." Quartz, November 15, 2016. https://qz.com/837237/people-are-getting-sick-of-working-in-the-sharing-economy/. Accessed October 15, 2017.

Heller, Nathan. "Is the Gig Economy Working?" *New Yorker*, May 15, 2017. https:// www.newyorker.com/magazine/2017/05/15/is-the-gig-economy-working. Accessed October 15, 2017.

Hunnicutt, Benjamin Kline. *Work Without End: Abandoning Shorter Hours for the Right to Work*. Philadelphia: Temple University Press, 1988.

Kessler-Harris, Alice. *Women Have Always Worked: A Historical Overview*. Old Westbury, NY: Feminist Press, 1981.

King, Martha. "Protecting and Representing Workers in the New Gig Economy: The Case of the Freelancers Union." In *New Labor in New York: Precarious Workers and the Future of the Labor Movement*, edited by Ruth Milkman and Ed Ott, 150–72. Ithaca, NY: Cornell University Press, 2014.

Lowrey, Annie. "What the Gig Economy Looks Like Around the World." *Atlantic Monthly*, April 13, 2017. https://www.theatlantic.com/business/archive/2017/04/gig-economy-global/522954/. Accessed October 15, 2017.

Mayer, Gerald, Benjamin Collins, and David H. Bradley. *The Fair Labor Standards Act (FLSA): An Overview*. Washington, DC: Congressional Research Service, 2013. https://fas.org/sgp/crs/misc/R42713.pdf. Accessed October 15, 2017.

Munnell, Alice H., and April Yanyuan Wu. "Do Older Workers Squeeze Out Younger Workers?" Working Paper 13-011. Stanford Institute for Economic Policy Research, Stanford, CA, December 2013. https://siepr.stanford.edu/research/publications/do-older-workers-squeeze-out-younger-workers. Accessed October 15, 2017.

Nemirow, Martin. "Work-Sharing Approaches: Past and Present." *Monthly Labor Review* 107, no. 9 (1984): 34–39. https://www.bls.gov/opub/mlr/1984/09/art6full.pdf. Accessed October 15, 2017.

Newlands, Gemma, Christoph Lutz, and Christian Fieseler. "Power in the Sharing Economy." EU H2020 Research Project Ps2Share: Participation, Privacy, and Power in the Sharing Economy, 2017. https://ssrn.com/abstract=2960938. Accessed October 15, 2017.

Ott, Ed. "Afterword: Lessons from the New Labor Movement for the Old." In *New Labor in New York: Precarious Workers and the Future of the Labor Movement*, edited by Ruth Milkman and Ed Ott, 289–94. Ithaca, NY: Cornell University Press, 2014.

Parilla, Joseph, and Alan Berube. "Lessons from Munich for America's Youth Employment Crisis." Washington, DC: Brookings Institution, March 31, 2014. https://www.brookings.edu/blog/the-avenue/2014/03/31/lessons-from-munich-for-americas-youth-employment-crisis/. Accessed October 15, 2017.

Ponnuru, Ramesh. "Work and the Democrats." *National Review*, July 9, 2015. http://www.nationalreview.com/corner/420955/work-and-democrats-ramesh-ponnuru. Accessed October 15, 2017.

Project: Time Off. *The State of American Vacation: How Vacation Became A Casualty of Our Work Culture*. Washington, DC: Project: Time Off, 2016. https://www.projecttimeoff.com/sites/default/files/PTO_SoAV%20Report_FINAL.pdf. Accessed October 15, 2017.

Ravenelle, Alexandrea J. "Sharing Economy Workers: Selling, Not Sharing." *Cambridge Journal of Regions, Economy and Society* 10, no. 2 (2017): 281–95.

Roediger, David R., and Philip S. Foner. *Our Own Time: A History of the American Labor Movement and the Working Day*. New York: Greenwood Press, 1989.

Rosenblum, Dan. "How to Hire a Housekeeper with a Clean Conscience." New York Nonprofit Media, June 6, 2017. http://nynmedia.com/news/how-to-hire-a-housekeeper-with-a-clean-conscience. Accessed November 6, 2017.

Scholz, Trebor. *Digital Labor: The Internet as Playground and Factory*. New York: Routledge, 2013.

———. "Platform Cooperativism vs. the Sharing Economy." Medium, December 5, 2014. https://medium.com/@trebors/platform-cooperativism-vs-the-sharing-economy-2ea737f1b5ad. Accessed October 15, 2017.

Schor, Juliet. "Debating the Sharing Economy." Great Transition Initiative, October 2014. http://greattransition.org/publication/debating-the-sharing-economy. Accessed October 15, 2017.

———. "Does the Sharing Economy Increase Inequality Within the Eighty Percent? Findings from a Qualitative Study of Platform Providers." *Cambridge Journal of Regions, Economy and Society* 10, no. 2 (2017): 263–79.

Smith, Aaron. "Shared, Collaborative, and On Demand: The New Digital Economy." Pew Research Center, May 19, 2016. http://www.pewinternet.org/2016/05/19/the-new-digital-economy/. Accessed October 15, 2017.

Spielman, Fran. "Labor, City Council Allies Propose Fair Workweek Ordinance." *Chicago Sun Times*, June 27, 2017. http://chicago.suntimes.com/news/labor-city-council-allies-propose-fair-work-week-ordinance/. Accessed October 15, 2017.

Standing, Guy. *The Precariat: The New Dangerous Class.* London: Bloomsbury Academic, 2011.

Stark, Fortney. "H.R.4961—Tax Equity and Fiscal Responsibility Act of 1982. 97th Congress (1981–1982)." Congress.gov, n.d. https://www.congress.gov/bill/97th-congress/house-bill/4961. Accessed May 12, 2015.

State of California Employment Development Department. "Work Sharing Program." 2017. http://www.edd.ca.gov/unemployment/Work_Sharing_Program.htm. Accessed October 25, 2017.

Stocksy. "About Us." 2017. https://www.stocksy.com/service/about/. Accessed October 15, 2017.

Storey, David, Tony Steadman, and Charles Davis. *Is the Gig Economy a Fleeting Fad, or an Enduring Legacy?* EY Contingent Workforce Study, 2016. http://www.ey.com/Publication/vwLUAssets/EY_Gig_economy_brochure/$FILE/gig-economy-brochure.pdf. Accessed October 26, 2017.

Tassinari, Arianna, and Vincenzo Maccarrone. "Striking the Startups." *Jacobin*, January 23, 2017. https://jacobinmag.com/2017/01/foodora-strike-turin-gig-economy-startups-uber/. Accessed October 15, 2017.

Trudo, Hanna. "Jeb Bush: 'People Need to Work Longer Hours.'" *Politico*, July 8, 2015. http://www.politico.com/story/2015/07/jeb-bush-people-should-work-longer-hours-119884. Accessed October 15, 2017.

Valletta, Robert, and Catherine van der List. "Involuntary Part-Time Work: Here to Stay?" *FRBSF Economic Letter* 1, no. 19 (2015). https://EconPapers.repec.org/RePEc:fip:fedfel:00059. Accessed November 7, 2017.

Van Grove, Jennifer. "Honeymoon Over for On-Demand Apps, Contract Workers." *San Diego-Union Tribune*, March 3, 2016a. http://www.sandiegouniontribune.com/business/technology/sdut-gig-economy-workers-political-legal-implications-2016mar03-htmlstory.html. Accessed October 15, 2017.

———. "California Bill Would Let Gig Workers Organize for Collective Bargaining." *Los Angeles Times*, March 11, 2016b. http://www.latimes.com/business/la-fi-gig-workers-bill-20160310-story.html. Accessed October 15, 2017.

Van Raaphorst, Donna L. *Union Maids Not Wanted: Organizing Domestic Workers, 1870–1940.* New York: Praeger, 1988.

Vroman, Wayne, and Vera Brusentsev. "Short-Time Compensation as a Policy to Stabilize Employment." Urban Institute, November 2009. http://www.urban.org/sites/default/files/publication/30751/411983-Short-Time-Compensation-as-a-Policy-to-Stabilize-Employment.PDF. Accessed October 27, 2017.

Walker, Michael, and Sarah Kaine. "Deliveroo Strike Win Shows Gig Workers Can Subvert the Rules Too." The Conversation, August 18, 2016. https://theconversation.com/deliveroo-strike-win-shows-gig-workers-can-subvert-the-rules-too-64049. Accessed October 15, 2017.

Weeks, Kathi. *Feminism, Marxism, Antiwork Politics, and Postwork Imaginaries.* Durham, NC: Duke University Press, 2011.

WeGoLook. "How the Gig Economy and Technology Can Save Retail." April 4, 2017. https://wegolook.com/blog/article/how-the-gig-economy-and-technology-can-save-retail/. Accessed October 19, 2017.

Wentworth, George, Claire McKenna, and Lynn Minick. *Lessons Learned: Maximizing the Potential of Work-Sharing in the United States.* New York: National Employment Law Project, 2014. http://www.nelp.org/content/uploads/2015/03/Lessons-Learned-Maximizing-Potential-Work-Sharing-in-US.pdf. Accessed October 15, 2017.

11

Youth Prospects and the Case for a Universal Basic Income

Sarah Reibstein and Andy Stern

INTRODUCTION

When the organizers of the Roosevelt House Public Policy Institute's 2015 Youth, Jobs, and the Future conference invited one of us—Andy Stern—to speak, they expected he would comment on the role of labor organizing in securing better jobs for working-class youth. As president emeritus of Service Employees Union International, Stern spent nearly a lifetime in labor unions. Thus, it created something of a splash when remarks expected to address the state of the union movement centered instead on the proposal of universal basic income (UBI), framed as an answer to the question "what are we going to do if there are not enough jobs for everyone?" Was this labor leader giving up on jobs?

By 2010, we argue in this chapter, the world had changed in fundamental and unpredictable ways. Unions, continuing to grow smaller and not stronger, no longer play the role they did in fighting inequality by distributing companies' financial success through collective bargaining. It is time to consider a radically different way of approaching the problem: a UBI. Hardly are we alone in believing that basic income is an idea now worth acting upon. Halfway across the world, another traditional labor stronghold—the Socialist Party of France—put forth Benoit Hamon, their presidential candidate in 2017 after extraordinarily unpopular François Hollande, as a bold candidate advocating basic income as a new answer to rapid socioeconomic transformations (Williamson 2017). Then, too, Elon Musk is one of a larger group of tech chief executive officers (Weller 2017c) who has lent his support to basic income; at the 2017 World Government Summit, he announced "It's going to be necessary" (Weller 2017a). Thus, what was once a niche radical idea is now so mainstream that taking a position *against* it also makes headlines (as Joe Biden [2016] has done). Lest we focus unduly on socialists, liberals, and Democrats, the same debates are happening with increasing regularity on Fox News (2017a, 2017b; Widerquist 2013).

Turning to the situation of young people in particular, statistics amply demonstrate that the idea of working—of labor—is not working for them in anything like the ways the "American dream" traditionally promised. Faced with the fact that something is amiss and different and that young people are feeling unprecedented levels of insecurity amid what has been labeled "precarity" (Kalleberg 2008) many scholarly and political actors turn to old solutions (i.e., to creating more jobs and better preparing young people to attain them) than they do to newer and more "out-of-the-box" solutions. Yet, while the preponderance of this work presumes that full employment is desirable and necessary for many people (see Chapter 12 for this position), we counterargue with the "taken-for-granted" character of this premise.

Instead, we consider the possibility that trends in the global economy— specifically, the decoupling of wages and jobs from growth and technology's impact on jobs—have reached a strategic inflection point such that radical rethinking of the problem and its solution is required. In so doing, we turn to the idea of UBI and argue for its relevance to this volume's focus on the problem of youth unemployment in the United States. On the one hand, then, we offer UBI as a contingency plan, that is, the most realistic option available as automation and technological unemployment continue and the instabilities and inequalities associated with living in a neoliberal capitalist world become too much to bear. On the other hand, simultaneously, we see this inflection point as an opportunity and UBI as a tool to rethink questions such as whether a "living" should have to be earned—why and how did that notion develop? In doing so, we investigate whether jobs are potentially not the answer but part of the problem. To be clear, we are not against jobs or active measures to make them available to people whenever and wherever possible: more precisely, this chapter contends that creating better and more jobs alone may not go far enough to remedy the insecurities and increased joblessness that the global economy is creating. In suggesting the immense current relevance of basic income, then, we are calling for a rethinking of old and now possibly stale assumptions about the character and culture of contemporary work.

WHY NOW?

Why the recent resurgence of interest in UBI? Again, more and more people, in and out of the United States, sense the existence, the persistence, of a problem; they have come to a visceral realization that good jobs are not out there as they once were. A key concept in formalizing this intuition is what Brynjolfsson and McAfee (2011) have called "the great decoupling" of jobs and wages from productivity and growth. When politicians say we need economic growth, they are unwittingly referring to a time when economic growth was a catchall for four integrated elements: GDP, productivity, wages, and job growth. During the 25-year post-war "golden age" of the American economy, these four indicators indeed rose together; over time, increasing labor productivity and GDP did translate into increasing employment (more jobs) and income (better jobs). But while productivity and growth have continued to steadily climb, private employment and median household income have broken off and begun to stagnate and even decline. Young people who entered the workforce in 1991 and 2001 are not experiencing the pattern of lifetime wage gains as did those who entered the workforce in the 1970s and 1980s. Moreover, labor force participation rate is at a 38-year low. This is in the context of a national economy that experienced an average annual growth rate of 5.5 percent from 1980 through 2016 (Bureau of Economic Analysis 2017).

Thus, growth of the economy is no longer a guarantee of economic or wage growth for people. Economists attribute these structural shifts to globalization and automation. In a global marketplace, the most profitable way to increase production involves cutting labor costs and growing capabilities to complement and substitute human labor with machines and software. The future, it appears, involves both fewer jobs and worse-paying ones (Stern 2016).

WHAT IS BASIC INCOME?

The idea of universal or guaranteed income proposes that governments provide cash transfers to ensure a livable income to all residents. In effect, this deals with the jobs crisis not by making sure that everyone has a job or by creating them but by making sure everyone does not *need* to have one. It is a policy worth considering if we accept that we have entered an age wherein producing prosperity is no longer the problem—but distributing prosperity is.

A Short History of Basic Income in Theory and Practice

As Stern (2016) noted in *Raising the Floor*, UBI is "an old idea that's a new idea." Thomas Paine (1797) argued for guaranteed income as a "natural inheritance" owed to every person living in a society, while Thomas Jefferson favored land grants (Stern 2016). Milton Friedman introduced the idea of a "negative income tax" in 1962, seeing it as a more efficient alternative to welfare (Chancer 1998). Friedrich Hayek agreed, and contemporary libertarian thinker Charles Murray has also become a visible proponent (Murray 2006). Perhaps most surprisingly, guaranteed annual income nearly became the law of the land with Richard Nixon's Family Assistance Plan, which passed the Senate only to be defeated in the House of Representatives in 1972 (Chancer 1998). The American government also invested tens of millions of dollars in the 1970s in negative income tax experiments, testing the policy in four major regions (Widerquist 2005).

Various forms of basic income have been piloted in Namibia (Haarmann and Haarmann 2007); Brazil (Suplicy 2007); India (Standing 2013); Germany (Knight 2015); Manitoba, Canada (Calnitsky 2016); and the United States (Widerquist 2005). Several countries and municipalities in Europe and North America are currently reconsidering the idea. Switzerland became the first country to hold a nationwide referendum on an unconditional income proposal in June 2016, gathering 100,000 signatures of support. While the measure was voted down, with only 23 percent voting in favor, organizing around the issue continues (BBC News 2016). Finland launched what it is calling a UBI trial in January 2017. The 2,000 participants, selected from those already receiving unemployment benefits or income supplements, will receive a monthly deposit of 560 Euros in place of other benefits through 2018 (Evans 2017). As of 2016, the Dutch city of Utrecht was also planning a UBI experiment, designed to test different conditions of requirements and incentives (Hamilton 2016), as was the province of Ontario, Canada (Ontario Ministry of Finance 2016). Related citizens' dividend and unconditional cash transfer programs have existed in Alaska (Barnes 2014), in Iran (Tabatai 2012), among the Seminole (Cattelino 2008) and Cherokee (Velasquez-Manoff 2014) Native Americans, and throughout the developing world (Baird et al. 2013). The Economic Security Project—an ambitious initiative to investigate UBI and other cash transfer programs as solutions to financial insecurity in the United States—launched in December 2016 with a group of high-profile signatories across academia, labor, business, technology, and the arts (Economic Security Project 2016).

Commonly Raised Concerns

Could the United States afford a basic income? Many who have looked at the issue think so. One plan, put forth by Andy Stern, would pay $1,000 per month to 18- to 64-year-olds and would cost between $1.75 trillion and $2.5 trillion a year—a sum that could be financed in several ways. Among realistic funding options would be ending many welfare programs (that currently cost the federal government $700 billion annually), while preserving Medicare and Social Security; adjusting retirement policy for future generations; instituting a cost-effective, non-employer-based healthcare system; redirecting some spending and tax expenditures, such as farm, oil, and gas subsidies and military spending; and raising additional revenue by instating financial transaction and wealth taxes, eliminating tax breaks, and charging fees for pollution (Stern 2016). Building a broad coalition for implementing UBI would entail making trade-offs, but this sketch of potential financing sources suggests that the overall goal is not fantastical.

Another commonly raised objection to the idea of guaranteed income is to raise the question "wouldn't everyone stop working?" How will socially necessary work get done if we all have the option to sit around all day watching television? Existing empirical evidence on the question, though, suggests that this is a highly overblown fear. Studies of the basic income pilots in the United States and Canada found that participants reduced their labor supply in response to the program by no more than 10 percent on average. Economists who have studied lottery winners find similar effects: despite the cultural myth that big-ticket lottery winners never have to work again, it seems that less than a quarter of them actually decide not to. There are important limitations of the pilot experiments that make it difficult to generalize from them, since the population of participants is often neither universal nor representative and the programs have had relatively short time horizons. Nevertheless, research suggests that a majority is likely to continue with paid work (Reibstein 2017).

Further, unlike existing means-tested welfare programs, there is no "welfare trap" to disincentivize paid work. UBI is meant to function as a "floor." Since payments are universal, additional labor income does not cancel benefits but simply augments earnings; paid labor remains a highly attractive option for those who wish to consume beyond subsistence levels (Murray 2006). And from a cultural perspective, it is possible that work will not be so easy for us to give up on altogether. From Weber's Protestant ethic (Weber 1930) to Fromm's socialist humanism (Fromm 1955), the idea of work has been central to a remarkably broad range of traditions in Western philosophy. While our argument is that paid work will play less of a role in the future and that there are reasons to embrace the decoupling of work from subsistence (as is fundamental to basic income), cultural change rarely happens overnight. In this and other respects, we find the chances of a societal *over*reaction to basic income—resulting in socially necessary jobs going unfilled—extraordinarily unlikely.

A third question we might ask preliminarily about the feasibility of guaranteed income is political: could this actually be passed, here in the United States, anytime soon? We believe the answer is yes. The election of Donald Trump to the American presidency has, as one of its myriad effects, unveiled stability in our political institutions as an illusory notion.

Regardless of Trump's intentions or ability to follow through on the populist promises of his campaign, elite agreements on key policy issues are being at least rhetorically challenged. The election has also made it unlikely that Democrats will make much meaningful change toward their agendas during the administration, especially if they continue to use the strategies they have come to rely on and which the Trump administration vows to repudiate. At the same time, progressives are beginning to engage in political activism at a scale unseen in recent years of American history, with the Women's March on January 21, 2017, drawing an estimated 3 million participants at least (Waddell 2017).

This combination could make it the right time for an unconventional policy approach. Reflecting on the 2016 election, Hillary Clinton has seemingly come to a similar conclusion and has cited UBI as one transformative policy prescription that could have helped her win. As Clinton noted, "Democrats should redouble our efforts to develop bold, creative ideas that offer broad-based benefits for the whole country" (Clinton 2017). And, again, basic income has enjoyed bipartisan support in the past. The "hands-off" approach inherent in granting cash to citizens to use as they please resonates with the libertarian streak running through American politics today, similar in form to the block grant approach to federal funding. And because the idea is "new again" in current political discourse, it has not become a polarizing issue like so many others.

WHY BASIC INCOME: NECESSITY

UBI may be an idea with a history and some momentum, but why is it a policy worth considering in the context of youth unemployment and precarity? We make the case, first, that a convergence of economic and political trends suggest that basic income is urgently needed because of crises in the labor market and (in the case of the United States) in welfare benefits provision.

Disappearing Jobs

Technology is undeniably a factor in youth unemployment and underemployment. New technologies disrupt labor markets by reducing the demand for workers, either because fewer of them are needed to accomplish the same task or because entire classes of jobs become obsolete. As technology continues to advance at exponential rates, both factors are of concern. A recent study found that labor-saving technology accounts for 88 percent of factory jobs lost in the United States from 2000 to 2010 (Hicks and Devaraj

2015). Real output of the United States' manufacturing sector was 70 percent higher in early 2018 than in 1987 (Federal Reserve Bank of St. Louis 2018a), while employment in that sector dropped by 28 percent over the same time period (Federal Reserve Bank of St. Louis 2018b). Perhaps more importantly, Frey and Osborne argue, machine learning and artificial intelligence in combination with big data are making it possible for computers to perform non-routine tasks; knowledge and service professions once thought to be immune to automation are increasingly under threat. By their estimation, 47 percent of American employment in 2010 is likely to be automated in the near future before the next round of engineering bottlenecks is hit (Frey and Osborne 2017). The situation in some developing countries is more dire, with the International Labour Organization reporting that jobs at risk of automation comprise 64 percent of employment in Indonesia, 86 percent in Vietnam, and 88 percent in Cambodia (Chang and Huynh 2016). The World Bank projects analogous figures of 69 percent in India, 77 percent in China, and 85 percent in Ethiopia (World Bank 2016). Of course, it is not likely to be the case that everything that can be automated will be; there are economic and social factors to consider in addition to technological ones. The Boston Consulting Group projects that in 2025, labor costs across the 25 largest exporting countries will be an average of 16 percent lower due to wider robotics use (Sirkin, Zinser, and Rose 2015). Technology research firm Gartner predicts that "software, robots, and smart machines" will replace one-third of US jobs by 2025 (Barajas 2014).

It is by no means guaranteed that innovation will create enough new jobs to fill the hole of those replaced by computerization. But even if it does, as we know from studying the period of the Industrial Revolution, negative consequences tend to be felt in advance. And they already are. Over the past few decades, automation has already replaced tasks done by middle-income workers such as legal research for lawyers, reading of X-rays for radiologists, translation for translators, medication dispensing for pharmacists, tax preparation for accountants, and writing annual corporate reports for writers. Moreover, all this has contributed to a polarization of the labor market. Young people who would have found good entry-level jobs in their parents' generation, say in the manufacturing sector, are now faced with low-paying service jobs.

And more and more young people are moving back to or delaying leaving their parents' homes. Up from 35 percent in 2000, recent data found that 51 percent of lower-skilled men in their 20s live with a parent or close relative (Hurst 2016). While the analogous figure is as high as 70 percent among men in this category who don't have jobs, we can surmise that some portion are simply working at jobs that are too insecure and underpaid to support an independent life.

Even highly educated young people, unless they are among the best connected who often have little trouble catapulting into top jobs, face similar frustrations. As an article in the *New York Times* revealed in 2012, Apple's highly skilled "Genius Bar" technicians made just $11.25 an hour, while the company sold $473,000 of goods per employee per year (Segal 2012). "You go into an Apple store and you see the future," says Jeff Faux, founder of the Economic Policy Institute. "The future of the labor force is all in those smart college-educated people with the T-shirts whose job is to be a retail clerk" (Stern 2016). We know what these low-paid jobs are going to look like, the basic income perspective argues—do we really want to create more of them?

In addition to causing fewer jobs and lower-paid jobs, technology is propelling the rise of contingent labor. Software makes it easy for employers to break up job responsibilities into discrete tasks and to farm those tasks out to a mobile and flexible workforce. This is evident in the highly visible companies of the "sharing economy": these are the Airbnbs and Ubers of the world that operate hospitality and taxi services without employing a single concierge or cab driver. We see it in the Amazon Mechanical Turk workers performing tasks for 1 to 10 cents. And it has also penetrated more traditional companies, with temp agencies enabling corporations to cut labor costs by replacing employees with short-term workers. Algorithmic scheduling has further empowered corporations to fit their employees into precisely the times and places they need them in order to generate the most revenue. This creates major challenges for workers with childcare responsibilities, long commutes, or multiple jobs (Stern 2016).

These changes are perhaps best understood not as a "broken" labor market but as a perfected capitalist labor market (Livingston 2016). If this perspective is correct, these are not trends that will reverse. And, importantly, calls for improving education and training are unlikely to be enough. While wage premiums associated with college and graduate degrees have generally been rising since 1980, the trend slowed down in the 1990s and 2000s, and there has been no growth since 2010 (Valletta 2016). The result is that the median income of a millennial holding a college degree in 2013 (just under $51,000) was only slightly higher than that of a baby boomer without a degree in 1989 (just over $49,000) (Allison 2017).

The crisis in jobs is the rallying point for supporters of UBI in the technology sector, whose arguments go something like the following: we cannot reverse these trends, and we should not try to do so. The best course of action is to be prepared to provide the support people will need to live in a jobless future.

Disappearing Social Safety Net

When asked about the problem that basic income solves, social worker and policy analyst Diane Pagen replied bluntly, "The United States doesn't have a safety net anymore" (2017). From this perspective, basic income is necessary now because far too many people in the richest country in the world are struggling to get by and there is little hope of current welfare policy fixing the problem. This basic point receives relatively little attention in theoretical academic discussions of UBI, perhaps because it is incontrovertible. However, we must not lose sight of the fact that one of the most immediate and direct benefits of the policy would be to rescue the extremely poor.

As Tach and Edin (2017) declare in their recent review of this subject, "It is hard to overstate the magnitude of the change in the US social safety net since the 1990s." In sum, their argument is that the Personal Responsibility and Work Opportunity Reconciliation Act that replaced Aid to Families with Dependent Children (AFDC) with the more restrictive Temporary Assistance to Needy Families (TANF), along with expansion of the Earned Income Tax Credit (EITC) and changes to the Supplemental Nutrition Assistance Program (SNAP), heralded a shift from a safety net where to be deserving of aid was based on need to one where to be deserving hinges on work. While the EITC and SNAP offer real advantages for poor working families, an increasing number of working and nonworking poor are falling through the cracks. Unlike AFDC, TANF has a 5-year lifetime limit on benefits, includes work requirements and incentives, and is funded via state block grants. As a result, the share of poor families eligible for cash benefits and the share of eligible families actually receiving cash benefits have dropped such that only 23 percent of poor families with children received cash welfare in 2014 (Tach and Edin 2017). As of early 2011, 1.5 million American households with 3 million children were living on no more than $2 per person per day—the World Bank's poverty measure for the developing world—and this number had doubled since 1996. The challenges they face can perhaps be readily imagined, ranging from hunger and homelessness to trauma and abuse (Edin and Shaefer 2015). Martin Luther King, Jr., wrote half a century ago that "The curse of poverty has no justification in our age" (King 1967). The moral imperative to end extreme poverty has not weakened since, and it is difficult to imagine how implementing UBI could fail to achieve this.

WHY BASIC INCOME: DESIRABILITY

Several factors render basic income well worth considering even in the absence of the urgency and necessity previously described. Following

Wright's methods of emancipatory social science (Wright 2010), we formulate this analysis of desirability by presenting a set of normative principles. Wright has articulated equality/fairness, democracy/freedom, and community/solidarity as three primary clusters of values in struggles for social justice (Wright 2016). Adapting this framework, we argue, first, that by liberating people from the demands of the capitalist employment relationship and the provider–client relationship of certain government programs, UBI inherently advances individual freedom or self-determination. Second, in making space for alternatives, UBI is likely to facilitate relations grounded in solidarity and the mutual benefit of the community. Third, and finally, consequences of UBI may include justice for particular marginalized groups, including those currently on welfare, women, and formerly incarcerated people.

Self-Determination

In focusing on the low remuneration and economic insecurity of contingent labor, we have largely taken a structural, materialist perspective thus far. But the situation is more complex when considered in light of cultural analysis. Part-time and independent work are not merely a necessity but also a choice that young people are increasingly making. By providing a floor of economic security, UBI makes this option much more feasible.

Individual freedom, personal control, and flexibility have deep roots in American society as "sacred modern values" (Klinenberg 2013); and working in the freelance, gig, and temp economies can be seen as a way of living these values. As Stern finds in his investigation of the new landscape of work, workers in these sectors narrate their choices in terms of the idea of being a free agent. A common refrain among young people affirms that the last thing they want is to "work for _____ (fill in the blank with IBM, Mobil, or any big company) and become a wage slave like my dad" (Stern 2016). While this kind of work is typically economically precarious, a basic income would change the game by enabling people to embrace the freedom that it entails—knowing there is a secure livelihood to fall back on.

UBI could also be a counter to the stifling, loyalist culture of Whyte's (1956) "organization man" for those who remain in traditional employment relationships. We see it as a sort of personal strike fund: imagine your employer knows that you and all your colleagues would be financially secure if you quit tomorrow. Bargaining for better working conditions, whether at contract negotiations or in day-to-day acts of resistance, suddenly seems more likely to result in wins for workers. Further promoting mobility, the costs of making a risky or expensive life change, like pursuing a new career or moving to a new place, become less insurmountable. As participatory democracy theorists have argued, when poorer people sign their rights over to richer people in an employment because there is no alternative, it can hardly be considered voluntary (Ellerman 1992; Pateman and Mills 2007). UBI could ideally enable truly voluntary work.

As Stern has argued, our current understanding of a "job" as an all-consuming personal identity is in fact relatively recent. For most of history, a job referred simply to a piece of work, coming from its initial meaning of "a cartload" (Stern 2016). Also historically contingent is the Hegelian conception of labor as the essence of a person on which Marx, Freud, and untold others have constructed social theory. Livingston argues that we might see the turning point of the modern era in Martin Luther's notion of work as a "calling," by which he meant an explicitly religious obligation to serve God through a vocation. On the contrary, before the Protestant Reformation, labor was seen as the lot of the unfree and self-ownership as key to freedom (Livingston 2016). Perhaps the modern construct of a "job" not only is incompatible with the present and future of the global economy but also has had unnecessarily adverse consequences for human development. From capitalism to socialism and everything outside and in between, there have always been some dissenting voices calling for the liberation from work as a means to human freedom.

Indeed, it is often forgotten that John Maynard Keynes, whose economic ideas constitute one of the most important paradigms of twentieth- and early twenty-first-century capitalism, saw the economic problem of providing for absolute needs as eminently solvable. He predicted that, by now, we would be setting our sights on the "permanent problem" of humanity—as Keynes put this, on "how to use his freedom from pressing economic cares, how to occupy the leisure, which science and compound interest will have won for him, to live wisely and agreeably and well" (Keynes 1930). On the other hand, within the history of Marxist thought, the autonomist movement has identified the subordination of life to work as the central feature of the capitalist system and promoted refusal of work as a core concept for resistance. This idea can even be traced back to Karl Marx's son-in-law, French revolutionary Paul Lafargue, who penned *The Right to Be Lazy* in 1880 as a damnation of "the capitalist creed of usefulness" (Weeks 2011). Poststructuralist critiques of Marxism, particularly Baudrillard's, also refute the logic of productivism as an ideological imposition of capitalism rather than a transhistorical reality (Baudrillard 1975). Moreover, progressives in the 1920s advocated for a "leisure ethic" to ensure that material progress remained a means to non-material ends (Aronowitz and Cutler 1998). Most recently, the idea of "economics as if people mattered" from Schumacher's 1973 *Small Is Beautiful* has been repopularized by Juliet Schor and others who argue that Americans overwork in order to overspend, all to the neglect of their non-material desires for leisure and wellness (Schor 1991, 1999). What these perspectives have in common is focusing on work as a means to human ends and useful only to the extent that it fulfills these ends. At the same time, none of these perspectives treat work as an a priori objective that is any more important than leisure and the pursuit of happiness. UBI puts this logic into action by divorcing the needs of survival from the demands of paid labor.

In a conservative libertarian sense, too, UBI supports freedom of choice. It is an appealing policy from this angle because it puts spending decisions in the hands of individuals as opposed to government spending on social programs that are meant to help the poor but only in ways dictated by the programs (Murray 2006). The details become important here, though, because a progressive case for UBI does not support this trade-off in the same way. While the progressive case does divert substantial decision-making power from the government to the people—things like food stamps, housing vouchers, and child support payments would most likely be replaced by the unconditional sum—it typically insists on preserving Medicare and Social Security and preserving more broadly the power of government to use social policy and spending to guide public well-being.

Community and Society

In addition to scholarship addressing the potential benefits of basic income for individual freedom, others have focused on collective impacts for community and society. In particular, the case is made that universal income would facilitate a rise in the kinds of work that are highly valued by society but less highly valued by the market. Consider the tedious service jobs that we argued earlier are becoming the new norm. What if the security of a guaranteed income could enable young people who take these jobs to pursue work aligned with their passions instead? Common sense in addition to theoretical and empirical research tell us that the work they would pursue would better contribute to a range of socially beneficial outcomes.

Rosso et al. have integrated decades worth of research in organizational behavior to identify four ideal type pathways to meaningful work, varying along the dimensions of agency/communion and self-/other-directed. Thus, people may find meaning in work through self-directed agency or *individuation*: gaining a sense of control, autonomy, and competence through the work they do. Others find it through other-directed agency or *contribution*: a sense of having significance and impact on others, or subordinating oneself to an organization's vision. Next there is self-directed communion or *self-connection*: finding an authentic or "true" self through work and affirming a consistent identity. And finally, there is other-directed communion or *unification*: developing interpersonal connectedness and belonging to a group and finding purpose through participating in a shared value system (Rosso, Dekas, and Wrzesniewski 2010). This suggests that a basic income would in fact result in more of the kinds of activities that basic income proponents assert it would: entrepreneurship, charity, cooperative production, the arts, education, spiritual development, and radical activism.

Evidence of the individuation motive in workers suggests that, if they had the means, more people would be self-employed or start their own ventures than currently do so. The drive for control and autonomy readily finds an outlet in entrepreneurship, yet this is a risky undertaking when there is no safety net; it is also difficult to achieve without access to capital. Venture capital is highly concentrated (even geographically, in California, New York, and Massachusetts), and the ability to fundraise through family and friends is sharply limited by class. Basic income would go a long way toward solving these problems. It would be fallback income for the individual whose venture may not be making a profit, and it would make banks more likely to loan to borrowers who have few assets (because at least those borrowers would have a steady income from which to repay). The benefits of entrepreneurship to a thriving economy and society—in terms of innovation, competition, and flexibility—have long been known.

Because of the contribution motive, basic income would also increase voluntary and charitable work. Basic income would make it possible to accept a lower wage, or no wage, to do the kinds of work that are not valued by the market: the work of educating the young, caring for the elderly, protecting animals and the environment, and much more. The desire for interconnection and self-abnegation to a group could also manifest in greater numbers of cooperatives and collectives; these would be organizations more likely than traditional firms to do socially conscious work. Basic income would also allow experimentation with worker cooperatives that, like entrepreneurship, are risky and not always lucrative.

The desire for self-connection is well suited to individually expressive activities like the arts. Art is widely connected with the drive for authenticity, and it is a well-known trope that a great number of would-be artists have to abandon that passion for jobs that pay the rent. We can certainly expect to see more people pursuing art in a world where subsistence income is guaranteed. In combination with the contribution motive, artist collectives are also likely to rise. The desire to commune with the self can also be powerfully explored through intellectual pursuits. Basic income might create more jobs in academia as more students can afford college. But it is also likely to produce alternative spaces for research and discovery. Intellectuals would be able to afford to teach in free schools and decentralized networks, publish in open journals, forsake patents, and choose a balance of research, teaching, and activism that may not be acceptable to most institutions. A revived thriving and democratic practice of arts and scholarship has the potential to contribute greatly to public life.

Finally, the unification motive is relevant to spiritual leaders with material concerns becoming less of an issue under a basic income; a heightened emphasis on pursuit of the spiritual is an obvious alternative that basic income might also enable for some. Social activism is also about communing with humanity, and it is hardly ever paid. We can expect more activism, both from individuals who do activism on the side of their paid work who might drop or reduce their paid work hours and from full-time "employed activists" in the non-profit sector. These employed activists in the non-profit sector would have the freedom to sever ties with foundations and corporations in order to pursue potentially more transformative work.

The reproductive work of care is an especially crucial area that gets undervalued by the market. First, women do more unpaid housework than men: from 1994 through 2003, married women did an average of 14.5 hours per week compared to men's 7 hours (Killewald and Gough 2010). Working mothers experience a double burden on their time and resources in performing this work on top of their paid employment (Hochschild 2003). As gender scholars point out, such care work is a public good. Parenting has benefits to capitalism in rearing generations of productive workers, and it has benefits to wider society in generating good spouses, neighbors, and citizens. Neoclassical economics suggest that, as it is impossible to exclude non-payers from reaping these benefits, the market will fail to provide an optimal supply of care. It has further been argued that the devaluation of care is seen within paid employment and accounts for some of the gender gap in wages. Jobs involving care tend to be female-dominated and to pay less (adjusting for differences in education and skill requirements and working conditions) than predominantly male jobs (England 2005).

UBI gives women and men the option to spend more time on care work and less on paid work; it thereby expands the choices of individuals, benefits society, and likely addresses inequality (as research has found that constraints on parenting time and resources, especially when children are young, contribute to a vicious cycle of reinforcing class differences) (Putnam 2016). It does not target the issue of wage differentials for paid care work quite as directly but is likely to have indirect consequences for this too. If the theory that the differential stems from a cultural devaluation of care is correct, then we can expect that UBI and its consequent changing narratives about work and worth will impact this. As performing the non-paid work of households becomes a valid choice that does not result in poverty or financial dependence on another, the sources of its devaluing are lessened.

Justice and Equality

Finally, UBI could help in addressing injustices of the labor market and developing new conceptions of "deservingness." Although Van Parijs' (1997) defense of UBI is couched in a notion he calls "real freedom," it is essentially a theory of justice he is advocating. This goes beyond a formal freedom *from* coercive restrictions and even moral dictates to argue in favor of structuring society so as to maximize broadly distributed opportunities—namely, freedom *to* pursue one's goals, while respecting formal freedoms. In other words, freedom requires a just distribution of resources.

We know that stratification in the labor market is highly dependent on demographic and structural factors out of any one individual's control; because inequality has risen, the consequences of the "birth lottery" (the parents to whom a child is born) have increased in recent years (Chetty et al. 2014). Yet poverty is stigmatized, and in cases where the unemployed and underemployed are able to receive welfare benefits to ensure their survival, the social punishment associated with being in such a position is not negligible (Newman and Massengill 2006). In contrast, the universality of a guaranteed income scheme would remove such stigma and perhaps contribute to lessening the racist attitudes that are associated with it. Fundamentally shifting the welfare debate from one of deservingness to one where the state has a responsibility to every citizen could further ideals of justice and equality. However, this requires confronting the idea that value is measured in labor lest resentment by the employed of the rest become intensified.

The relationships between immigration, racial and ethnic diversity, and attitudes toward the welfare state are such that a UBI could lessen tensions. But it would have to be implemented thoughtfully in the context of rising populist and in some cases nativist ideologies in the United States and Europe. An experiment in Norway found that while a majority of participants reacted positively to the idea of universal income guarantees for Norwegian citizens, framing the question to include residents who are not Norwegian made people less supportive, particularly among those who also reported a restrictive attitude toward immigrants (Bay and Pedersen 2006). Yet a UBI that excludes immigrants would exacerbate injustices faced by these populations. In the case of the Alaska Permanent Fund, Griffin shows how the Alaska Supreme Court, in determining eligibility for the dividend derived from this sovereign wealth fund, defines outsiders and insiders of the state's political community (Griffin 2012). Universal benefits make salient the question of "who counts" and could create further interest in protectionism; indeed, Jordan and Düvell advocate for the radical solution of a universal *global* basic income to ensure international social justice (see Seglow 2005).

An underexplored area concerns the relation between UBI and identity politics. Politically speaking, the seeming lack of identity politics in the conception of UBI is likely to be conducive to generating broad bipartisan appeal. But sociologists should not necessarily see UBI as a repudiation of identity politics and the related frames of privilege and intersectionality that the approach has helped to grasp. Social policy in the United States has long used an ethic of "universalism" to maintain a social order in which resources and respect are in fact dominated by white, male, working citizens (Katznelson 2005; Mettler 1998; Glenn 2004). The promise of guaranteed income universalism can only be fulfilled by acknowledging and avoiding the trap of false universalism. The Movement for Black Lives includes a UBI in its policy platform, arguing that it can provide a measure of economic justice in a context where structural racism has long limited access to labor market and wealth-building opportunities for Black Americans. Yet they argue that a basic income "plus" – containing additional targeted revenues for African Americans, to be funded by divesting from criminal justice – is needed for the policy to function as reparations for harms (Warren 2016).

A feminist perspective also suggests that UBI could redress gender inequality by altering power dynamics in relationships. Domestic violence is aided by women's financial dependence on men and is particularly prevalent among families receiving welfare (Tolman and Rosen 2001). Granting a livable income to all would enable women to escape abusive situations without fear of going hungry as a result. Even in less extreme circumstances, increasing financial autonomy for women has positive effects for women's empowerment; it erodes the harmful effects of prescribed gender roles, as feminists have argued since *The Second Sex* (de Beauvoir 2010). This has also been shown empirically by recent studies of cash transfer programs in the developing world, albeit with qualifications and limitations (Molyneux and Thomson 2011).

Formerly incarcerated individuals are another population who could benefit from UBI. A recent study found that 77 percent of state prisoners released in 2005 were arrested again by 2010 (Breitwieser et al. 2016); having a job immediately after release substantially reduces the likelihood of recidivism (Cove and Bowes 2015). Yet, given the challenges of finding jobs in the future coupled with the reality that those with prison records generally are passed over for other qualified applicants with no criminal records, a UBI seems like a rare opportunity to allow the imprisoned to re-enter society with a "stake," stability, and less pressure to turn to illicit money-producing enterprises. Of course, this presumes that there are not restrictions on eligibility for UBI based on past or present incarceration status, as there are, for example, with the Alaska Permanent Fund Dividend (Alaska Department of Revenue 2018).

LOOKING AHEAD

UBI is a radical policy proposal in many ways. It turns the ideal of "hard work" that has been deeply embedded in the rhetoric of US social policy and rooted in core capitalist notions of value, on its head. In other ways, though, it is not incompatible with the system we have, nor does its attainment seem impossible.

The state of Alaska has what scholars have referred to as a partial basic income (Widerquist and Howard 2012) in the Alaska Permanent Fund Dividend (PFD). The Alaska Permanent Fund Corporation is a sovereign wealth fund endowed with state oil and mineral revenues that has, since 1992, paid out a dividend annually to nearly all residents of the state. While the PFD is much smaller in dollar amount than any reasonable proposal for a full guaranteed income—ranging from over $300 to over $2,000 per year—it is not insignificant. A recent survey finds that 40 percent of Alaska voters say "the yearly dividends have made a great deal or quite a bit of difference in their lives over the past five years" (Harstad 2017). Contrary to fears that government cash transfers without work requirements or means testing would be politically unpalatable, support for this program is strong. Two-thirds of Alaska voters prefer to preserve the PFD even if it means beginning to pay state income taxes (which Alaskans currently do not do). Most importantly, this support seems to be related to precisely the elements of the PFD that most resemble UBI. "It treats all of us Alaskans equally" was one of the leading reasons for support expressed, as found in the survey (Harstad 2017). While the long-running program has not tended to get a lot of attention on the national stage, this may be changing. In fact, Hillary Clinton's memoir of the 2016 presidential election reveals that the campaign was at one point considering a universal carbon dividend program based on the PFD; she refers to it as "Alaska for America" (Clinton 2017). Mark Zuckerberg also touted the program after a trip to Alaska in July 2017 in the context of his already established support for UBI (Weller 2017b).

Also, in the summer of 2017, Hawaii became the first US state to pass legislation supporting the idea of a UBI. The bill declares "that all families in Hawaii deserve basic financial security" and establishes a working group to assess job market exposure to automation and analyze and evaluate UBI and related policy options (Galeon 2017).

On the other side of the Atlantic, Benoît Hamon handily won the French Socialist Party's presidential nomination in 2017 running on a platform that centered on UBI. Hamon's income plan itself, endorsed at least in part by Thomas Piketty and a number of other prominent French researchers, is informative. He advocates for a three-stage rollout: increasing welfare payments for the country's poorest (to €600), extending those payments to all 18- to 25-year-olds, and finally rolling out an increased monthly payment (€750) to all citizens (Williamson 2017). The plan addresses concerns about overhauling welfare in one fell swoop, and it puts youth at the center. Further, his presidential platform included UBI in the context of other reforms that squarely address the questions of work and automation we have discussed in this chapter: a tax levied on companies using robots to replace workers and a reduction of the working week from 35 to 32 hours (Nelson 2017). Beating the centrist frontrunner former prime minister Manuel Valls for the party nomination, Hamon is further proof that this message is resonating.

With conversations about UBI cropping up in so many corners of the world, and across the political spectrum, it is time to organize around this issue. Stern (2016) has proposed working toward a constitutional amendment for UBI or a demand for UBI at the ballot box in the 23 states that allow for citizens' initiatives; he has also recommended that a presidential candidate run on a UBI platform in 2020 or 2024. But imagination is also very much needed. The Economic Security Project has launched a speculative fiction contest to seek creative responses to these questions: What would a world look like where everyone's basic financial needs were met (Defabio 2017)? How would we like to organize work and life outside the 40-hour workweek? If we can answer these questions, then we will really have something to rally behind. And if past trends are any indication, the new models will come from the youth.

REFERENCES

Alaska Department of Revenue. "Eligibility Requirements." 2018. https://pfd.alaska. gov/Eligibility/Requirements. Accessed May 17, 2018.

Allison, Tom. "Financial Health of Young America: Measuring Generational Declines between Baby Boomers & Millennials." Young Invincibles, 2017. http:// younginvincibles.org/wp-content/uploads/2017/04/FHYA-Final2017-1-1.pdf. Accessed May 16, 2018.

Aronowitz, Stanley, and Jonathan Cutler. *Post-Work: The Wages of Cybernation.* New York: Routledge, 1998.

Baird, Sarah, Francisco H. G. Ferreira, Berk Özler, and Michael Woolcock. *Relative Effectiveness of Conditional and Unconditional Cash Transfers for Schooling Outcomes in Developing Countries: A Systematic Review.* Oslo, Norway: Campbell Collaboration, 2013.

Barajas, Joshua. "Smart Robots Will Take Over a Third of Jobs by 2025, Gartner Says." *PBS News Hour*, October 7, 2014. https://www.pbs.org/newshour/economy/smart-robots-will-take-third-jobs-2025-gartner-says

Barnes, Peter. *With Liberty and Dividends for All: How to Save Our Middle-Class When Jobs Don't Pay Enough*. San Francisco: Berrett-Koehler Publishers, 2014.

Baudrillard, Jean. *The Mirror of Production*. St. Louis, MO: Telos Press, 1975.

Bay, Ann-Helén, and Axel West Pedersen. "The Limits of Social Solidarity: Basic Income, Immigration and the Legitimacy of the Universal Welfare State." *Acta Sociologica* 49, no. 4 (2006): 419–36.

BBC News. "Switzerland's Voters Reject Basic Income Plan." June 5, 2016. http://www.bbc.com/news/world-europe-36454060. Accessed January 23, 2017.

Biden, Joe. "Let's Choose a Future That Puts Work First." *Biden Institute Blog*. Biden Institute at the University of Delaware School of Public Policy and Administration, 2016. https://www.sppa.udel.edu/bideninstitute/research-policy/biden-institute-blog/Let%E2%80%99s-Choose-a-Future-That-Puts-Work-First. Accessed September 18, 2017.

Breitwieser, Audrey, Diane Whitmore Schanzenbach, Greg Nantz, Lauren Bauer, Megan Mumford, and Ryan Nunn. *Twelve Facts About Incarceration and Prisoner Reentry*. Washington, DC: Brookings Institution, 2016.

Brynjolfsson, Erik, and Andrew McAfee. *Race Against the Machine: How the Digital Revolution Is Accelerating Innovation, Driving Productivity, and Irreversibly Transforming Employment and the Economy*. Lexington, MA: Digital Frontier Press, 2011.

Bureau of Economic Analysis. "Gross Domestic Product: Percent change from preceding period." 2017. https://www.bea.gov/national/xls/gdpchg.xlsx. Accessed May 1, 2017.

Calnitsky, David. "'More Normal than Welfare': The Mincome Experiment, Stigma, and Community Experience." *Canadian Review of Sociology* 53, no. 1 (2016): 26–71.

Cattelino, Jessica R. *High Stakes: Florida Seminole Gaming and Sovereignty*. Durham, NC: Duke University Press, 2008.

Chancer, Lynn. "Benefitting from Pragmatic Vision: The Case for Guaranteed Income in Principle." In *Post-Work: The Wages of Cybernation*, edited by Stanley Aronowitz and Jonathan Cutler, 81–128. New York and London: Routledge, 1998.

Chang, Jae-Hee, and Phu Huynh. *ASEAN in Transformation: The Future of Jobs at Risk of Automation*. Geneva, Switzerland: International Labour Organization, 2016.

Chetty, Raj, Nathaniel Hendren, Patrick Kline, Emmanuel Saez, and Nicholas Turner. "Is the United States Still a Land of Opportunity? Recent Trends in Intergenerational Mobility." NBER Working Paper 19844. Cambridge, MA: National Bureau of Economic Research, 2014.

Clinton, Hillary Rodham. *What Happened*. New York: Simon & Schuster, 2017.

Cove, Peter, and Lee Bowes. "Immediate Access to Employment Reduces Recidivism." Real Clear Politics, June 11, 2015. https://www.realclearpolitics.com/articles/2015/06/11/immediate_access_to_employment_reduces_recidivism_126939.html. Accessed February 14, 2017.

de Beauvoir, Simone. *The Second Sex*, translated by Constance Borde and Sheila Malovany-Chevallier. New York: Alfred A. Knopf, 2010.

Defabio, Cara Rose. "Into the Black: A Short Fiction Contest with a Big Prize." Medium, September 6, 2017. Accessed September 12, 2017.

Economic Security Project. 2016. http://economicsecurityproject.org/. Accessed September 26, 2017.

Edin, Kathryn J., and H. Luke Shaefer. *$2.00 a Day: Living on Almost Nothing in America*. New York: Houghton Mifflin Harcourt, 2015.

Ellerman, David. *Property and Contract in Economics: The Case for Economic Democracy*. Cambridge, MA: Basil Blackwell, 1992.

England, Paula. "Emerging Theories of Care Work." *Annual Review of Sociology* 31, no. 1 (2005): 381–99.

Evans, Kristina. "Universal Basic Income Is a Go in Finland." TrigTent, January 5, 2017. https://www.trigtent.com/content/universal-basic-income-go-finland. Accessed February 10, 2017.

Federal Reserve Bank of St. Louis. "Manufacturing Sector: Real Output." 2018a. https://fred.stlouisfed.org/series/OUTMS. Accessed May 16, 2018.

Federal Reserve Bank of St. Louis. "Manufacturing Sector: Employment." 2018b. https://fred.stlouisfed.org/series/PRS30006013. Accessed May 16, 2018.

Fox News. "Push for a Universal Basic Income Gains Traction." September 17, 2017a. http://video.foxnews.com/v/5579038773001/? - sp=show-clips.

Fox News. "Universal Basic Income Gaining Popularity Amid Jobs Debate." June 28, 2017b. http://video.foxnews.com/v/5486383947001/? - sp=show-clips.

Frey, Carl Benedikt, and Michael A. Osborne. "The Future of Employment: How Susceptible Are Jobs to Computerisation?" *Technological Forecasting and Social Change* 114 (2017): 254–80.

Fromm, Erich. *The Sane Society*. New York: Rinehart, 1955.

Galeon, Dom. "Hawaii Just Became the First US State to Pass a Bill Supporting Basic Income." Business Insider, June 15, 2017. http://www.businessinsider.com/hawaii-basic-income-bill-2017-6. Accessed September 12, 2017.

Glenn, Evelyn Nakano. *Unequal Freedom: How Race and Gender Shaped American Citizenship and Labor*. Cambridge: Harvard University Press, 2004.

Griffin, Christopher L., Jr. "The Alaska Permanent Fund Dividend and Membership in the State's Political Community." *Alaska Law Review* 29, no. 1 (2012): 79–92.

Haarmann, Claudia, and Dirk Haarmann. "From Survival to Decent Employment: Basic Income Security in Namibia." *Basic Income Studies* 2, no. 1 (2007): doi:https://doi.org/10.2202/1932-0183.1066.

Hamilton, Tracy Brown. "The Netherlands' Upcoming Money-for-Nothing Experiment." *The Atlantic*, June 21, 2016. https://www.theatlantic.com/business/archive/2016/06/netherlands-utrecht-universal-basic-income-experiment/487883/. Accessed February 10, 2017

Harstad, Paul. "Executive Summary of Findings from a Survey of Alaska Voters on the PFD." Economic Security Project, June 22, 2017. https://www.scribd.com/document/352375988/ESP-Alaska-PFD-Phone-Survey-Executive-Summary-Spring-2017. Accessed July 6, 2017

Hicks, Michael J., and Srikant Devaraj. *The Myth and Reality of Manufacturing in America*. Muncie, IN: Ball State University, 2015.

Hochschild, Arlie. *The Second Shift*. With Anne Machung. New York and London: Penguin Books, 2003.

Hurst, Erik. "Video Killed the Radio Star: How Games, Phones, and Other Tech Innovations Are Changing the Labor Force." Chicago Booth Review, September 1, 2016. http://review.chicagobooth.edu/economics/2016/article/video-killed-radio-star. Accessed March 12, 2017.

Kalleberg, Arne. "Precarious Work, Insecure Workers: Employment Relations in Transition." *American Sociological Review* 74 (2009): 1–22.

Katznelson, Ira. *When Affirmative Action Was White: An Untold History of Racial Inequality in Twentieth-Century America.* New York: W. W. Norton & Company, 2005.

Keynes, John Maynard. *Essays in Persuasion.* New York: W.W. Norton & Co., 1963, pp. 358–373. http://georgemaciunas.com/wp-content/uploads/2012/06/Economic-Possibilities-of-Our-Grandchildren.pdf. Accessed February 11, 2017.

Killewald, Alexandra, and Margaret Gough. "Money Isn't Everything: Wives' Earnings and Housework Time." *Social Science Research* 39 (2010): 987–1003.

King, Martin Luther. *Where Do We Go from Here: Chaos or Community?* New York: Harper & Row, 1967.

Klinenberg, Eric. *Going Solo: The Extraordinary Rise and Surprising Appeal of Living Alone.* London: Penguin Books, 2013.

Knight, Ben. "Free Money—Germany's Basic Income Lottery." Deutsche Welle, June 10, 2015. http://www.dw.com/en/free-money-germanys-basic-income-lottery/a-18764779. Accessed January 13, 2017.

Livingston, James. *No More Work: Why Full Employment Is a Bad Idea.* Chapel Hill: University of North Carolina Press, 2016.

Mettler, Suzanne. *Dividing Citizens: Gender and Federalism in New Deal Public Policy.* Ithaca: Cornell University Press, 1998.

Molyneux, Maxine, and Marilyn Thomson. "Cash Transfers, Gender Equity and Women's Empowerment in Peru, Ecuador and Bolivia." *Gender and Development* 19, no. 2 (2011): 195–212.

Murray, Charles. *In Our Hands: A Plan to Replace the Welfare State.* Washington, DC: AEI Press, 2006.

Nelson, Eshe. "France's Socialist Presidential Candidate Is Calling for a Universal Basic Income, Robot Tax, and Legal Weed." Quartz, January 31, 2017. https://qz.com/897942/frances-socialist-presidential-candidate-is-calling-for-a-universal-basic-income-robot-tax-and-legal-weed/. Accessed October 18, 2017.

Newman, Katherine S., and Rebekah Peeples Massengill. "The Texture of Hardship: Qualitative Sociology of Poverty, 1995–2005." *Annual Review of Sociology* 32 (2006): 423–46.

Ontario Ministry of Finance. "2016 Ontario Budget." 2016. http://www.fin.gov.on.ca/en/budget/ontariobudgets/2016/ch1e.html. Accessed February 10, 2017.

Pagen, Diane. "16th Annual U.S. Basic Income Guarantee Congress Opening Session." Roosevelt House Public Policy Institute at Hunter College, June 15, 2017. http://www.roosevelthouse.hunter.cuny.edu/events/16th-annual-u-s-basic-income-guarantee-congress-opening-panel/. Accessed July 15, 2017.

Paine, Thomas. "Agrarian Justice." Project Gutenberg. 1797. http://www.gutenberg.org/files/31271/31271-h/31271-h.htm. Accessed November 23, 2015.

Pateman, Carole, and Charles W. Mills. *Contract and Domination.* Cambridge: Polity Press, 2007.

Putnam, Robert D. *Our Kids: The American Dream in Crisis*. New York: Simon and Schuster, 2016.

Reibstein, Sarah. "Is Universal Basic Income a Disincentive to Work? An Empirical Review." Presented at the American Sociological Association 2017 Annual Meeting (August 13, Montreal), 2017. http://tinyurl.com/kfa9a8n.

Rosso, Brent D., Kathryn H. Dekas, and Amy Wrzesniewski. "On the Meaning of Work: A Theoretical Integration and Review." *Research in Organizational Behavior* 30 (2010): 91–127.

Schor, Juliet. *The Overspent American: Why We Want What We Don't Need*. New York : HarperPerennial, 1999.

———. *The Overworked American: The Unexpected Decline of Leisure*. New York: Basic Books, 1991.

Segal, David. "Apple's Retail Army, Long on Loyalty but Short on Pay." *New York Times*, June 23, 2012.

Seglow, Jonathan. "The Ethics of Immigration." *Political Studies Review* 3 (2005): 317–34.

Sirkin, Harold L., Michael Zinser, and Justin Ryan Rose. "The Robotics Revolution: The Next Great Leap in Manufacturing." The Boston Consulting Group, 2015. https://circabc.europa.eu/sd/a/b3067f4e-ea5e-4864-9693-0645e5cbc053/BCG_The_Robotics_Revolution_Sep_2015_tcm80-197133.pdf. Accessed May 16, 2018.

Standing, Guy. "Unconditional Basic Income: Two Pilots in Madhya Pradesh." Prepared for the Delhi Conference, May 30–31, 2013. https://www.guystanding.com/files/documents/Basic_Income_Pilots_in_India_note_for_inaugural.pdf. Accessed February 12, 2017.

Stern, Andy. *Raising the Floor: How a Universal Basic Income Can Renew Our Economy and Rebuild the American Dream*. With Lee Kravitz. New York: PublicAffairs, 2016.

Suplicy, Eduardo Matarazzo. "Basic Income and Employment in Brazil." Basic Income Studies 2, no. 1 (2007): doi:https://doi.org/10.2202/1932-0183.1067.

Tabatai, Hamid. "From Price Subsidies to Basic Income: The Iran Model and Its Lessons." In *Exporting the Alaska Model: Adapting the Permanent Fund Dividend for Reform Around the World*, edited by Karl Widerquist and Michael W. Howard, 17–32. New York: Palgrave Macmillan, 2012.

Tach, Laura, and Kathryn Edin. "The Social Safety Net After Welfare Reform: Recent Developments and Consequences for Household Dynamics." *Annual Review of Sociology* 43 (2017): 541–61.

Tolman, Richard M., and Daniel Rosen. "Domestic Violence in the Lives of Women Receiving Welfare: Mental Health, Substance Dependence, and Economic Well-Being." *Violence Against Women* 7, no. 2 (2001): 141–58.

Valletta, Robert G. "Recent Flattening in the Higher Education Wage Premium: Polarization, Skill Downgrading, or Both?" NBER Working Paper 22935. National Bureau of Economic Research, Cambridge, MA, 2016.

Van Parijs, Philippe. *Real Freedom for All: What (if Anything) Can Justify Capitalism?* New York: Oxford University Press, 1997.

Velasquez-Manoff, Moises. "What Happens When the Poor Receive a Stipend?" *New York Times*, January 18, 2014.

Waddell, Kaveh. "The Exhausting Work of Tallying America's Largest Protest." *The Atlantic*, January 23, 2017.

Warren, Dorian T. "Reparations for the Continued Divestment from, Discrimination toward, and Exploitation of Our Communities in the Form of a Guaranteed Minimum Livable Income for All Black People, with Clearly Articulated Corporate Regulations." In *A Vision for Black Lives: Policy Demands for Black Power, Freedom, and Justice. The Movement for Black Lives*, August 1, 2016. http://www.ibtimes.com/heres-what-black-lives-matter-wants-6-reforms-detailed-social-justice-movements-2396502. Accessed May 17, 2018.

Weber, Max. *The Protestant Ethic and the Spirit of Capitalism*, translated by Talcott Parsons. New York: Scribner, 1930.

Weeks, Kathi. *The Problem with Work: Feminism, Marxism, Antiwork Politics, and Postwork Imaginaries*. Durham, NC: Duke University Press, 2011.

Weller, Chris. "Elon Musk Doubles Down on Universal Basic Income: 'It's Going to Be Necessary.'" Business Insider, February 13, 2017a. http://www.businessinsider.com/elon-musk-universal-basic-income-2017-2. Accessed October 18, 2017.

———. "Mark Zuckerberg Doubles Down on Universal Basic Income After a Trip to Alaska." Business Insider, July 5, 2017b. http://www.businessinsider.com/mark-zuckerberg-universal-basic-income-alaska-2017-7. Accessed September 12, 2017.

———. "Richard Branson Just Endorsed Basic Income—Here Are 10 Other Tech Moguls Who Support the Radical Idea." Business Insider, August 21, 2017c. http://www.businessinsider.com/entrepreneurs-endorsing-universal-basic-income-2017-3. Accessed October 18, 2017.

Whyte, William Hollingsworth. *The Organization Man*. New York: Simon and Schuster, 1956.

Widerquist, Karl. "A Failure to Communicate: What (if anything) Can We Learn from the Negative Income Tax Experiments?" *Journal of Socio-Economics* 34, no. 1 (2005): 49–81.

———. "VIDEO: Fox News Calls Basic Income 'A Great Idea.'" Basic Income News, 2013. http://basicincome.org/news/2013/11/video-fox-news-calls-basic-income-a-great-idea/. Accessed October 18, 2017.

Widerquist, Karl, and Michael Howard, eds. *Alaska's Permanent Fund Dividend: Examining Its Suitability as a Model*. New York: Palgrave Macmillan, 2012.

Williamson, Lucy. "France's Benoit Hamon Rouses Socialists with Basic Income Plan." BBC News, January 24, 2017. http://www.bbc.com/news/world-europe-38723219. Accessed October 18, 2017.

World Bank. *World Development Report 2016: Digital Dividends*. Washington, DC: World Bank, 2016. http://documents.worldbank.org/curated/en/896971468194972881/pdf/102725-PUB-Replacement-PUBLIC.pdf. Accessed May 10, 2017.

Wright, Erik Olin. *Envisioning Real Utopias*. New York: Verso Books, 2010.

———. "Real Utopias and the Dilemmas of Institutional Transformation." *Justice, Power and Resistance* 1, no. 1 (2016): 33–52.

12

The Enduring Case for Full Employment

Robert Kuttner

A SPLIT-LEVEL ECONOMY

America is suffering from a split-level economy—especially for the young. It is really a three-class economy. A tiny fraction of young people grow up to become part of the super-rich—the 1 percent—through either inheritance or access to elite institutions such as Harvard Business School, which emerges via genuine entrepreneurship or financial manipulation. They become part of the far more unequal society that America has become.

Other young people are helped by parental endowments of wealth and position to become part of the professional class—this can be thought of as the family welfare state—that provides a family head start. This class is made up of intergenerational transfers that stay inside a household: parents pay tuition so that kids do not have to incur college debt; parents subsidize unpaid internships to help offspring become networked on career ladders; they provide down payments or help with rent; later on, they subsidize expensive pre-K for the third generation. Like so much else, social investments that were once public have now been privatized and stay within the family. And, consequently, positional advantage is inherited in this economy to a far greater degree than it was during the post-war boom.

Meanwhile, the vast majority of young people, whose families cannot give them inherited privilege, struggle to gain a foothold. All of this operates in the context of the erosion of payroll jobs in favor of the "gig economy" (namely short-term, on-demand jobs that involve what labor economists call non-standard employment), of rising costs of education and housing relative to income, and of the absence of policies to bridge work and family. As a result of these developments all told, negative effects cascade down the generations.

THE PROBLEM: FROM REGULAR JOBS TO CASUAL LABOR AND PRECARITY

First, the labor market has turned against workers generally and especially against the young. This has little to do with technology or skills but mainly involves changes in power relationships. A generation ago, most jobs were regular payroll jobs or ones that might have been organized as casual labor. Indeed, the effort by employers to reduce regular work to casual labor is a very old story, dating back centuries. In 1902, approximately 30,000 New York subway workers—mostly Italian immigrants who had been recruited by labor bosses known as *padroni*, who had themselves been hired by construction companies—went on strike for the right to be paid as salaried employees rather than casual day laborers. Close to exactly the same thing also occurred in the garment industry.

This shift, from payroll jobs and career ladders to the on-demand economy and casual day labor, amounted to a transfer of power from working people to managers and financiers. It was a change in the social contract that had come into being after World War II; in the era of the blue-collar middle class, we had a different social contract anchored in a different politics. The change has been toward a precarious labor market whose enthusiasts try to prettify it with the term "the sharing economy" as if it were voluntary or somehow reflective of a preference on the part of the Millennial generation for greater flexibility. This is mostly a convenient fable, though. With different rules, and different politics, it does not have to be this way.

What about skills and education? Presently, we have a better-educated population than the one we had during the era of much more equal earnings when most Americans did not go to college. Of course, better schooling opportunities at all levels are valuable in their own right to produce a broadly educated citizenry and a more productive economy. But better education and training do not address the slide into a contingent labor force. This is a structural reality that has little, if anything, to do with education levels.

I have an English friend whose 20-something son has been having trouble getting traction in his career. Last time I visited I said, "How's your boy doing?" "Fine," said my friend, Charles is a barrister. "Wonderful," I replied. Barrister, as you know, is the English term for lawyer. "Actually," said my friend, "I think that's pronounced barista."

A SOLUTION: THE HISTORY OF FULL EMPLOYMENT AS REMEDY

Second, it is essential to keep in mind the importance of full employment as a remedy that often falls into the national memory hole. With full employment, though, all is possible. Without it, the best structural policies still lead to a game of musical chairs in which some are left out. Without full employment, there is insufficient bargaining power to raise wages, no matter how many overeducated young people we graduate. My young barista friend is a college graduate.

There is a story promoted by financial elites to the effect that the young are getting a raw deal because too much is spent on the old vis-à-vis Social Security and Medicare and because our deficits and debts to pay for these programs slow the rate of economic growth. The Peter G. Peterson Foundation has spent over a billion dollars to promote this story, which has also been peddled by groups like the Bowles-Simpson Commission, the Bipartisan Policy Center, Third Way, No Labels, and the Committee for a Responsible Federal Budget. Close to conventional wisdom in many elite policy circles is to just cut Social Security and Medicare and reduce the deficit, and somehow growth rates will increase and good jobs will flow to young people.

This story falls apart, though, on close examination. I have written a book about it entitled *Debtors' Prison* (Kuttner 2013). The punchline is very simple: you cannot deflate your way to high growth. Nor are any of the sponsors of the story genuine advocates of serious investment in the young. They are fiscal conservatives who do not like government and are trying to define generational justice in a way that requires further cuts in social investment. To be clear, we do need better training and education policies for poor kids. But better human capital does not allow the economy to bootstrap its way to full employment.

There is a long-standing debate about targeting versus universalism. Do we help the poor more with policies aimed explicitly at the poor and at communities of color, or do we fashion universal policies that help minorities and the poor disproportionately because that is where the need is greatest? I think we need both. William Julius Wilson, in the first issue of *The American Prospect*, made a case for race-neutral policies and what Theda Skocpol, referring to Wilson, calls "targeting within universalism" in the next issue when referring to less privileged people receiving extra benefits without stigma (Wilson 1990; Skocpol 1990). But if you think of this debate, full employment is the ultimate case of targeting within universalism. Tight labor markets help all wage earners, but during the rare periods of full employment the greatest gains have gone to the young, the unskilled, and people of color.

It is also worth recalling the history of full employment as a concept and as a politics. In 1940, after nearly 8 years of the New Deal, the unemployment rate was still around 14 percent. Wages were stagnant. By early 1942, unemployment fell to 3 percent, and then 2 percent. So, what happened? Workers did not suddenly become better trained or more diligent.

Pearl Harbor happened. The US government entered about $100 billion of war production orders in the first 6 months of 1942. American output rose by 50 percent between 1939 and 1942, financed by massively increasing surtaxes and by government borrowing. The public deficit was about 25 percent of GDP per year for the 4 years of the war. It was also financed by very high taxes on people of high incomes, with top marginal rates as high as 94 percent.

Moreover, the war was a massive job-training program; it involved enormous public investments in science and technology as well as a recapitalization of industry that had been undercapitalized throughout the depressed economy of the 1930s. Even though about a third of what was produced was made and then soon blown up, wages increased so much during the war that despite rationing, civilian living standards were a great deal higher in 1945 than in 1940.

The point is that we did not train people first: we created massive government-driven demand, which in turn produced jobs, and then people were trained on the job. People who had never worked in a factory as well as people who were functionally illiterate became skilled employees. Women and African Americans took well-paying jobs from which they had been excluded. The first on-site, high-quality day-care programs were created for war production workers.

The war occurred after the 13-year experience of the Great Depression, a time when many economists had convinced themselves that we were just stuck at a permanent plateau of high unemployment and stagnant wages known as "secular" stagnation. Supposedly, automation and the satisfaction of basic wants meant that there just was not enough work to go around. This turned out to be profoundly wrong. In fact, we had a shortfall of demand that in turn led to underinvestment and to an economy performing far below its threshold of possibility. The economy settled at an equilibrium that was well below the output of which it was capable.

For that cohort of leaders, high unemployment was a curse. It condemned a whole generation to economic hardship and promoted the rise of dictators. Nazi Germany, which used rearmament as a stimulus policy, was the first to get out of the Great Depression. Writing in 1938, Keynes noted that it was hard to expect that a democracy would give government the fiscal authority needed to surmount a great depression in peacetime. But this was exactly what occurred once the war came.

Following the war, planners resolved that high unemployment must never return: they became obsessed with full employment. A great deal happened immediately post-war and in 1944 alone. Full employment was alluded to in Roosevelt's Four Freedoms speech and in his call for a second Bill of Rights. In 1944, too, the Bretton Woods conference aimed at creating an international monetary system in which nations could run high-employment economies without worry about the austerity demands of private financial speculators.

Still in 1944, the second of Lord William Beveridge's great wartime reports was all about the centrality of full employment. In this report, entitled "The Purpose of Employment," Beveridge wrote, "Idleness is not the same as want, but a separate evil, which men do not escape by having an income. They must also have the feeling of rendering useful service" (Beveridge 1982: 339). Indeed, unemployment in the United Kingdom never fell below 10 percent throughout the two decades between World War I and World War II and averaged 14 percent. As Beveridge commented, too, "In the un-planned market economy of Britain between the two wars, a substantial proportion of the productive capacity of the country stood idle or ran to waste" (Beveridge 1982). His answer was a public investment budget that included social investment such as the National Health Service and public works outlays so as to keep the economy at full employment. Britain stayed at full employment for two decades after the war.

In the United States, the Wagner-Murray Full Employment Bill written in 1944 sought to officially commit to full employment with policy instruments to match. The Wagner-Murray bill spelled out the federal government's role in assuring full employment. The president was to transmit an annual national production and employment budget to Congress. This would include estimates of the size of the labor force, total national production needed to provide jobs for the labor force, and total anticipated output in the absence of special measures by the federal government. But if anticipated production was insufficient, the federal government was to encourage sufficient additional nonfederal investment and expenditures to stimulate creation of private sector jobs; if necessary, federal expenditures were to close the remaining gap to assure full employment.

The bill passed the Senate overwhelmingly. However, in late 1945, it was killed in the more conservative House where the New Deal majority in Congress was not as strong. The eventual Employment Act of 1946 was substantially weakened, offering a set of goals rather than a concrete planning document. It committed the government to "maximum employment, production, and purchasing power" but did not include a planning process to assure that outcome (Murray 1946).

For much of the post-war boom, we stayed reasonably close to full employment. There were some mild recessions, but labor markets and labor bargaining power were tight enough that wages rose with productivity. The bottom quintile actually gained income share faster than the top quintile. This was what the economists Claudia Goldin and Robert A. Margo (1992) called the "Great Compression"—namely, the compression of the wage structure. It was all the more remarkable because discrimination against blacks and women was still the norm.

Robust Keynesianism was gradually diluted into a very modest counter-cyclical policy using tax cuts rather than a commitment to true full employ-ment via public investment or public employment. President Kennedy, who had campaigned on a promise to get the country moving again, came out for a major tax cut in 1962. Congress approved the cut in early 1964, 3 months after Kennedy's death. But Kennedy's Council of Economic Advisers in-cluded leading self-described Keynesians Walter Heller and James Tobin. An informal adviser was the most famous Keynesian of all, John Kenneth Galbraith. Galbraith urged a deficit-financed increase in public investment. The policy would do double duty. The deficit itself would be a tonic, and so would the public improvements.

More centrist neo-Keynesians on Kennedy's Council of Economic Advisers argued that if the goal was stimulus, though, a dollar of tax cut was as good as a dollar of public spending. That premise has subsequently been disproven. A dollar of tax cut is less efficient as stimulus, especially when some of it goes to the rich because the rich do not spend all of it. By contrast, when you increase public spending by a dollar, every penny gets injected into the economy. And "stimulus," as we learned from President Obama's Recovery Act, is not the same as a full commitment to full employment.

In Kennedy's day, the politics was more important than the economics. With Congress narrowly divided and business lobbying intense, a tax cut was a far easier sell than an increase in public investment. The moderate neo-Keynesians won the debate, and Galbraith was sent packing as Kennedy's ambassador to India.

Full employment arose again, though, in the context of President Johnson's War on Poverty. With the War on Poverty, a four-way debate took place between the full employment people, the human capital people, the culture-of-poverty people like Harvard professor and future senator Daniel Patrick Moynihan, and the community empowerment people who included Michael Harrington (the latter also very much a believer in full employment).

Moynihan, who ridiculed the idea of involvement of the poor as "max-imum feasible misunderstanding," was on at least three sides of the de-bate at different times (Moynihan 1969). Harrington also acknowledged that there was a culture of poverty but not in the sense of blaming the victim (Harrington 1962). The actual anti-poverty program enacted in 1964 was a stew of these diverse elements.

But even the full employment people were divided into two camps: the centrist neo-Keynesians on the Council of Economic Advisers, who thought it was possible to get there mainly with fiscal and monetary policy, and more radical advocates. Within the latter camp were John Kenneth Galbraith,

A. Phillip Randolph, Walter Reuther, Gunnar Myrdal, and Hyman Minsky advocating for more public investment and direct public employment. This group correctly worried that if macroeconomic policy alone was relied upon, inflation might result and lead to the policy likely being reversed by the Fed before full employment was ever reached.

This trap had been averted during World War II with wage and price controls and rationing—something not possible in peacetime. But the scale of public works spending proposed by Randolph and Myrdal would have cost $10 billion a year, and the entire War on Poverty amounted to $1 billion. This group then became the loyal opposition of the War on Poverty.

This debate is largely forgotten history, yet it is highly instructive for our own time. Conventional economics disputes Keynes' idea that high unemployment was mainly a shortfall of aggregate demand and investment. By emphasizing human capital, you could make unemployment the fault of deficiencies in the poor themselves. You could duck the question of the scale of public outlay needed to keep the economy at full employment and emphasize training, as it was far less controversial.

A third dimension of the War on Poverty was community empowerment. This was useful in its own right. Poor people surely lacked political power, and it was helpful to deepen and strengthen indigenous economic and social institutions. Community Action Program (CAP) agencies, Head Start as not just preschool but also a rival power center to the white power structure especially in the Deep South, Neighborhood Legal Services, VISTA—all these did useful work. Among other things, they helped to incubate a generation of African American and Hispanic political leaders in the big cities. But this aspect of the War on Poverty also sidestepped full employment, and CAP agencies did not get us to full employment.

And there was soon a backlash against community empowerment, not just by Republican conservatives but by Democratic mayors who saw Washington's Office of Economic Opportunity underwriting independent power bases in opposition to themselves. Even before the Nixon administration, much of the community empowerment aspect of the War on Poverty was diluted as too radical. A true commitment to full employment would have been a more enduring and helpful form of economic radicalism. In the absence of full employment, relying on either community power or human capital to get people into decent jobs was a game of musical chairs.

By the 1960s, Keynes was long gone; but one of his greatest disciples, the economist Hyman Minsky, pointed out that you could not get to full employment by way of human capital. As Minsky argued, "The war on poverty was born out of neoclassical theory in which it is the poor—not the economy—that is to blame for poverty. The war on poverty tried to change the poor, not the economy" (Minsky 1971). He added that "We have to reverse the thrust of policy of the past 40 years and move towards a system in which labor force attachment is encouraged. But to do that we must make jobs available; any policy strategy which does not take job creation as its first and primary objective is but a continuation of the impoverishing strategy of the past decade" (Minsky 1975). Minsky correctly argued that policy was needed to meet the poor where they are and that tight fiscal policy could only take you part of the way: government's role as employer of last resort was needed do the rest.

Most of the income gains that accrued to people of color and the poor in the 1960s were the result of very tight labor markets combined with the gradual enforcement of anti-discrimination measures. These were, first, the two executive orders on affirmative action by Presidents Kennedy and Johnson and, second, the Civil Rights Act of 1964 with its fair employment titles.

Basically, by the end of this contemporary history, the full employment people had lost this debate. President Johnson and Congress poured money into a wide range of anti-poverty programs, some of which did a great deal of good. However, rising real incomes of that era were primarily the result of labor markets so tight that even people with relatively low skills were able to find jobs and increase their earnings over time. Direct government employment, with the exception of a small jobs corps, VISTA, and employment in the anti-poverty program itself, was deemed too expensive. By the time the government did sponsor billions of dollars in more outlay for direct employment, the jobs—hundreds of thousands of very dangerous and expensive ones—were in Vietnam.

Instead of a civilian full employment program, then, we got the Vietnam War and military Keynesianism—leading to very tight labor markets indeed. So long as wartime full employment lasted, we had rising incomes at the bottom. For the entire period 1947 to 1973, the bottom quintile gained income at a faster rate than the top or the middle. While the late 1960s was a period of wage growth, the cause was full employment and expanded civil rights more than the official War on Poverty.

The next chapter of the full employment story occurred in 1977 and 1978 when the full employment people finally got their views enacted partly into law with the Humphrey-Hawkins Act of 1978. This committed the government to a goal of 4 percent unemployment and 4 percent inflation and authorized a public employment program if unemployment exceeded this. The most important "sleeper" provision, though, directed the Federal Reserve to pursue high growth and high employment—known as the "dual mandate"—along with price stability. This was very important in countering the internal Fed culture where, traditionally, the central bank's prime job is to keep inflation at bay. This was in fact a sleeper until the Yellen administration was in charge at the Fed, when, in fending off pressures to prematurely raise rates, Yellen cited the dual mandate codified in the Humphrey-Hawkins Act that was intended to promote full employment.

One other period demonstrated the centrality of tight labor markets to full employment: the late 1990s. Since the end of the post-war boom in the early 1970s, this is the only period when the bottom of the income distribution enjoyed significant gains in earnings. Expansion of the earned income tax credit helped; the cutting of other social investments, such as Temporary Assistance for Needy Families (TANF), hurt. But one cannot tell a persuasive story about wage gains in the late 1990s that attributes income growth mainly to sectoral policies. Rather, again, most of the gains were the result of very tight labor markets.

In the late 1990s, unemployment bottomed out at 4 percent. The incomes of black workers actually rose faster than those of white workers between 1995 and 2000. Black unemployment and white unemployment rates converged to some degree: the jobless rate was 3.5 percent for whites and 7.6 percent for blacks. During the 1990s, the increase for blacks was 2.7 times greater than that for whites (4.3 percent versus 1.6 percent). This is not surprising because when jobs are plentiful and workers are scarce, rather than vice versa, employers will hire and even train people whom they would not otherwise hire. With very tight labor markets, workers have some bargaining power.

Structurally, and even as recently as the late 1990s, we had a very different economy. Uber and TaskRabbit had not yet been invented. There was some contingent employment, but it was far from the norm. Unions were losing members but were much stronger than they are in the late 2010s. TANF had not taken full effect. Thus, workers had more bargaining power to defend a reservation wage than they do presently. Five percent unemployment means something very different in terms of wage gains in 2017 or 2018 than it did in 1998, much less 1968.

Moreover, currently, labor statistics are very misleading. The nominal unemployment rate is below 5 percent. However, the rate of labor force participation is down, and an increasing share of jobs are substandard jobs—"gigs" rather than payroll employment. Not surprisingly, when labor markets are slack, there is no pressure to raise wages—and least of all to raise them for workers in the lower-skilled occupations where most young people from low-income communities start out.

Full employment costs money. As Minsky recognized, if you try to achieve full employment only through fiscal policy—large deficits—eventually, you run the risk of inflation or of the Fed pulling the plug. By contrast, it needs to be done substantially with tax and invest.

BACK TO THE PRESENT: WHERE ARE WE NOW?

Where has this history left us in the late 2010s? In addition to all the other factors depressing earnings growth, we face an intensification of automation and robots. As an explanation for what is occurring, I think this is mostly a red herring. With the right policies, automation is a blessing that allows more output with less human toil. The challenge, then, is to devise policies that spread that wealth around, as President Obama so memorably told Joe the plumber.

Nor is this a new story. More than 40 years ago at a time of another automation scare, the Nobel laureate Vassily Leontief liked to tell the parable of the last industrial worker. What happens, he asked, when so much production is automated that there is just one human factory worker and her job is to flip the switch? The answer, he said, is that the whole economic question becomes distributive. Who gets the fruits of that productivity? Owners? Workers? Society as a whole? And what is the new distribution of work, income, and leisure?

There is no shortage of work to be done. At present, persistent unemployment coexists with wages that are so low that people not uncommonly take two and three jobs and work 80 hours a week in order to make ends meet. And this "work without end" ethic is not happening only at the low end of the socioeconomic spectrum. In Silicon Valley, we have people working far more hours than they want to or even need to because some obsessive workaholic is willing to work longer hours than another person and is hungry for that person's job (Jacobs and Gerson 2004). And this is not a function of skills, as the case of university adjuncts makes clear.

Thus, full employment does not mean that everyone works 80 hours a week or that family life is destroyed. On the contrary, in an economy as productive as ours, we should be shortening working time. This would be doable if we had decent jobs at decent wages for all.

At this point, then, let me connect the two parts of my story. The rise of the gig economy is in part the result of slack labor markets and diminishing regular jobs. People work as TaskRabbits, Mechanical Turks, and packers in Amazon warehouses not because they love these precarious and exploitative jobs but because better jobs and careers are not on offer. Far fewer people would drive for Uber if the economy had more real jobs.

The Uber economy, defined as an economy of freelance workers, is not a technological imperative. It is a business model. Uber defines fares and sets the terms of work. Some people would call that an employer. In fact, the California secretary of labor recently categorized Uber as an employer despite the company's claim that it is merely an Internet matching platform. The Internal Revenue Service has gone after FedEx for disguising regular employees as independent contractors. The general counsel of the National Labor Relations Board has defined the corporate parent as well as the local franchise owner of a McDonald's or Burger King as a co-employer. University adjuncts are getting unionized.

With a different constellation of political power and a more robust set of regulations, much, if not most, of the gig economy could be defined as payroll jobs and regulated accordingly. And with full employment, fewer people would be available to take low-paid, unreliable gigs. Even TaskRabbits would have to be paid decently. The option to be a freelancer or an entrepreneur would still be there, as it always has been.

BUT IS FULL EMPLOYMENT POLITICALLY FEASIBLE?

What about full employment, then? Is it even possible? I have written that one strategy would be to ensure that all human service work pays a living, middle-class wage—say, $35,000 a year and up. That would cost between $50 billion and $100 billion a year depending on the details. This is a field that is only going to keep growing. We can define jobs as taking care of the young, the old, the sick; as low-wage custodial care; or as skilled, decently paid professions.

And we need a massive public infrastructure/green transition program. This means increasing public outlay by maybe 5 percentage points of GDP. This would entail about $750 billion a year, most of it tax-supported not deficit-supported. That would be sufficient to create very tight labor markets and lots of good jobs.

According to the American Society of Civil Engineers, the United States has a deficit of $3.4 trillion in basic infrastructure: roads, bridges, tunnels, water and sewer systems, and public buildings. This does not even include the new imperative to invest in systems to protect coasts against storm surges or to create twenty-first-century infrastructure such as smart grid electrical systems, greener waste disposal, building retrofitting for energy savings, and universal high-speed broadband. A multi-trillion-dollar public investment would provide good domestic jobs while improving the productivity and growth rate of the economy. Tight labor markets, all by themselves, improve labor's bargaining power. One of the reasons wages are so low today is persistent high unemployment. People are forced to accept chores as TaskRabbits because they cannot find better jobs.

The Obama stimulus package is a classic example of how not to take advantage of a historical moment. Stimulus is a macroeconomic term, as in countercyclical stimulus. The rhetoric of the White House—really the rhetoric of the Office of Management and Budget—was that the stimulus would be timely, targeted, and temporary, as if they were uncomfortable, almost apologetic, about investing all that public money. The program would then be scrapped, it was promised, as soon as the worst emergency was behind us. But timely, targeted, and temporary was wrong, wrong, and wrong. It meant that only "shovel-ready" projects could be considered. It was the opposite of the kind of planning process envisioned by Beveridge, Minsky, and Senators Warner and Murray in 1944 and Senator Hubert Humphrey and Congressman Gus Hawkins in 1977.

The American Recovery and Reinvestment Act of 2009—the Obama stimulus—should have opened the door to a permanent program of investment in deferred basic infrastructure and green transition. It should have begun a national conversation about redeeming the value of public and social investment per se as an ongoing need, not as a regrettable temporary patch.

I have been harsh here about the value of human capital strategies as substitutes for full employment or as a route to full employment. I do not mean to be dismissive. Many investments in workers, especially young workers, are worth making. Community colleges are one good example. The 6-year completion rate at community colleges is only about 39 percent because most people attending community college are also working, and many are juggling work and family. Consequently, they study "catch as catch can," miss classes, and keep deferring the completion of their degrees or certificates. But community colleges can be a route to decent jobs. Students should be offered a stipend for living expenses, just as the post-war GI Bill did, which in our present context would be a phenomenally efficient investment.

We have a shortage of nurses in this country. We outsource training of registered nurses to Nigeria and the Philippines. When I looked into the source of the bottleneck, it turns out that there are not enough master's-level instructors in community colleges to meet the demand; they can make more money in hospitals. So, for failure to spend a few hundred million dollars to adequately fund training programs, we are denying American kids the chance to become well-paid professionals.

All of this is to say that I am all in favor of well-targeted education and training programs. But these work best in tandem with a national commitment to full employment and a national commitment to regularizing work. This is the strategy of Denmark's famous active labor market: full employment plus continuous investment in upgrading of the labor force. It works.

Until recently, something close to a consensus existed among conservative economists that widening income inequality was a story of skills mismatch: the technical term for this is skill-biased technological change. Some people are paid more because they have the skills the economy demands; others do not have these skills and are paid less. Lately, many of the proponents of this view have walked it back. The timing is wrong; the data do not fit the hypothesis. In this regard, Larry Mishel and Ruy A. Teixeira (1991) of the Economic Policy Institute deserve great credit for their research persuading the skills camp to give ground. Skills are part of the story, but a bigger part is the one-sided abrogation of a social compact that once provided decent living standards even for the lower-skilled.

And, of course, one can't tell this story without acknowledging the special role of race. The post-war social contract was for white men. They enjoyed a degree of job security and decent earnings as so-called heads of households, meaning that there was a gender discrimination aspect, too. I do not wish to glamorize the "good old days" that had much to be ashamed of except to point out that full employment is better than high unemployment and that regularized payroll jobs are better than day labor. Just as people of color and women were gaining more access to mainstream jobs, the ground rules changed, and the entire economy became more precarious. In fashioning a more just economy, we need to be alert to changes in the family, and we need to design labor markets accordingly.

There is one other caveat. Economic historians have a very useful concept known as "path dependence." The classic case is the QWERTY keyboard that is less efficient than alternatives, but we use QWERTY because we have always used it. Path dependence also describes policy. We are now stuck with TANF as a block grant because its sponsors put us on that path. We are stuck with health insurance provided by private insurers because we started on that path in the 1930s and 1940s and have never quite had the political power to change it.

This is a moment when we do not have a great deal of political power to make drastic changes. But, as we pursue policy changes that are necessarily incremental for now, it is crucially important to be mindful of which policy shifts move us in the direction of a better path and which ones buy a little gain but at the cost of reinforcing the perverse path we are on.

I wish to end this chapter with a quote from David Rolf. David is the organizer who brought the $15 per hour minimum wage to Seattle and who jump-started the national movement for a $15 per hour minimum wage. At a recent conference, Rolf remarked, "Policy is frozen politics." As far as I can tell, that wonderful observation is original to Rolf. What did he mean by policy is frozen politics? Our current decent policies—namely Social Security, Medicare, the Wagner Act, community colleges, civil rights, progressive taxation—are the frozen fruit codified into law of yesterday's live political struggles. But good policy erodes over time unless nourished by live, liquid, hot politics. And sometimes, policy goes the wrong way: TANF, the assault on public institutions, the attack on collective bargaining, and the obsession with budget cutting are also the legacy of politics. This is all the more reason for a vigorous politics on behalf of a decent society that draws the right lessons from history.

The story of extreme inequality in America is very substantially a labor-market story in two core respects. First, our labor markets are too slack, too far from full employment; and second, they are too irregular and getting more irregular every day. None of this is mainly the result of technology or of changing cultural values or of deficient skills. It is the result of politics, and it will only be changed by politics.

REFERENCES

Beveridge, William. 1982. "The Foundations of the Welfare State." In *The Foundations of the Welfare State*, edited by Pat Thane and Jo Campling, 339. New York: Pearson Education Limited.

"David Rolf, president, Workers Lab, Service Employees International Union, Local 775" (Albert Shanker Institute), YouTube, January 19, 2015, https://www.youtube.com/watch?v=005d8e5Swec.

Goldin, Claudia, and Robert A. Margo. "The Great Compression: The Wage Structure in the United States at Mid-Century." *Quarterly Journal of Economics* 107, no. 1 (1992): 1–34.

Harrington, Michael. *The Other America: Poverty in the United States*. New York: Simon & Schuster, 1962.

Jacobs, Jerry A., and Kathleen Gerson. *The Time Divide: Work, Family, and Gender Inequality*. Cambridge, MA: Harvard University Press, 2004.

Kuttner, Robert. *Debtors' Prison: The Politics of Austerity Versus Possibility*. New York: Knopf, 2013.

Minsky, Hyman P. "The Poverty of Economic Policy." Unpublished paper, presented at the Graduate Institute of Cooperative Leadership, New York, July 14, 1975.

———. "Where Did the American Economy—and Economists—Go Wrong?" Unpublished manuscript, 1971. http://digitalcommons.bard.edu/cgi/viewcontent.cgi?article=1427&context=hm_archive.

Mishel, Lawrence, and Ruy A. Teixeira. *The Myth of the Coming Labor Shortage: Jobs, Skills, and the Incomes of America's Workforce 2000*. Washington, DC: Economic Policy Institute, 1991. http://files.eric.ed.gov/fulltext/ED346265.pdf.

Moynihan, Daniel P. *Maximum Feasible Misunderstanding: Community Action in the War on Poverty*. New York: Free Press, 1969.

Murray, James E. Employment Act of 1946, Pub. L. No. 79–304, 15 U.S.C. § 1021 (1946).

Skocpol, Theda. "Sustainable Social Policy: Fighting Poverty Without Poverty Programs." *American Prospect* (Summer 1990). http://prospect.org/article/sustainable-social-policy-fighting-poverty-without-poverty-programs.

Wilson, William Julius. "Race-Neutral Policies and the Democratic Coalition." *American Prospect* (Spring 1990). http://prospect.org/article/race-neutral-policies-and-democratic-coalition.

Index

Note: Tables and figures are indicated by "t" or "f" following the page number. Endnote material is indicated with an "n" followed by the note number.